BRITISH GOVERNMENT IN INDIA

Curzon of Kedleston 1903

Lord Curzon of Kedleston as Viceroy, 1903

BRITISH GOVERNMENT IN INDIA

The Story of the Viceroys and Government Houses

By

THE MARQUIS CURZON OF KEDLESTON, K.G.

Viceroy and Governor General of India
Jan. 1899–May 1904, and Dec. 1904–Nov. 1905

VOLUME TWO

CASSELL AND COMPANY, LTD
London, New York, Toronto and Melbourne

Published 1925

Printed in Great Britain

CONTENTS OF VOLUME TWO

CHAPTER X

BARRACKPORE GOVERNMENT HOUSE

CHAPTER XI

SOME NOTES ON THE VICEROYALTY AND GOVERNOR GENERAL-SHIP OF INDIA

PART I

CONTENTS

PART II

CHAPTER XII

NOTES ON SOME VICEROYS AND GOVERNORS GENERAL

PART I. CLIVE TO BENTINCK, 1765–1835

CONTENTS

CHAPTER XII

Part II.   Auckland to Minto, 1836–1910

LIST OF ILLUSTRATIONS

x   LIST OF ILLUSTRATIONS

BRITISH GOVERNMENT IN INDIA

CHAPTER X

BARRACKPORE GOVERNMENT HOUSE

"Barrackpore is delicious and takes the sting out of India."—1st EARL OF MINTO.

"Which of you, intending to build a tower sitteth not down first, and counteth the cost, whether he have sufficient to finish it?"—LUKE XIV, 28.

IN my First Volume I have dealt in the main with the memories and antiquities of Calcutta, and have provided some material and, I hope, solved some problems for the archæologist and the historian. Before I pass to the examination of the more strictly political questions which I have foreshadowed in this volume, let me leave the city in which I have tarried so long, and in company with my readers seek a brief relaxation amid the enchanted glades of Barrackpore.

Nearly all visitors to Calcutta, and the majority of European residents, have been up the river to this country retreat of the Governor General, have wandered in the bamboo avenues, or perhaps lunched under the shady colonnades of the great banian, have admired the flaming bougainvillia, or played golf in the Park. But few who have thus enjoyed the hospitality of the Viceroy, or later of the Governor of Bengal, have any idea of the history—a history of deep interest and romance—that the place possesses, or pause to think of the scenes that it has witnessed. For more than a century Barrackpore was the rural resort of the Governor General, where he could throw off some of the restraints, if few of the cares, of State, and where his wife or himself could find in the delights of the garden or in the amusements of the menagerie, the elephant stud, and the links, some relief from the ceaseless persecution of official routine. But it was almost equally a seat of Government. Thither up the river or by the road has moved

2—B

I

a long procession of all the best and bravest in India—every statesman, or general, or divine, every illustrious visitor to Calcutta ; along its terrace and under its leafy shades anxious men have paced up and down ; in its sunny verandahs or in its darkened rooms, conferences have been held, decisions taken,[1] Minutes written pregnant with vast consequences to India ; many Governors General have resided there for months on end ; there too tragedies have been enacted, and perils incurred, as great as any that mark the troubled page of British dominion in the East.

The name Barrackpore is a characteristic barbarism, that sufficiently indicates the origin of the European station. English troops were first quartered there in 1775 ; and till the Mutiny it was the principal garrison station of Calcutta. The Cantonment no longer possesses its old importance ; and the greatly reduced garrison now maintained consists only of about 500 British Infantry and a small artillery unit with a few guns.

According to legend, Barrackpore had been a place of British settlement for a century before its occupation for military purposes. An oral tradition declares that Job Charnock built a bungalow on this spot, and that a native bazaar grew up under his protection, before he moved down stream and settled at Calcutta. This may be so ; but I cannot help thinking that the Charnock legend owed its origin solely to the native name of Chanak ; for, most certainly, as I shall show, the latter has not been derived from, but was anterior to and entirely independent of the legend. The tradition is thus cited by Rainey :—

" Even the natives whom Governor Charnock is reputed to have treated with great severity, have perpetuated his name by calling Barrackpore, where he had a *bangalah* and a small bazaar, after him, Charnock or Chanock "[2];

and the story is told, in somewhat similar language, in the pages of Orme, W. Hamilton, and Hunter.

But as a matter of fact Chanak is not only a common village name in Bengal (which it is thought may perhaps have been derived from Chanakya, the famous Minister of the great King Chandra Gupta), but it appears to have been the actual name of a native village on this very site, at a period when Job Charnock was still living far away at Patna,

---

[1] We have a record of a Council held at Barrackpore by Lord Wellesley in August 1801, just before his departure for the Upper Provinces ; and probably this is not a solitary case.

[2] " Historical and Topographical Sketch of Calcutta," 1876, p. 16.

and before he had moved to Lower Bengal. A letter from the Court of Directors in England to Fort St. George, dated 14th December, 1677, is conclusive on this point :

" It is ordered that if any ships shall go up the said river as high as Hughley, *or at least as far as Channock*," etc.

Other and earlier evidence supports the same conclusion. The learned Pundit Hara Prasad Shastri read a paper before the Asiatic Society of Calcutta in December 1892, about an old Bengali MS. of the year 1495 A.D. describing a journey made by one Chand Sagar on the Ganges at that date. With a fleet of seven vessels he descended the river, and at this spot he is described as passing " Chanak." The same name appears as Tsjannok in much the same locality in a Dutch atlas of Bengal which I have seen, of the year 1678 ; and in an English map of Barrackpore, in the early part of the 19th century, the name Achanak is printed immediately south of the present railway station of Barrackpore. We may be confident, therefore, that this is the original name of the place, and that Job Charnock, even if he ever called and traded here, is at any rate not its eponymous hero.

When the British Cantonment was founded at Barrackpore in 1775, bungalows built by Englishmen followed ; the first of these was erected in February 1775, at a spot about 150 yards distant from the present Flagstaff, and 14 miles as the crow flies from Calcutta. Ten years later, Government appeared upon the scene as owner ; for Captain John Macintyre having offered, in April 1785, to sell a property of 220 *bighas* or 70 acres and two bungalows to the Government, either for the extension of the Cantonment or the convenience of the Commander-in-Chief, they were purchased with the approval of the Acting Governor General, Sir John Macpherson, for the substantial sum of Rs. 25,000 or over £3,000 in August of the same year, and the bungalows were handed over for occupation to the Commander-in-Chief. This house and grounds were the nucleus of the present Barrackpore Park.

Lord Valentia makes the statement that the Government House at Barrackpore (*i.e.* Captain Macintyre's bungalow) was the country seat of Sir John Macpherson, February 1785–September 1786, and continued so under Lord Cornwallis, that Sir John Shore (Lord Teignmouth), Governor General 1793-1798, gave it up to the Commander-in-Chief, receiving instead Rs. 5000 p.a. to hire a residence for himself ; and that Lord Wellesley having been made the head of the army, took back Barrackpore, and gave the Rs. 5,000 a year to the Commander-in-Chief.[1] There is some truth, but a good deal more of error, in these statements, and what really happened appears to have been as follows. Sir John Macpherson never occupied the bungalow, for it was with his approval that it was purchased for the Commander-in-Chief. Lord Cornwallis, who succeeded Macpherson, was both Governor General and Commander-in-Chief, and it seems to have been in the latter capacity that he became possessed of the house. There is nothing to show that Sir John Shore ever lived there ; and the Rs. 500 a month, or £750 a year, was the allowance granted by the Court of Directors to the Governor General for a country residence—an allowance which would naturally have lapsed when Cornwallis occupied the Barrackpore bungalow, and have been resumed by Shore who was never Commander-in-Chief. Then Lord Wellesley appropriated the place, as the property of the Governor General in Council, on the retirement of Sir Alured Clarke, the Commander-in-Chief, in 1801.

The belief has been generally entertained that it was by virtue of his military title as " Captain General and Commanding in Chief of all the Forces of the Crown in the East Indies "—which had been conferred upon him by Pitt on 7th August, 1800, after the Mysore Campaign, that Wellesley effected the seizure of Barrackpore. This appointment had been intended partly as a compliment to Wellesley, but still more in order to secure unity of action in the various campaigns that were then impending in India. The fortunate acquisition, however, at the sale of the Wellesley MSS. (belonging to a descendant of the family) at Christie's, in February 1918, of the original autograph letter in which Lord Wellesley had given notice to his Commander-in-Chief, in December 1800, of his intended act,[2] has enabled me to solve all doubts and to place the transaction upon a historical basis. I give the text in full.

[1] The Commission is printed in Pearce's " Memoirs of Marquis Wellesley," Vol. I, pp. 357-361. It reached India 26th February, 1801. The post of General Commanding in Chief of the Forces in Bengal, held at that time by General Sir Alured Clarke, was in the gift of the Horse Guards and was not strictly under the orders of the Company. This office was held, together with the Governor Generalship, by Lord Cornwallis in both his terms of office, by Lord Hastings 1813-1823, and by Lord William Bentinck for the period from May 1833 to May 1835.

[2] This letter, along with several other autograph letters of Lord Wellesley, and one of the Duke of Wellington, is now in the Victoria Memorial Hall at Calcutta, for which I acquired it.

Private.

" My dear Sir,

I entirely forgot to speak to you yesterday on a subject, which had been a matter of communication between us last year, but was dropped by me under the apprehension of interfering with your private convenience. I refer to the Country Residence of Barrackpore, which I have long thought the most eligible situation for the Garden House of the Governor-General. I remember that you entertained some doubts with respect to the claims and convenience of your Successors in the Command. I have examined the whole question with attention, and I am perfectly satisfied that the Country Residence at Barrackpore in entirely at the disposal of the Government, that it has accidentally passed into the hands of the Commander-in-Chief, and that it is resumable at the pleasure of the Governor General in Council. It is therefore evident to me that no right of the Commander-in-Chief would be affected by the resumption of the Place, whenever any person holding my station might think fit to resume it. With respect to the convenience of any future Commander-in-Chief, it might be easy to provide for that, either by erecting another Bungalow in the neighbourhood of the Cantonment, or by assigning a proper Garden House for his use. While the separate command of the Governor General over the Cantonment of Barrackpore shall continue, no other reason, than the superior healthiness of the air, seems to recommend the vicinity of Barrackpore for the Residence of the Commander-in-Chief. I have stated these considerations merely for the purpose of apprizing you of the general reasons, which have determined me (whenever you shall embark for Europe and your personal convenience shall no longer be in question), to resume the Residence at Barrackpore ; and to annex it permanently to the Government General ; making such an arrangement for the accommodation of your Successor as he may judge most eligible. My determination will absolve you from all embarrassment with regard to those motives of delicacy, which I know you always feel with respect to any supposed claims or rights belonging to your Command ; since my mind is entirely decided on the question, although no consideration would ever have induced me to press it upon your attention, if you had remained in Bengal. Under all these circumstances I am desirous of stating a request to you, on which I must further entreat you to decide with reference to your personal convenience. It is my intention to pass the approaching Hot Season at Barrackpore, and with this view, it would be extremely convenient to me to obtain possession of the place as soon as possible, for the purpose of preparing the House more effectually against the Heat. If it should not be inconvenient to you to allow the Place to pass into my hands, I should return you many thanks for such a mark of kindness. Whatever property may now be in the house or grounds, of which you wish to dispose, might be transferred immediately at a just valuation. On this question I again request you to decide entirely according to your convenience, which I should be deeply concerned to disturb for a moment. My determination to occupy the Place immediately after your departure necessarily excludes all question respecting the rights of your successor : you may be assured that I will take care to render him ample justice, and to provide him with every suitable accommodation in the room of that which I propose to appropriate to the Governor General.

" Believe me, Dear Sir, Always Yours
Sincerely,
(Signed)   Wellesley.

" H.E. Sir A. Clarke, K.B.,"
    etc.,   etc.,   etc.

The Governor General was successful both in his request and in the date fixed by him for its fulfilment. On the first day in the New Year the Commander-in-Chief hastened to express his acquiescence ; and the following Minute is to be found in the Records of the Public Department of the Government of India dated 25th June, 1801.

" The House at Barrackpore the property of the Company, which has hitherto been occupied by the Commander-in-Chief as a Garden House, having been appropriated from the 1st February last to the use of the Governor General, His Excellency the Most Noble the Governor General in Council orders that the monthly sum of Rupees 500 . . . hitherto received by the Governor General for a Garden House do cease to be drawn by the Governor General from the 1st February last, and that the amount be paid from that date to the Commander-in-Chief for the purposes of providing His Excellency with a garden house in the room of the house at Barrackpore.

(Signed)   Wellesley."

Two days later the successful Governor General wrote a letter, dated 27th June, 1801, to the fascinating Lady Anne Barnard, the authoress of " Robin Adair," so familiar to any reader who has studied the story of the British connection with the Cape more than a century ago, in which he thus alludes to his ready-won spoil :

" I have been very well since Henry's[1] arrival, residing almost entirely at Barrackpore, a charming spot which, in my usual spirit of tyranny, I have plucked from the Commander in Chief."[2]

Such, in contradistinction to the popular version of the guide books, was the real history of events at Barrackpore.

[1] His youngest brother, who went out to India as his Private Secretary, and after his return to England in 1805, became in turn Minister in Spain, and Ambassador at Vienna and Paris, being created Lord Cowley in 1828.
[2] " Lives of the Lindsays."

So far we have heard of a Garden House and a Park. We now have to trace the steps by which the former was transformed into the Government House of a later day, while the latter became the beautiful pleasaunce that modern Calcutta knows so well. Lord Wellesley, in his final Defence to the Directors, said that the house which he took over was "an old cottage in a state of considerable decay." Captain Wyatt, the architect of Government House, Calcutta, was employed to execute the necessary repairs, so as to admit of immediate occupation; and what the house was like at that time, and what was the manner of life lived there, may be gathered from the illustration drawn for Lord Valentia by his travelling companion and artist, Mr. Salt, which is reproduced here, and from the narrative of the former :—

"February 4th 1803.—In consequence of a general invitation, I, yesterday proceeded to Barrackpore, Lord Wellesley's country residence; Mr. Graham and Mr. Salt accompanied me. We arrived before breakfast, and I found His Excellency just returned from his ride. The situation of the house is much more pleasing than anything I have yet seen. It is considerably elevated above the Hooghly river, on a very extended reach of which it stands : directly opposite is the Danish settlement of Serampore : on the sides are pagodas, villages, and groves of lofty trees. The water is much clearer than at Calcutta, and covered with the State barges and cutters of the Governor-General. These, painted green, and ornamented with gold, contrasted with the scarlet dresses of the rowers, were a great addition to the scene. The park is laid out in the English style; and the house, at present unfinished, is well adapted to the climate, having a beautiful verandah on every side, and the rooms being on a very ample scale. This place originally belonged to the Commander-in-Chief; and Lord Wellesley took possession of it on being appointed Captain General, and has improved it with his usual taste. Several of the bungalows belonging to the lines have been taken into the Park, and are fitted up for the reception of the Secretaries, Aides-de-Camp, and visitors. His Excellency had ordered one to be prepared for me, of which I immediately took possession. After breakfast at the house, we returned to our own habitations till dinner; His Lordship being busily employed with his different Secretaries in preparing despatches for England. At dinner, however, I had the pleasure of several hours' conversation with him respecting India, and the several important additions which he had made to that part of our Empire. It was with great regret that I felt myself obliged this night to return to Calcutta; but the hot weather was most rapidly approaching, and, as a new comer, I was fearful of exposing myself too much to it during a journey of eight hundred miles. At His Excellency's request I left Mr. Salt behind me to take views of the place; and after dinner, embarked, accompanied by Mr. Graham, in a state barge. It is about fourteen miles by land or water from Barrackpore to Calcutta :

we stopped, however, about three miles from the town, where we were met by Mr. Graham's carriage." [1]

The next stages may be described in the words of Lord Wellesley :

" The house continued in this (*i.e.* unfurnished) state until the commencement of 1804, when the old parts of the building were found upon examination to be unsafe. The old building was accordingly surveyed by Captain Aubury, who had succeeded Captain Wyatt as Superintendent of Public Works, and was, by him, reported to be incapable of repair. It appeared that even if the building could have been repaired the expense would have been as great as that of erecting a new habitation on the same spot ; and it was apprehended that the mixture of the old with new work, would not form a durable building, and would require perpetual repairs. It appeared therefore, advisable to erect a new building on the site, and of the same dimensions as the former, applying such parts of the building as had been more recently erected, to the construction of the new habitation." [2]

These words have greatly confused the few writers who have seen them, and they most imperfectly represent Lord Wellesley's real intentions. They do not relate to the present Government House at Barrackpore at all ; but to another and much vaster construction which the ambitious founder—his hands and brain now free from the anxieties of the Calcutta Government House—was planning at Barrackpore as the crowning act of his imperial Aedileship. It is in fact clear, both from his own language and from a phrase that appears in a subsequent letter of the first Lord Minto—(" A better and more regular house will certainly be proper. Such an one there was, but it was pulled down to make room for the projected palace, of which the ground floor walls are finished ")—that Wellesley demolished the then existing bungalow, and commenced to build another structure on its site ; and, further, that he must at the same time have constructed the nucleus of the present Government House, which is higher up the river, to act as an *ad interim* residence for the Governor General.

His ideas of the new palace were hardly of the " country villa " type, unless it were a villa of the Cæsars. The building was to have cost from 3 to 4 lacs (*i.e.* up to £50,000) ; while a part of his scheme is said to have been the bringing up of all the public offices from Calcutta, and planting them in Barrackpore Park. This must, I think,

---

[1] " Voyages and Travels," Vol. I, pp. 64-6.
[2] " Miscellany of the Asiatic Annual Register " 1807, pp. 66-7.

be an exaggeration, although quarters for a certain number of officials were doubtless a part of the plan. He is further said to have contemplated connecting the two Government Houses by a straight avenue leading from one to the other, but to have abandoned this as too costly.[1]

With Wellesley to plan was to execute, with or without sanction, and accordingly we are not surprised to learn that, once condemned, the old building straightway disappeared, the materials for the new one were collected, and the erection begun. The lower storey was in fact already built when, in August 1805, its magnificent founder retired from the scene. The buildings which he had managed to erect during his short period of unimpeded autocracy were thus described in a Report dated 2nd April, 1806, which was prepared for his successor :

(1) A stable with stalls for 36 horses and standing for 4 carriages and a bungalow for the coachman.
(2) A bridge over the Nullah leading to the Cantonments.
(3) An aviary for the large birds in the Menagerie.
(4) A bungalow for the Band.
(5) Repairs to the existing Bungalow.
(6) A new bungalow for temporary occupation.
(7) The New House (which the Governor General had euphemistically described as " a new Bungalow " !).

Tom Raw (Sir C. D'Oyly) is very caustic at the expense of Lord Wellesley's unfinished structure :

" Here from the cares of Government released
Our Indian Governors their ease enjoy,
In pleasures by the contrast much increased
Their intermediate moments they employ.
Wellesley first stampt it his. He was the boy
For making ducks and drakes with public cash,
Planned a great house that time might not destroy ;
Built the first floor, prepared brick, beam, and sash,
And then returned, and left it in this dismal hash." [2]

Lord Cornwallis, however, who came out with very different ideas from his predecessors, at once ordered the work to be discontinued ; although, with a view to preserving the materials, and in order to avoid a complete sacrifice of the money already expended, he gave instruc-

[1] J. H Blochmann, "Calcutta during the Last Century," 1867.
[2] "Tom Raw the Griffin," p. 199.

tions for the unroofed building to be covered in. Shortly afterwards he sickened and died. His acting successor, Sir George Barlow, whose policy was the opposite of Lord Wellesley's in almost every particular, received very explicit directions from the Court of Directors, which he readily obeyed.

" To what purpose this building can be now converted we are at a loss to conceive, having no plan or estimates to form an opinion upon the subject ; but we positively direct that no further expense be incurred upon it without our previous sanction, trusting that our present Governor General will be particularly mindful of our repeated injunctions with regard to Public Works and Buildings in future, and at the same time studiously endeavour to diminish the expense we have hitherto incurred on this account." [1]

The subsequent fate of the building was not less tragic than its interrupted beginnings. A good many of the materials were destroyed by a fire in the depot where they were stored in Calcutta, and the remainder, consisting of beams, doors, and windows, were sold by public auction for very small prices by the first Lord Minto (1807-1813), who, much as he liked Barrackpore, was very anxious to be quit of such an encumbrance. Lady Nugent mentioned the relics of the structure in July 1812. [2] The next Governor General, Lord Hastings (1813-1823), is said at one time to have contemplated finishing the structure on a reduced scale ; but, if so, he soon abandoned the idea, and devoted himself to the enlargement and completion of the present house. In his day the empty shell was finally pulled down, and Lady Hastings built a greenhouse or conservatory on the site.

Where exactly this abortive palace of Lord Wellesley stood has been one of the puzzles that have agitated Calcutta topographers for the last half century. Mrs. Graham, who came up the river to visit Barrackpore in 1810, said :

" When we came to the port of Barrackpore the tamarind, acacia, and peepil tree, through whose branches the moon threw her flickering beams on the river, seemed to hang over our heads, and formed a strong contrast to the white buildings of Serampore which shone on the opposite shore. We landed at the palace begun by the Marquis Wellesley, but discontinued by the frugality of the Indian Company ; its unfinished arches showed by the moonlight like an ancient ruin and completed the beauty of the scenery." [3]

[1] Despatches from the Court of Directors, dated 23rd July, 1806.
[2] "Journal," Vol. I, p. 153.
[3] "Journal of a Residence in India," 1812, pp. 142-3.

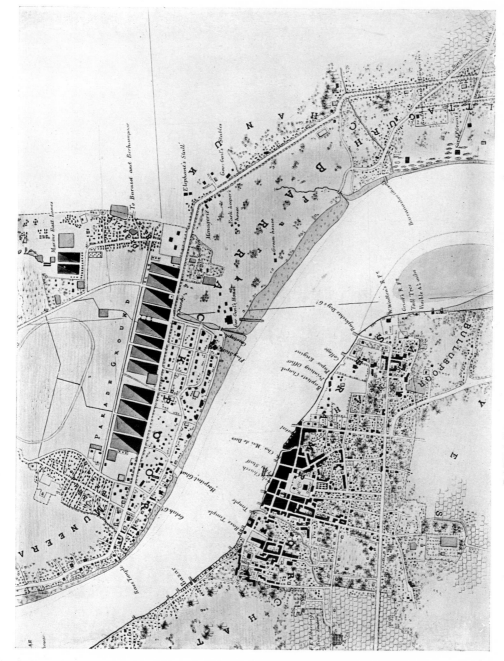

BARRACKPORE PARK AND CANTONMENT (1841)

Reference is made in the Calcutta Records to a map on which the site of the "Green House" is marked ; but this map, along with all the early plans of the Government House, as altered by Lord Wellesley and his successors, and of the new palace as projected by the former, could not be found at Calcutta in spite of the most patient search. The last mention of the "Green House" that I have come across is in Lady Amherst's description of the Barrackpore Meeting of 1824, where she says that on 30th October Sir E. Paget, the Commander-in-Chief, and his staff bivouacked in the Green House.[1] This, too, has long ago vanished. That its site, however—*i.e.*, the site of Wellesley's projected palace—was on the bank of the river and therefore accessible to its breezes at a point some way to the South-east of the present house, and probably in the neighbourhood of the lower landing-place, seems to be beyond doubt. It could hardly, in fact, have been anywhere else.

I have left the above paragraph standing exactly as I first wrote it, in the hope that I may be forgiven the mild satisfaction of having found my own confident conjecture verified before these pages go to print. Since they were written, a search at the India Office has revealed a copy of the map of 1841, by Charles Joseph, which could not be traced at Calcutta. A reproduction of it is given here, and it shows the Green House, marked at a spot on the river bank almost identical with the existing Band Stand in the Park and immediately below the lower landing-place. This then was the actual site of such vaulting ambition and such sad disaster.

We will now revert to Lord Wellesley and his scheme. No sooner had he acquired the Commander-in-Chief's house and the surrounding land in 1801, than he set about enlarging the latter, which he afterwards described as " covered with jungle or swamps," and converting it into the Park that has been the pride of the neighbourhood and of Calcutta for so many years. What exactly was the additional area that he purchased we do not know, although the extent of the ground originally sold by Captain Macintyre to the Company in 1785 has already been given at 220 *bighas* or about 70 acres. We have a paper in 1801, requesting the Board of Revenue to appoint someone to mark out the boundaries of the property required, and to fix the compensation, and nominating Captain Wyatt to take part in the adjudication.

[1] " Lord Amherst " (Rulers of India Series), 1894, p. 151.

Thornton, in his Gazetteer, gives the total area of the Park and grounds as 210 acres. But this is a mistake; since the measurements show it to be not less than 1,006 *bighas*, or nearly 350 acres—a total which, no doubt, was the result of subsequent acquisitions.

Among the papers in the India Office is a series (entitled " Extracts from Bengal Public Consultations of the Years 1805 and 1806 ") relating to the sums actually paid in compensation to the owners whose property had been compulsorily acquired. These show that the total finally paid by Government amounted to Sicca Rupees 76.619 or £9,577. When first taken over, the ground now contained in the Park was as flat as a billiard table—as flat, in fact, as the entire alluvial plain of the Gangetic Delta.

But Lord Wellesley was resolved to have not merely an English country seat but also an English park around it ; and therefore, under his strenuous direction, the surface of the ground was shaped in to hillocks and undulations, the soil excavated from the large ornamental tanks being utilised, and convict labour being employed [1] for the purpose.

With the passage of time, the illusion has become complete, and the landscape of the Park has always won the enthusiastic admiration of visitors. " Naufragus " in 1810 remarked in best guide-book style :

" The grounds around this retreat are laid out with infinite taste in imitation of our parks in England, and produce a splendid effect on the eye." [2]

Miss Emma Roberts excelled herself in the rhapsody of her transports :

" Although, with the exception of the park, which has been raised into sweeping undulations by artificial means, the cantonments and their vicinity present a flat surface, the combinations of wood, water, and greensward, in numberless vistas, nooks, and small open spaces, yield scenes of tranquil beauty, which eyes, however cold, can scarcely contemplate unmoved.

[1] Lord Wellesley in his Minute of 4th May, 1805, thus described the work : " Some expense was also incurred in repairing and draining part of the ground. This labour, however, was chiefly performed by convicts, without any additional expense to Government, in pursuance of an experiment, recently commenced, for applying the labour of convicts to public works and to the general improvement of the country, in digging tanks, constructing roads and bridges, draining ground, and removing jungle and other nuisances in the vicinity of the Residency, and of the station of Barrackpore. At the commencement of the experiment the convicts performed only a certain description of work, and the remainder was occasionally executed by day labourers. As soon as the convicts became more expert they were substituted altogether in the place of the day labourers, and they now continue to perform what remains of the whole proposed work."

[2] " Adventures," p. 135.

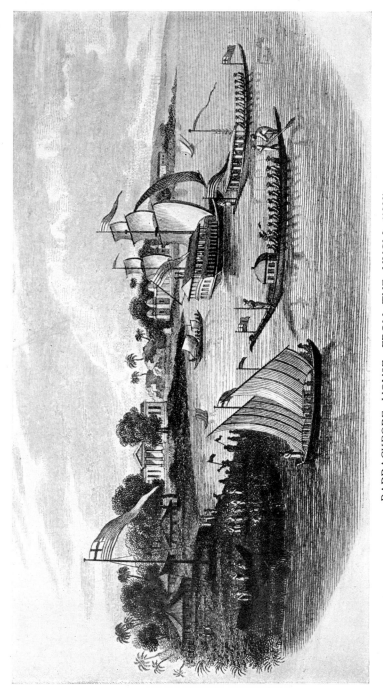

BARRACKPORE HOUSE, FROM THE HUGLI (1803)

"Though an authoritative mandate from the Court of Directors, dictated by unaffected alarm, put an effective stop to the completion of one of the Marquess of Wellesley's most splendid projects, Barrackpore is still indebted to him for a park which is justly considered one of the finest specimens of dressed and ornamented nature which taste has ever produced. Enough has been done to the mansion to render it a very elegant and commodious residence, and the gardens attached to it are unrivalled both in beauty and stateliness, combining the grandeur of Asiatic proportions with the picturesqueness of European design. The gravelled avenues are wide enough to allow wheel carriages to pass off. These ample paths wind through broad parterres, and shrubberies of the most brilliant flowers, sometimes skirting along high walls of creeping plants trained against lofty trees ; at others overlooking large tanks so completely covered with pink blossoms of the lotus as to conceal the element in which this splendid aquatic plant delights." [1]

Whether or not Lord Wellesley ever contemplated, as has been said, a straight avenue connecting his two Government Houses, in the approved manner of the railway line from St. Petersburg to Moscow, he at any rate laid out the existing road from Calcutta, which, as the first section of the Grand Trunk Road, runs in almost a bee-line from the Western suburbs of Calcutta to Barrackpore, and he caused it to be planted, as " Naufragus " tells us, with rows of trees at the distance of twelve or fifteen feet from each other, without intermission, the whole way. By a strange coincidence this road was opened for the public use in the very week in which Wellesley handed over charge of his high office—namely 29th July, 1805. A notification in the " Calcutta Gazette " of that date ran thus :

"All persons are desired to be careful not to injure the young trees planted on the sides of the road.

"Travellers whether on horseback, foot, or in carriages are requested to keep on the central or brick part of the road and pass through the side avenues.

"All elephants, bullocks, and hackeries are strictly prohibited from passing on the side of the roads." [2]

Ten years later, so great was the communication between Calcutta and Barrackpore—at that time a large Cantonment—that a Royal Mail Coach, as it was officially described, was established by order of

---

[1] " Scenes and Characteristics of Hindostan," Vol. III, pp. 273-7.
[2] A prohibition which now, as then, is consistently disregarded. I have never been able to understand why an Indian with his bullock cart will never use a *pukka* or made road if he can, but will always diverge into the heavy dust and sand at its side. He thinks, I fancy, that somehow he is vindicating mmemorial custom, and perhaps scoring off Government.

Government to run between the two places, carrying six passengers inside, and six out. How successfully Wellesley had planted may be seen half a century later, when Lady Canning, describing her first visits to Barrackpore, wrote thus (19th March, 1856):

" The last ten or twelve miles of the road are as straight as an arrow, and bordered all the way with beautiful trees, planted in Lord Wellesley's time, mango, banyan, india-rubber, peepul—like white poplars—teak, with enormous leaves, laurel of several sorts, mimosas, tamarinds, etc. But it all looks poisonously green, and gives a notion of unwholesome damp, yet this is not at all an unwholesome part of the country. The roads are of pounded red brick, and the country brighter and richer in colour than anything European. We have a half-way house to which our horses are sent, and where we change the escorts, and the red and gold servants and soldiers looked bright and gay at this place." [1]

A few years later the disastrous cyclone of 1864 smote the avenue with terrific force, and created many of the gaps which were visible in my day, but have since been replanted.

Such were the proceedings of Lord Wellesley at Barrackpore. Reviewing the papers that exist in the India Office and at Calcutta, it is impossible to resist the conclusion that he acted in respect of the new palace there with as complete a lack of sanction as he had already done in the case of Government House at Calcutta. Indeed, his own Defence, originally put forward in his Minute of 4th May, 1805, and subsequently repeated in the Letter to the Court of 4th July, 1805, is positively misleading. For who that reads of " a new building on the site and old foundations and of the same dimensions as the former, applying such parts of the building as had been more recently erected to the construction of the new habitation," could have realised (1) that the existing residence, as depicted in Lord Valentia's illustration, had been entirely swept away, (2) that a new and costly structure, on an evidently much more ambitious scale, had begun to rise in its place, (3) that a great store of fresh material had been collected for this, and (4) that meanwhile a third residence (the nucleus of the present Government House) must have been erected, or, if already existing, greatly enlarged, on another site ? Neither does any estimate of cost appear to have been sent to London. On the contrary, both in the Minute and the Despatch, Lord Wellesley excused himself mainly on the ground

---

[1] " Story of Two Noble Lives," Vol. II, p. 60. The same custom prevailed in my time.

that Captain Aubury, the engineer officer, had volunteered for the campaign at Bhurtpore. The first that the Directors appear to have heard of it was the figures contained in the annual accounts sent home, of which we catch a glimpse in two paragraphs of the famous cancelled Despatch No. 128 of April 1805 :

" 73. We observe also that a considerable sum has been disbursed for the Governor General's House and Park at Barrackpore, and for making a new road thither. What we see already charged on this account amounts to about Sicca Rupees 46.000 or £5,300.

" 74. Among other articles of the Durbar accounts of the year 1802-3 that have contributed to the increase of the expense, we find . . . near Sicca Rupees 50.000 or £5,800 for the Governor General's garden at Barrackpore."

Small wonder that when the Court realised what had been done, and found a President of the Board of Control willing to pass a strong Despatch, their long-pent-up anger should have burst forth in a furious though futile expostulation, the culprit being by this time safely back in England, and quite indifferent to any censure that might be posted to Calcutta. In their Despatch of 23rd July, 1806, the Court wrote thus :

" Our surprise and astonishment (*i.e.* at the Calcutta proceedings) have been much increased by the communication made to us (on the Bengal Public Letter of 4th July, 1805) by which we learn, notwithstanding the heavy expense already incurred on account of the Government House at Calcutta, that a Building of considerable extent has been commenced at Barrackpore for the residence of the Governor General ; this too at a time when our Finances are in a state of the utmost embarrassment, and when we are called upon to make the greatest exertions to supply you with funds from Europe to assist in defraying the extraordinary expenses of the war. How to account for the inconsistency of such a proceeding we know not."

It is now the fashion to describe as prescience what must undoubtedly have struck the Directors of those days as presumption, not redeemed even by candour ; and those who for a century have revelled in the Barrackpore of Lord Wellesley's creation—for, in spite of the fiasco on the river bank, he and no other was its real founder—may not be too eager to sit in judgment upon his lapses from administrative rectitude or personal veracity. I fear, however, that the orthodox moralist will not tolerate any such palliation, and that the proceedings both at Barrackpore and Calcutta will never fail to elicit his pained reprobation.

It is only fair to Lord Wellesley to add that he never failed to justify his acts of extravagance by considerations of public advantage : though we are left in some little doubt as to how far these were made the excuse or were really the motive for his policy. Thus in the case of Barrackpore, a long Minute of the Governor General is extant, dated 1st June, 1805, saying that upon the first laying out of the place he had intended to establish an institution for the improvement of agriculture in India : and that he now proposed to establish an experimental farm in Bengal in order to improve the breed of cattle, introduce a better system of agriculture, and reduce expenses (this I am sure was intended to flatter the Court) by the use of machinery. The quantity of land required, by a curious coincidence, was 900 *bighas* or 300 acres, and accordingly a better place could not be found than Barrackpore, where the park might be used as a pasture for the cattle. The Minute proceeded to describe all the proposed arrangements, and it was to be sent to the Court with a request for the sanction of two European experts. By this time the Court was not likely to grant any request for fresh expenditure emanating from Lord Wellesley, and the project was stillborn. [1] Barrackpore was also to be the site of an establishment for the study of the Natural History of India : and this scheme so far took effect that it became the germ of the Zoological Collection that existed in the Park for three-quarters of a century, and will be noticed presently. [2]

And now, saying good-bye for the moment to this splendid and quite impenitent sinner, let us follow the history of the Barrackpore house that *was* built by him, and was the parent of the present mansion. Described by Lord Minto as " only a makeshift while the great house was erecting," it consisted, when Lord Wellesley left India, of three large rooms opening into a verandah. Sir George Barlow, who acted from 1805 to 1807 on the death of Lord Cornwallis, by converting each corner of the verandah into a small room, greatly improved the comfort of the residence. Then came the first Lord Minto, who loved the place, and whose testimony, already referred to, demands a fuller citation :

" Barrackpore surpasses all my expectations, in the beauty of the ground, the beauty of the situation, and the comfort of its ways, compared to Calcutta. The grounds are a mixture of park and pleasure-grounds. They are laid out

---

[1] " Despatches, etc., by the Marquis Wellesley " (ed. Montgomery Martin), Vol. IV, p. 676.
[2] *Ibid.*, p. 674.

with the greatest judgment and taste, and their extent is very considerable. There is a great variety of fine timber and curious ornamental shrubs and flowering trees. Pools of water of very pretty forms and certain inequalities of surface have been artificially produced, but the real beauties consist in the rich verdure which covers the whole, the magnificent timber, and the fine river which forms one side of the place from end to end. Although it is a tide river, there is no mud on the sides ; the grass extends to low watermark. The breadth of the Ganges here is sufficient for grandeur, and not too much for beauty. It is all alive with a brisk navigation of boats and vessels of different build and dimensions, and all of the most picturesque forms and fashions. The present house is what is called a bungalow or cottage, and was intended only as a makeshift while the great house was erecting. It is a cottage indeed, but a very considerable building compared with the European scale. . . . The verandah next the room is a charming apartment. It affords a long, shaded, airy walk with a most beautiful prospect, and we find it an excellent eating-room.[1] It is within forty or fifty paces off the water's edge.

" Besides this principal bungalow there are a number of smaller ones like neat Swiss cottages scattered about the lawn. These afford accommodation for Aides-de-Camp, guests, etc., etc. A better and more regular house will certainly be proper. Such an one there was, but it was pulled down to make room for the projected palace, of which the ground-floor walls are finished. It would have been magnificent, I have no doubt, but in perfect contradiction with every purpose of the place. It would have been to come from Calcutta to Calcutta again ; and you must have had the same multitude of troublesome attendants, and have lived the same full-dress, intolerable life at your country house as in town. I am extremely glad it has been stopped, and am selling off the material which had been laid in, hoping there will be no change in my time. The road from Calcutta to Barrackpore is beautiful the whole way."[2]

A year later (April 1808) Lord Minto is still enamoured of Barrackpore, where he spends the middle of every week. There, as he says, he can read his Despatches in peace and quiet, and write without interruption. At sunset he walks out alone to catch the breeze along the river bank (his son and the younger members of the party being occupied in hunting jackals). His only complaint is that there is no one to talk to, except on business—for, as will be remembered, his wife had stayed at home and never joined him in India. Indeed, they were never to meet again.

It was reserved for Lord Hastings, who was in India as Governor General for ten years (1813-1823), to make the substantial additions

---

[1] It has been used so, in hot weather, ever since.
[2] " Lord Minto in India," by the Countess of Minto, 1846, pp. 31-2.

2—C

and improvements that converted the house into its present form,[1] more than doubling its size, and rendering it capable of accommodating a limited number of guests, as well as the family of the Governor General.

It must be remembered that in those days the Governor General, except when on tour, spent the entire summer months in Bengal, the first hint of the Simla exodus not being given until Lord Amherst went there, for one hot weather only, in 1829, while on the march in Northern India—and the practice not becoming an annual custom till the time of Sir John Lawrence in 1864. Accordingly Barrackpore was the habitual summer residence of the Governor General, and we hear much more about it in contemporary correspondence and memoirs than in later days, when it became, so to speak, after the English model, the week-end retreat of the Viceroy. This fact, and the diminution in the strength of the garrison, are the reasons for which, in modern times, we rarely hear of the big parties and balls that were not uncommon in Barrackpore Government House in the first half of the 19th century.

Lord Amherst is our next witness. Lord Colchester's Diary contains a letter from him dated 15th March, 1824, which shows that his appreciation was not behind that of his predecessors :

" I am writing to you from our country house, sixteen miles from Calcutta, a most delightful spot with fine spread of trees, and the Hooghly branch of the Ganges flowing under our windows. There is certainly more variety in the grounds than in the rest of Bengal. I do believe some of our *mountains* may be 15 or 20 feet above the valleys." [2]

Bishop Heber, who came to Barrackpore on 28th October, 1828, as the guest of Lord and Lady Amherst, adds to the chorus a note of not wholly uncritical admiration :

" The house itself of Barrackpore is handsome, containing three fine sitting-rooms, though but few bedchambers. Indeed, as in this climate no sleeping rooms are even tolerable unless they admit the Southern breeze,[3] there can be but few in any house. Accordingly that of Barrackpore barely accommodates Lord Amherst's family, and his Aides-de-Camp and visitors sleep in bungalows, built at some little distance from it in the park. ' Bungalow,' a

---

[1] There is a passage in the " Hastings Journal " which states that the house was to have been completed by April 1815, but was still unfinished when he came back from the Upper Provinces in October.

[2] " Diary," Vol. III, pp. 316-18.

[3] This cannot be said to apply to the cold weather, since I lived for the week-ends of seven seasons on the North side of the house, without recourse, except in the daytime, to a punkah.

corruption of Bengalee,[1] is the general name in this country for any structure in the cottage style, and only of one floor. Some of these are spacious and comfortable dwellings, generally with high thatched roofs, surrounded with a verandah, and containing three or four good apartments, with bath-rooms and dressing-rooms enclosed from the Eastern, Western, or Northern verandahs. The South is always left open." [2]

Miss Emma Roberts, who took a rather spiteful pleasure in recording anything unfavourable to the régime of Lord and Lady W. Bentinck, is our next witness (1835):

" Barrackpore is frequently resorted to by the chief person in the state, as a retreat from the toils of business and the scarcely less fatiguing duties entailed upon him at public entertainments. Few balls or fêtes of any kind are given at the Park, possibly to avoid the offence which the exclusion of visitors from Calcutta might give, and the great inconvenience resulting from their attendance. The last affair of the kind proved a complete failure, in consequence of an unexpected gale from the South West ; a contingency from which Bengal only for the short period of the cold season is altogether free. A very large proportion of the guests determined to go up by water, anticipating a delightful excursion by starlight ; but the horrors of the storm burst upon them ere they could reach their destination ; the Hoogly ran mountains high, washing over the decks of the frail little summer-vessels, and driving many on shore, to the consternation of the passengers and the utter ruin of their ball-dresses. The travellers by land were not better off : the horses took fright at the lightning ; the road was rendered impassable by trees torn up by the roots ; ladies, terrified out of their senses, made an attempt to walk, and the party, when collected at last, presented a most lugubrious spectacle, a concourse of wet, weary, miserable guests, eagerly impatient to return to their homes, yet compelled to await more favourable weather."

In the following year Lord Auckland and his two sisters arrived in India, and in March 1836 paid their first visit to Barrackpore. Their impressions were those of the normal visitor for the first time. The house is " a charming place," said one : it is " the perfection of comfort," said the other. There in the first year of their residence they spent every Thursday to Monday, dedicating the smaller half of the week to Calcutta. Later, as their brother's preoccupations grew, they often only managed a week-end at Barrackpore. But anyone who desires to form an idea of what the hot weather at Calcutta and Barrack-

---

[1] The generally accepted theory is that this type of house was first built in Bengal, and, when reproduced in other parts of the country, was known as *Bangala* or Bengal-style house.
[2] "Narrative of a Journey in India," Vol. I, p. 36.

pore can be, or at least was in those days, cannot do better than read
Miss Emily Eden's entertaining letters. After the experience of her
first summer, she sighs for the abortive palace of Lord Wellesley.

" It certainly was a shame to stop Lord Wellesley when he was running up
another good Government House at Barrackpore, and to stop the finish of this
provisional house.[1] As it is, there are no glass windows in the lower storey, and
I only wonder the servants can bear the heat so well as they do ; and then, as
there are no doors whatever to the interior of our part of the house[2]—nothing
but open jalousies—the hot wind comes hurtling upstairs and through all the
jalousies and spoils our comfort."[3]

Mention has been made by more than one of our authorities of the
bungalows in the grounds. Lord Valentia, who slept in one of them,
says that originally they belonged to the officers of the Cantonment
and were taken over with the Park. Victor Jacquemont, the French
Naturalist, who spent some time at Barrackpore as the guest of Lord
and Lady William Bentinck in 1829, was similarly accommodated, and
used to work there with great comfort in the morning.[4] Lord Minto's
comparison of them to Swiss cottages was an allusion to the thatch with
which they were originally roofed, and which remained until the time
of the first Lord Elgin, in 1863, when his Military Secretary, the late
Sir Seymour Blane, told me that he persuaded his Chief to pull down
the ancient buildings, which had become dilapidated, and to replace
them by *pukka* constructions—information which I find confirmed by
the entry of sums, amounting to Rs. 81.000 for this purpose, in the
accounts of 1863 and the two following years. The original thatched
bungalows, if Lord Valentia's picture is to be trusted, were not on the
site of their later successors, but were on the river bank in the neighbourhood of the present Government House.

Not the least of the many distinguished occupants of the bungalows
in Barrackpore grounds—for in olden days guests seem never to have
stayed in the house—was the Afghan exile Dost Mohammed, who spent
some days in one of them, as Lord Auckland's guest, in June 1841,
just before the awful disasters at Kabul. He made himself very agreeable, attended a ball given in his honour in Barrackpore House, sat to

[1] Miss Eden seems to have been unaware that it was completed by Lord Hastings.
[2] An omission long since rectified.
[3] " Letters from India," Vol. I, pp. 347-8.
[4] *Ibid.*, 1834, Vol. I, p. 279.

BARRACKPORE HOUSE (1856)

Miss Emily Eden for his picture, and was immensely taken with the giraffe in the Menagerie in the Park.

In Lord Canning's time we hear of the guests being fetched backwards and forwards between the bungalows and the house in *tonjons*, a form of palanquin or portable chair with a hood which was used by persons of station, and of which there is an illustration, with a red tasselled canopy, in one of Fraser's published drawings. Tommy Atkins converted this name with characteristic directness into Tom John.[1]   Lady Lytton was, I believe, the last châtelaine of Barrackpore House who used this form of conveyance, which had been replaced in my day by a *jinricsha* for ladies in the heat.   The old *tonions* were still to be seen in the basement at Barrackpore some years before my time, but, when I inquired for them, they had disappeared.

To revert to the narrative of the house and its occupants, Lord Dalhousie, like all his predecessors, succumbed at once to the charms of Barrackpore. Within three weeks of his arrival in Calcutta in February 1848, we find him writing to Sir George Couper :

" It is charming, and reconciles me to a residence in Bengal more than anything else has yet done.   The rooms are large but liveable, the furniture not smart, but not so scandalous and blackguard as that at the Government House ; a pretty pleasure ground, beautiful garden, an aviary, a menagerie, and all situated on the bank of the river, and surrounded by a park quite home-like in its character, and as English as anything can be, where you have banians and cocoanuts, and palms and mangoes, for oaks and elms, larch and beech." [2]

After his first hot weather he describes his life there :

" I spent Sunday, Monday, Tuesday and Wednesday at Barrackpore with Lady Dalhousie, went into Calcutta very early on Thursday morning, remained there Thursday, Friday and Saturday, and returned to the country on Saturday night ' at e'en.'   We used to have a dinner party of twenty-five at Barrackpore on Tuesdays, one of fifty at Calcutta on Fridays.   My Lady during the summer months had an evening dancing party once a month, and we had three very large balls at Calcutta, and one at Barrackpore."

What the hard-working Governor General thought of these functions leaks out in one of the Private Letters since published :

---

[1] The name *tonjon* must not be mistaken, as it often has been, for *jompon* (*anglice* John Pon), which is the *jampan* or portable chair of Upper India, a name to which has variously been ascribed a Malay, a Japanese, and a Kashmiri origin.
[2] " Private Letters " (ed. J. G. Baird), London, 1910, p. 21.

" They are irritably formal. It is a ' palace dinner ' ; and whether it be His Sacred Majesty that is host or His Honour the Governor of Heligoland, formality cannot be got rid of in such places. In short, my life is the concentrated essence of dullness socially at present."

We shall hear later what he had to say about the furniture.

While his wife was living, Lord Dalhousie spent many happy hours at Barrackpore. When she died at sea on her way home to England in 1853, he was so sore-stricken that for two years he never went near the spot, directing all his letters, when in Bengal, from Government House, Calcutta. At length on 20th November, 1854, he wrote to his friend Couper :

" Last week I went to Barrackpore for a day. It was a miserable visit. I had not been there for nearly two years. I spent there the last days of my happiness, and the contrast was truly wretched. However, as it is a more pleasant residence for most people than this town, I mean to take my daughter there,[1] and I wished to break myself into it. With her company I hope it may be different—without her I would not go again for half Bengal."[2]

Among other features of the Barrackpore of earlier days was the Menagerie in the Park. The memory of this had completely died out when I was in India, and people did not even know where the animal-houses had stood. But this is easily determined by maps ; and no visitor to the place in the first half of the last century, and even later, failed to dilate upon the Menagerie and its contents.

It seems to have been generally believed that the collection of animals was due to the whim of some early Governor General, assisted by the presents which Indian Chiefs are or were in the habit of making to the head of the Government. Such was not the way in which the Menagerie was founded, though it afterwards formed a principal source of its replenishment. As has been shown, it was one of the universal projects of Lord Wellesley. He had proposed to attach a Natural History Institution to his ill-fated College of Fort William, the original site of which was intended to be in Garden Reach. For this purpose a number of animals had been collected, and between the years 1800 and 1804 £350 was spent upon their upkeep. The College having been vetoed, the undefeated Governor General turned to Barrackpore ;

[1] Lady Susan Ramsay, afterwards Lady Connemara.
[2] " Private Letters," p. 330.

THE MENAGERIE IN BARRACKPORE PARK (1820)

and another lengthy Minute[1] recorded the appointment of Dr. Francis Buchanan to undertake the official study of the Natural History of India, and the creation of an establishment at Barrackpore " where the quadrupeds and birds which may be collected for Dr. Buchanan will be kept until they have been described and drawn." The civil and military offices in the Bengal Presidency were circularised and enjoined to assist the Medical Officers in procuring suitable specimens, and similar orders were issued to Madras, Bombay, Ceylon and the Straits Settlements. We have the figures of the monthly outlay that was sanctioned for the new establishment.

	Sicca Rupees
For the upkeep of quadrupeds and birds ...	500
For the painter	100
For the writer	40
For stationery and colours	60
For the collection of animals and birds	300
	Rs. 1,000

The greater part of these schemes came to nothing and perished when their author left India. But the Menagerie survived, and continued for three-quarters of a century to provide amusement to the Governor General's guests, and to figure in the pages of travellers.

When Mrs. Graham visited Barrackpore in 1810, it contained a pelican, a syrus or sarsa (a species of stork), a flamingo, an ostrich, a cassowary, a Java pigeon, as well as two tigers and two bears. Lady Nugent in 1914 noted among the inmates a black leopard and the ostrich. Between 1817 and 1819 a new aviary was constructed at a cost of Sicca Rupees 6.030, and in 1822 a new Menagerie—*i.e.* both in the time of Lord Hastings. These were on the North-east side of the Park, just inside the East gate leading from the Calcutta road, on a site to the North of where the Coachman's bungalow now stands. A passage in one of Lady Canning's letters had rather puzzled me—viz., that the water birds were living in her time " in Gothic arcades over tanks," until, in the published drawings of Sir Ch. D'Oyly, I found an illustration of the cages, etc., as they existed in his time, *circa* 1820-1830, when the animals seem to have been confined in structures

---

[1] " Dispatches," etc. (ed. Montgomery Martin), Vol. IV, p. 674.

partly of Gothic and partly of classical style. I reproduce the illustration here.

Our authorities already quoted keep us in touch with the growth or decline of the collection. Lord Amherst told Bishop Heber in 1823 that the Menagerie contained a *ghyal* or Tibetan bison and a South African ass in the park, while in cages were lynxes, tigers, leopards, bears, a porcupine, a kangaroo, monkeys, and mouse deer and birds. When Jacquemont visited it in 1829 the wild donkey, the two bears and a lynx, monkey, and ostrich were still there ; but the tiger, some African lions, and the cheetahs had been given away by the Governor General to some Rajas. A little later the French Naturalist reported that Lord W. Bentinck took no interest in the collection, which had sunk to two miserable bears, and that " Anglo-Indian society thought this the end of Empire." [1]

The true explanation is forthcoming in the narrative of Miss Emma Roberts, from which it appears that the disappearance of the Menagerie was a part of the policy of retrenchment being relentlessly pursued by Lord W. Bentinck with the approval of the Company.

" The present Government, too economical in its arrangements to sanction an expense of 500 Rupees per month, the cost of the establishment, gave away birds and beasts without remorse, and permitted the buildings to fall into decay." [2]

A swift reaction took place in the reign of Lord Auckland, whose sisters as well as himself took the liveliest interest in this miniature Zoo, which henceforth flourished greatly.

We find in Miss Eden's Letters repeated references to the Menagerie ; and in 1837 it is described as " quite full." Among its contents at that time were two rhinos, a tiger, two black bears, two cheetahs, a white monkey, three sloths, a baboon, and a giraffe, as well as any number of birds. Lord Auckland and his sisters even started a new aviary for some golden pheasants from China, making use of a sham ruin in the garden for the purpose.

Ten years later, in Lady Canning's time, we are introduced once more to all our old friends, the tigers, leopards, bears, ostriches, monkeys, rhino, and Dost Mohammed's giraffe. There were also a number of

---

[1] " Letters from India," Vol. I, pp. 171, 212.
[2] " Scenes and Characteristics of Hindostan," 3 Vols., 1835 : Vol. I, p. 130.

ELEPHANTS AND BODY GUARD IN BARRACKPORE PARK (1820)

water birds, white egrets, flamingos, China pigeons, *monal* pheasants, etc. But after that a period of decline ensued ; and my last news of the Menagerie is in the days of Lord Lytton, who, finding the residue of survivors more than miserable, followed an example already set by Lord Northbrook by handing them over to the Calcutta Zoo, which had been opened at Alipur a few years before (1874-1877) chiefly owing to the energy of Sir Richard Temple, then Lieutenant Governor of Bengal. The cages at Barrackpore were afterwards taken down.[1]

Mention of the Menagerie leads me by a natural transition to the elephants, which were also an inseparable feature of Barrackpore Park in olden times. A number of these animals, from eight to a dozen, the property of the Governor General, were always kept there for his personal use : and with their magnificent hangings of scarlet and gold were eagerly mounted by the guests, many of whom enjoyed their first elephant ride under these conditions. So did many a Governor General from Lord Cornwallis onwards, and so did our gossiping witnesses Mrs. Graham, Bishop Heber, M. Jacquemont (who prided himself that Lady W. Bentinck " seemed so pleased with our group on the top of this moving mountain that she never had any other companion but myself "), and Miss Roberts. The last-named, however, easily carries off the palm in the rhetorical competition :

" A large stud of elephants is kept at Barrackpore, and these noble animals, decorated with flowing *jhools* of scarlet cloth edged with gold, and bearing fair freight of ladies belonging to the Viceregal Court, may be seen pacing along the flowing labyrinths, to European eyes strange guests in a private garden. These blooming plantations afford excellent parrot-shooting—a sport to which some of the great men of the Presidency are said to be much addicted, but which it grieves persons possessed of the slightest degree of sentiment to see carried on in the secluded haunts of a pleasure-ground, and against those bright-winged visitants whose gem-like plumage adds so much of ornament to the scene." [2]

Lord Auckland and his sisters and their guests seem to have taken almost daily elephant rides at Barrackpore. Lord and Lady Canning sometimes indulged in the same amusement, if it can be so described ; and we can picture no prettier scene in the kaleidoscopic drama of which Barrackpore has been the stage than that of sweet Lady Canning and

[1] They consisted originally of four separate houses as well as a bear-pit and a giraffe stable.
[2] I never heard elsewhere of the parrot-shooting, and am glad to say that it was not practised at a ater time.

the war-seamed Sir Colin Campbell taking a ride together on an elephant in Barrackpore Park, in sheer delight at the news that had arrived that day (26th September, 1857) of the recapture of Delhi from the Mutineers.

In Sir Ch. D'Oyly's excellent " Views of Calcutta and Environs " is a coloured plate of the Governor General's party mounted on elephants in the Park at Barrackpore, and attended by the mounted Body Guard—a rather incongruous combination—as they must often have been seen in the second quarter of the 19th century.   It is reproduced here.

As a matter of fact the Barrackpore stud of elephants was only a fraction of the number assigned to the Governor General in days when they were the recognised method of locomotion, while on the march, in many parts of the country, and were also used for purposes of State ceremonial as well as of *shikar*.   In 1852 the Hatikhana of the Governor General consisted of one hundred and forty-six elephants.   Gradually, as travel by rail superseded marching, as the necessary display on State occasions was more suitably provided by imposing Cavalry escorts, and as the needs of *shikar* could be supplied locally, the stud was allowed to dwindle.   When Lord Dufferin arrived in 1885, there were still thirty-five elephants in the Hatikhana, though these were used for commercial purposes only.   In Lord Lansdowne's time the number of the Viceroy's stud had shrunk to three animals alone, one of which, said to have been ridden by Warren Hastings, one hundred and twenty years before, was drowned while crossing the Ganges.   Upon Lord Elgin's arrival only one survived : and as the cost of re-establishing the Hatikhana with tuskers, even on a modest scale, was estimated at two and a half lacs, or £16,000, it was decided to abolish it altogether. This was done in January 1895, when all the howdahs and equipment were sold by auction, with the exception of ten shooting howdahs which were retained and kept henceforward at Bareilly.   On the same occasion the great silver howdah which had been used on State occasions by the Viceroy was sent with the embroidered *jhools* to Viceregal Lodge at Simla, where they now adorn the Entrance Hall.

I may here add a few words about this Howdah.   Remembering the attacks that were made upon Lord Dalhousie for his order of a silver howdah to meet Gholab Singh of Jammu at Wazirabad in December 1850, and which he repelled in the following indignant terms :

BARRACKPORE HOUSE, NORTH FRONT (1870)

" The howdah of the Governor General was one of wood painted like a street cab, so that the very *mahout* was ashamed to sit in front of it. Accordingly one was ordered at Calcutta, and on this extravagance, amounting to £1,500 sterling, I am pilloried to the English public as fond of parade—silver howdahs and so forth—at the expense of the Company—" [1]

I used to wonder what had become of this structure, and whether any portion of it lingered in the successor at Simla. The emblematic and armorial adornments of the latter suggested that it was for the most part of later date ; but Messrs. Hamilton of Calcutta, who did the work to the order of Lord Northbrook in 1875, were of opinion, when I consulted them, that as their ledgers spoke of renovation, it was upon the framework or body of Lord Dalhousie's howdah that they had worked. That this was the case is conclusively proved by a passage in the " Life of Lord Dalhousie," where the howdah in which the Governor General rode to meet the Maharaja is described as having had upon it the two figures of Justice and Peace supporting the Imperial Crown. No doubt these were the figures that afterwards reappeared as or were transformed into the heathen goddesses.[2] I remember Lord Northbrook telling me, when I went out to India, that on the first occasion when he used this howdah in an elephant procession at Agra, the big Imperial Crown, perched on a cushion in front, kept wobbling to and fro, and, with every lurch of the elephant, threatened to tumble off. As the accompanying illustration shows, the howdah was a very handsome seat. On the front panel were silver figures of Ceres and Minerva chased in high relief, one on either side. In the centre of this panel, under the shaky Imperial Crown, were engraved the Star of India and the Chariot of Helios, in high relief. The Royal Arms were chased on the side panels, and in the border above the tasselled fringe the Rose, Shamrock, and Thistle were combined. The general effect produced by the silver-gilt reliefs on a background of burnished silver was very splendid. This howdah was used by the Prince of Wales (King Edward VII) on several occasions in 1875-6, and by Lord Lytton at the Imperial Assemblage at Delhi in 1877. Lady Curzon and I rode in it at the Delhi Durbar in 1903. Finding, however, that the figures of Ceres and Minerva, as originally modelled, were very coarse and ugly, both in design and shape, I had them melted down

---

[1] " Private Letters " (ed. J. G. Baird), p. 174.
[2] " Life of Lord Dalhousie," by Sir W. Lee Warner, Vol. I, p. 366.

and replaced by fresh and more artistic figures in 1902. There being no Elephant Procession in the present King's Durbar in 1911, the howdah was not then brought into use ; but it was occupied by Lord Hardinge when the attempt was made upon his life at Delhi in December 1912. On that occasion the bomb thrown at the Viceroy from the verandah or roof of a native house in the Chandni Chowk, as the Procession passed, struck the thick metal-plated stick of the State umbrella, which it broke, and then partly shattered the back panel of the Viceroy's seat, the stout woodwork and stuffing of which probably saved his life. The howdah has since gone back to its resting-place on the platform at Simla, and there, now that the old traditional form of Viceregal progression has wellnigh disappeared, it will tend to repose as a relic of a half-forgotten past, to be utilised merely as a sit-out retreat by dancing couples at the balls at Viceregal Lodge.

At the Durbar of 1st January, 1903—to celebrate the Coronation of King Edward VII—finding that, though I had the howdah, I had, as before explained, no elephant on which to place it, and ascertaining by enquiry that among the beasts still attached to the Army there was not a single tusker of suitable size or manners, I was driven to borrow from the Indian Princes, and the Maharajas of Jaipur and Benares supplied the splendid animals which headed the procession on that occasion. When the present King proclaimed his own Coronation at Delhi, in December 1911, he did not mount an elephant on that or any other State occasion.

Thus the decline and fall of this noble animal, which has played so large a part in the ceremonial history of the British Government in India, is complete ; and I have only interpolated this digression upon his progressive disappearance here, because the narrative may be held to possess some interest, and is not indirectly connected with Barrackpore, which was for so long his official headquarters.

It is true that the Radical Press in England, in their amiable desire to exaggerate the " show " of Viceroyalty in my day—though it did not differ in any respect from that fixed by long tradition, and practised equally by my predecessors and my successors—were fond of depicting me and my family as riding promiscuously and habitually on elephants in India. Fifty years earlier the harmless gibe would have been an accurate statement of fact. The modern Viceroy cannot, however, disport himself on an elephant, for the simple reason that he does

STATE HOWDAH

STATE HOWDAH

not possess such an animal. As a matter of fact, while in India I never mounted an elephant, whose gait I abominated, except for purposes of *shikar*, or where no other means of locomotion existed in distant parts of the country, and on the solitary occasion of the State entry at Delhi. But of course a daily elephant ride in full uniform suggested a scenic picture which no enterprising journalist could afford to despise.

In the first half of the 19th century we find records of another fashion that has similarly declined. More than once we hear of the Barrackpore jackal hunt, pursued with a pack of English hounds. This seems to have been a regimental institution. There are references to it in the times of the first Lord Minto and of Lord Amherst. At a later date the experiment was revived by Lord Herbrand Russell (now Duke of Bedford), when a member of Lord Dufferin's staff ; and by the late Lord Suffolk, when a member of my own. Barrackpore Park was certainly never deficient in the quarry, if one might judge from the diabolical howls that disturbed our slumbers at midnight, at any rate until we started a campaign of extirpation against these abominable pests.

The memory of another and nobler sport has been bequeathed to Barrackpore—for in a shady corner of the grounds rest the remains of a famous horse, the property of Lord William Beresford, Military Secretary to Lord Ripon and Lord Lansdowne, with an inscription to the effect that it twice won for him the Viceroy's Cup at Calcutta.

Miss Eden's Letters more than once mention the annual dragging of the big ponds in the Park for fish, and this was done too in my time. Probably the ponds are much more assiduously fished now than in former days, and the capture is therefore less ; but the nets brought up a very considerable spoil.

I will deal with the Gardens a little later on. But I may here revert to the bungalows as they existed in my time. These single-storey whitewashed residences, the earlier history of which I have previously described, were then known, and had been for years, as the Flag Staff Bungalow (from its proximity to the Flag Staff on the river bank), usually occupied by the Private Secretary ; Bungalows Nos. 1 and 2 ; and the Military Secretary's Bungalow. The three last named are situated a little to the North of Government House, and the third has obtained the popular local sobriquet of Honeymoon Hall, owing to the frequency with which it has been lent by successive Viceroys for that purpose. I remember on one occasion seeing one of my guests, then an official of the highest rank, wander away in a pensive vein in the direction of this bungalow, and on my subsequently enquiring the reason, I learned that he was revisiting for the first time the abode which had played so important a part in his own life over thirty years before.[1] Close to the Flag Staff Bungalow still stands one of the tall masonry towers which were erected as semaphore stations for the use of the Governor General, at intervals of eight miles along the Great Trunk Road from Calcutta, between 1820 and 1830. They were intended to be erected the entire distance to Bombay, but I believe never got beyond the Hugli district of Lower Bengal. A little later the electric telegraph took their place.

So far, I have said little about the interior of Barrackpore, because there was little to be said. When Government House at Calcutta was as ill-furnished as I have shown it to be, in the earlier and middle parts of the last century, it was not likely that Barrackpore, which was only regarded as a country villa, and had for long, as we have seen, neither glass windows nor interior doors, would fare much better at the hands of a body who looked so closely to economy as the Directors of the East India Company.

A frequent but futile growl was heard from the lady occupants ; as, for instance, when Miss Emily Eden in her first season (1836) complained that " the house is in a wretched state, the sofas are wretchedly hard. The furniture is worse than that of any London hotel." Nor was it any better when she left. " Barrackpore is altogether in a ramshackle state ; and it will be better for the next Governor General not to try any repairs ; . . . and if it tumbles down, he can build himself a house with good doors and windows."

Miss Eden was not far wrong in her forecast of what some future tenant would think and say. After the two short reigns of Lord Ellenborough and Lord Hardinge, Lord Dalhousie appeared upon the scene, and, as we have seen, was a frequent resident at Barrackpore. He did not waste much time in forming an opinion about its internal equipment ; and when his Furniture Committee turned their attention to this house they dealt with it in a manner that was worthy of their master. I take the following from their Report :

[1] In the " Life and Letters of Macaulay," Vol. I, p. 396, it is mentioned that his sister Hannah, who married young Trevelyan in 1835, was another of these happy guests.

GOTHIC RUIN IN BARRACKPORE GARDEN (c. 1870)

" The entrance to the house is from the North, and at the head of the stair-case is a landing-place, out of which opens the central and principal apartment, used now as a drawing-room, which is of very noble proportions. To the East of this room is the dining-room, and beyond this latter a billiard-room.[1] On the West side, corresponding with these in size, are the private apartments : and to the South and North of these sides are the bedrooms and dressing-rooms. The house is not well constructed for ventilation, and the accommodation in it is not more than sufficient for the Governor General himself, and one or two guests ; so that the staff reside principally in bungalows adjoining the house, of which there are three of the better sort, and another called the flag-staff bungalow, which is in reality a substantial brick-built lower-roomed house, reserved for the use of the Governor General's guests.

" The only room in the house which needs to be furnished as a reception-room is the large central apartment we have described. It may be enough to say that the furniture of this room, though all possible pains have been taken to make it appear to the best advantage, is more below what should be the standard for the drawing-room of the Governor General's country house than the furniture of the drawing-room of the Calcutta house is below its proper standard. Some of the principal articles require to be concealed with covers to avoid exciting ridicule. One of these, a round table, we are thoroughly convinced, would not realise three Rupees at auction if sold to-morrow, and many of the other things are little better. We submit that it cannot be right to furnish a Governor General's house in this style.

" The lighting of this really magnificent apartment is by three small chandeliers of the same poor pattern as those in Calcutta. Corner lights on pedestals have been added ; but it is necessary still to retain the original very unsightly wall-shades. We believe that it is now many years since such things have been seen in any other house. Provision for handsomely lighting this hand-some room is, we are of opinion, indispensably necessary.

" The dining-room has no dining-table belonging to it ; a set of camp-tables are used for dining upon. These are the camp-tables that have served the Governor General in his recent tour in the Punjab and the North-Western Provinces, and have been brought down from as far as Peshawur, bearing, of course, many visible marks of the unavoidable damage incident to so long a journey. The table service is no better than the table. It consists princi-pally of the camp equipage of the Governor General. The chairs are much the same as those in the drawing-room ; the lighting is worse.

" The private rooms occupied by the Governor General are fitted with a few articles of modern furniture, recently purchased, plain in their character, but of good quality.

" The furniture of the rest of the bedrooms and sitting-rooms is so very bad that we are at a loss properly to describe its character, so as to convey a

---

[1] In later times this was used as a Serving Room, and the billiard table was placed in the room beyond the big drawing-room, and opening on to the North verandah.

true idea of it to persons who have not seen it. None of the articles in any room match with each other; they are all very old, and many of them are hardly serviceable. We are sure that, as a whole, nothing so bad can be found in the residence of any private gentleman of but moderate means in Calcutta."

These very caustic remarks in nowise exaggerated the facts, for they are borne out by the almost contemporaneous testimony of an article in the " Calcutta Review" (1845):

" The house is also remarkable for its antique furniture, which continues to resist all the innovations of modern taste. The side sofas of the plainest form, the chairs, the marble tables with their antiquated legs, the long mirrors in old-fashioned frames, and even the chandeliers, remain unaltered after the lapse of more than thirty years (i.e. since put in by Lord Hastings). In one of the side drawing-rooms is to be seen almost the last specimen of the single-branch wall-shade, which the progress of improvement has long since banished from all other houses. That primitive wall-shade, with its still more primitive bracket, was to be seen in the house in the days of Lord Minto, and while the new men of only twenty years' standing in the service regard it as an emblem of the shabbiness of the Court of Directors, who are deaf to all entreaties for new and more respectable furniture, there are others who can gaze on it with the deepest antiquarian interest."

The tables, the mirrors, and the primitive wall-shade were all there in my time, more than half a century later, invested, if not with a still dwindling respectability, at any rate with increasing antiquarian interest. Perhaps I owed them to the fact that none of my predecessors had been given the money, or had found the inclination, to renovate the interior of Barrackpore. We made it as comfortable as we could with the existing resources, and with a few modern arm-chairs; and left it to our successors, the later Lord and Lady Minto, to move forward where we had stood still.

Lord Dalhousie had set an example of like reserve, for in his Memorandum, following upon the Report of his Furniture Committee, he said that he proposed to postpone dealing with Barrackpore till Government House, Calcutta, had been completely equipped. Nor do I think that he can have done much (although no doubt the camp furniture did not survive the invective of the Committee), because we find Lady Canning at the commencement of her reign describing Barrackpore as a délabré villa, and writing thus to Lady Sydney:

THE BANYAN TREE, BARRACKPORE (1870)

" I am rather miserable at this exceedingly ill *monté* house ; the dinner, with its cotton tablecloth and Bohemian glass and candlesticks, looks exactly like a *table d'hôte*. . . . Lord Dalhousie furnished a long room where we dine, and it is handsomely done, though with red damask and velvet-pile carpet ! "

She subsequently explained that with the aid of 450 yards of rose chintz, and a considerable addition of arm-chairs, small tables, framed drawings, and flower pots, she had made the house " look rather nice even as an English country house." [1]   That is the highest standard to which Barrackpore had ever until my time aspired to rise ; although Lord Minto, by installing the electric light with ormolu sconces, laying a teak floor in the principal room, collecting a good deal of old furniture, and redecorating the entire house, subsequently brought the interior to a level which must have made our predecessors sigh with envy in their graves.   Since the place, however, ceased to be occupied by the Viceroy, there has been a lamentable relapse ; and I learn that in 1918-19 the whole of the furniture was removed to Belvedere, when the Governor General took over that residence in exchange for Barrackpore.   The latter is therefore once more a shell.

In my chapter on Government House, Calcutta, I have mentioned that the Mysore series of oil paintings by T. Hickey hung originally at Barrackpore, but were moved to the capital by Lord Dufferin.   A statement in the 'Calcutta Review' of 1845 that there were excellent portraits of the Royal Family of Oude by Home at Barrackpore is apparently a confusion with Hickey's Mysore paintings.   Elsewhere I have seen the Barrackpore paintings described as those of " some Pindaree Chieftains."

The departmental records of Barrackpore Government House are not very full or illuminating, and they relate to the exterior rather than to the interior.   After Lord Hastings had completed the building, but few alterations were made to it by his successors.   Lord Auckland added the verandah on the Western side, and Lord Lytton the exterior staircase on the South or river front, replacing a mean iron staircase that had previously existed there.   Lady Lytton made a number of internal improvements ; but fresh chintz has been the main contribution of successive occupants, from Lady Canning onwards.

It is the Garden, much more than the interior, that has absorbed

---

[1] " Story of Two Noble Lives," Vol. II, pp. 63, 99.

the attention and inspired the taste of Viceroys or their wives ; and its gradual evolution to its extraordinary beauty and charm as I knew them was the result of many activities, perhaps chiefly those of Lady Canning, who lies not unfitly buried at the threshold of the place she loved so well. Of Lady Hastings' vanished Green House I have spoken. Lord Auckland and his sisters converted an old thatched bungalow in the Flower Garden into a plant and seed house, which still exists, and Miss Eden planted a flower garden.

Lord Ellenborough laid out the broad terrace walk that runs along the old river bank from the lower landing-stage to the house. Lady Canning constructed the raised walk leading straight down from the South front of the house to the main landing-stage, and planted poinsettias along it and placed a stone bench at the end, and she also made the terrace and pillared balustrade round the small Italian Garden on the same side, and planted the bamboos and the blue convolvulus behind it.

I had never seen any explanation of the inlaid marble basin and fountain that adorns this Garden. But I had very little doubt that it must have been brought down from Agra, and that it once adorned a palace of the Great Moghul ; and in the course of my reading I subsequently found a clue in the following passage in the Private Journal of Lord Hastings—brought out by his daughter Lady Bute in 1858. Lord Hastings visited Agra in February 1815, and, although he left orders for works of general repair to be carried out both at Sikandra and at the Taj, he did not shrink from ordering the removal of the marble fittings of the Royal baths in the Palace in the Fort :

" I directed the marble of this Chamber, as *well as the white marble basin of a fountain*, which I found in the artillery yard, full of all kinds of lumber, to be raised and shipped for Calcutta, where they may somehow or other be employed as ornaments to the city." [1]

I was unable to discover any of these trophies in Calcutta ; but I feel tolerably sure that the white marble basin found a resting-place in the Governor General's own Garden at Barrackpore, and that it is the trophy to which I have referred.

Lady Canning also opened out the big banian-tree (previously closed in by shrubs) which lends so much beauty to the Garden,

[1] " Private Journal of the Marquess of Hastings," Vol. II, p. 20.

BAMBOO AVENUE AT BARRACKPORE (1904)

providing as it does an open-air sitting-room and dining-room combined, that can be used either in the heat of the day or at night, ready decorated by the creepers and orchids that hang in festoons from its pillared arcades.

During the twenty-five years before I was in India, a new feature had arisen, owing to the marked inclination of the main current of the Hugli River to swing over to the right or Serampore bank, thus receding from the Barrackpore shore, and gradually forming below it a broad alluvial belt which, as it solidified and became coated with grass, was converted into a rich meadow. The maps of the first half of the 19th century show that the Flag Staff Ghat, higher up than Government House, was then in regular use. Lady Canning, as we have seen, made the ghat immediately fronting the house, across the alluvial meadow, then only fifty yards in width.

Lady Ripon planted this *bund* or raised road with the bamboo avenue or *berceau* that now converts it into a tunnel of green shade, and Lord Dufferin commemorated her achievement by a stone with an inscription, still to be seen. But in 1888-9, owing to the receding of the channel, a new landing-stage had to be made with a constantly extending pontoon, six hundred yards lower down, and from this point the second Lord Elgin in 1894 planted another bamboo avenue or tunnel below Lord Ellenborough's terrace, inside which the scorching walk to or from the boat could be accomplished with comfort in the hottest sunshine. This avenue, however, was cut down by Lord Minto, because it was thought to obscure the view.

In my last year, 1904-5, the main channel of the Hugli showed signs of returning to the left bank, and we succeeded in using once again the landing-place of Lady Canning and the avenue of Lady Ripon.

But the retirement of the river enabled me to plan an improvement of a more important nature. The broad belt of foreshore, over one hundred yards in width, that had gradually accumulated between the upper and the lower landing-stages, and which we used for a time as a polo ground, had acquired sufficient consistency to admit of being treated as an additional garden.[1]

I drew the plans which were to convert this place into a great stretch

---

[1] Fifty years earlier we read of it as entirely covered by the river at high tides, when it was converted into a broad and placid lake.

of sward with broad gravelled walks and patterned flower-beds, and a pool and fountain in the centre. This scheme, owing to the fear of floods, was abandoned by my successor.

A rosary seems to have been one of Lady Ripon's happy legacies to Barrackpore, and anyone who saw the way in which roses flourished in that rich soil would have understood why it was that between 1899 and 1905 we greatly developed this feature of the Garden, converting the entire vegetable garden (as marked in earlier plans) into a nursery for roses, whence we could at any moment transport the 3,000 blooms that were required for the decoration of Government House on the occasion of a State Ball at Calcutta. These improvements owed a great deal to the energy and taste of my Military Secretary, Colonel Everard Baring. They were greatly extended by Lord and Lady Minto, who added many beds and pergolas, and a stone basin with a fountain.

A further improvement effected in my time was the draining and turfing of the dried bottom of the long tank between the North front of Barrackpore House and the Cantonment Church, known as the Moti Jheel, a prolific breeding-ground of mosquitoes and malaria for the inhabitants of the neighbouring bungalows. This *jheel* was still further filled up by Lord Minto. There was one improvement, however, which, strongly as it was recommended to me, I did not make. Among the many amusing letters from native correspondents which fill the Viceroy's postbag, I received none more original than this:

" Your Excellency,
" The following humble petition most respectfully sheweth that the following matter has for a long time eluded the attention of the Government officials. That a place very near to Barrackpore Park may be used as a wonderful water park suggested by your humble petitioner. That the place being bounded on three sides by the river Hooghly is most beautifully situated, and the fittest place for making the wonderful plan. That it can be isolated from the land by cutting a canal only on one side of it and converted into a beautiful little island. That it will be the most soothing place for Your Excellency's most purious brain which is cardenshal with the cares of so vast an Empire, is the conviction of your humble servant. I am waiting for your kind notice because I hope to see the year 1900 as the era of this memorable event."

Alas, 1900 has long gone by, and the waterpark has never been made, and no longer does the Viceroy's purious brain require any such solace, that official having deserted Barrackpore altogether.

TEMPLE OF FAME AT BARRACKPORE

In addition to the staff bungalows and the numerous smaller houses for bandmaster, cook, guards, and other attendants, that are strewn about the grounds, the visitor will notice in the Garden or Park of Barrackpore House three other structures of which something must be said. The first of these is a small but decorative white plastered building in the design of a Greek temple, with portico and pillars, standing above the old river bank between Government House and the Flag Staff Bungalow. This edifice, which has been variously described as the Temple of Fame, the Cenotaph, and the Memorial Hall, and contains on its façade a dedication

TO THE MEMORY OF THE BRAVE

was erected by the first Lord Minto in commemoration of 24 officers who had fallen in the conquest of Java and the Isle of France (Mauritius) in the years 1810 and 1811, and whose names are inscribed upon tablets affixed to the walls. The building is entirely empty save for the marble tablets containing the names and inscriptions that adorn the walls. To them in 1844 Lord Ellenborough added a tablet with an inscription and the names of nine officers who had fallen at Maharajpore and Punniar in the previous year. There never seemed to me to have been any point in erecting this military monument in the private grounds of the Governor General, where its existence is unseen and almost unknown, and since Lord Ellenborough's day no attempt has been made to add to its contents. I am told that it is now used by the military authorities as a mess.

The second structure is the pathetic monument erected over the remains of Lady Canning, the gifted wife of that sorely tried statesman. She died in Calcutta, at the early age of forty-four, on 18th November, 1861, of malarial fever, caught while passing through the fever-haunted Terai on her return from a visit to Darjeeling. The Viceroy decided to bury her at Barrackpore, which she had loved so dearly, and for the beautifying of which she had done so much, and to enclose a sufficient space of ground (seventy yards by thirty) for the use of his successors. Fortunately none of them has found occasion to take advantage of it, and its inauguration remains a unique, as it is assuredly the most tragic, episode in the history of Barrackpore.

Lady Canning had died at Government House, Calcutta ; and there at midnight on the day of her death the four A.D.C.s of the Viceroy, one of whom long afterwards told me the tale, lifted her body into the coffin, which was carried on a gun-carriage, drawn by six black horses, to Barrackpore in the dead of the Indian night.   In the breaking dawn of the next morning, while the full moon was setting in one quarter of the heavens, and the first rays of the sun struggled up the Eastern sky and faintly flushed the silent stream, the body was carried down the terrace walk from Government House on the shoulders of twelve English soldiers, the A.D.C.s holding the fringe of the pall.   Lord Canning walked immediately after, the stricken figure of a doomed man ; eleven persons only were present at the ceremony, which was conducted by the Archdeacon of Calcutta.   A solid masonry vault had been constructed by Captain (afterwards Sir Henry) Yule, Secretary of the Public Works Department, by the side of the terrace walk, at a spot where Lady Canning had loved to sit ; and there the body of this beautiful and ill-fated woman was laid to rest.   The afflicted husband walked back alone after the ceremony and locked himself indoors for the entire day.   Every morning at dawn and also in the darkness of the night he would be found at the graveside, where a light was kept burning.   Three days later he poured forth the anguish of his soul in the following tribute, subsequently carved upon the headstone of the grave :

" Honours and praises written on a tomb are at best a vain glory ; but that her charity, humility, meekness, and watchful faith in her Saviour will, for that Saviour's sake, be accepted of God, and be to her a glory everlasting, is the firm trust of those who knew her best, and most dearly loved her in life, and who cherish the memory of her, departed.   Sacred to the Memory of Charlotte Elizabeth, eldest daughter of Lord Stuart De Rothsay, wife of Charles John, Viscount and Earl Canning, first Viceroy of India.   Born at Paris 31st March 1817.   Died at Calcutta 18th November 1861."

By the time that these words were chiselled upon the tombstone the hand that had penned them was also cold in death ; and to the inscription of the bereaved husband had to be added the postscript :

" The above words were written on the 22nd November 1861 by Earl Canning, who survived his wife but seven months.   He left India on the 18th March, died in London on the 17th June, aged forty-nine, and was buried in Westminster Abbey on the 21st June 1862."

TOMB OF LADY CANNING AT BARRACKPORE

The enclosure of the tomb was protected by an iron railing, formed of the intertwined initials of Lady Canning (C.C), at the cost of the Government of India, and in March 1862, a few days before the widowed husband sailed for England, and only three months before his own death, the ground was consecrated in his presence by Bishop Cotton. But the monument originally erected, which was designed by Lady Canning's gifted sister, Louisa Lady Waterford, and consisted of an immense marble platform ornamented with inlaid mosaic in the Agra fashion, and with a headstone rising at one end, was found to suffer so badly from the monsoon rains that some years later there was a talk of sheltering it with a canopy of timber or stone.

This idea, however, was abandoned, and in 1873 the original monument was transferred by Lord Northbrook, with the assent of the family, to the Cathedral at Calcutta, in the Southern transept of which it stood till 1913. A simpler reproduction without the inlaid work, but with the same inscription, was erected above the grave, and this is the tomb which the visitor passes on every occasion that he walks to or from the lower landing-stage at Barrackpore. The story has obtained currency in some quarters that the body was afterwards removed to this country. But such was not the case, and by the side of the mighty Ganges, in a distant land, far removed from her husband and her people, Charlotte Canning sleeps her last sleep.

In 1913 the cenotaph made a further migration. For the Cathedral authorities, finding that its great size blocked the South transept, which they desired to use as a chapel, obtained the permission of the representatives of Lord Canning's family to move it yet once more, and it was shifted to the North portico of St. John's Church (the earlier Cathedral Church), where it now stands in the verandah.

The third building to which I referred, but little noticed in comparison with the two memorials above described, is a native village school at the Southern extremity of the Park, known as the Eden school, because of its foundation by Lord Auckland at his own expense in 1836. His sister's letters are full of allusions to this scheme.

I mention it here, because the school was supposed to be under the special patronage of the Viceroy, who once during his term of office entertained the boys in the grounds of Government House, and distributed the prizes to them with or without the allocation that is customary on such occasions, and not a word of which in all probability did his youthful hearers understand.

An earlier Governor General's wife had made a similar experiment, for we read in Lord Hastings' Private Journal[1] that a native school was founded at Barrackpore by Lady Hastings for eighty native boys and sixteen European and Eurasian girls, and that she prepared for them a textbook of moral precepts and stories translated into Bengali and Hindustani. As Lord Auckland and his sister had to begin again, I can only conclude that Lady Hastings' venture had met the fate of so many Viceregal undertakings.

Very little has been said, so far, of the Park at Barrackpore. Originally there seems to have been little or no distinction between the Park and Gardens; but as the public were increasingly admitted to the former and as the cultivation of the latter developed, so did they gradually acquire in some measure a separate existence, although in parts there was no boundary line between the two, and roads to which the public were admitted ran through both. The first Lord Elgin complained (1862) that there was only one private walk left to him, namely that along the river bank to Lady Canning's grave, and that the whole of the Garden as well as the Park was open to the public. At some subsequent period the Viceregal ownership was more definitely reasserted: and during the last half-century the process has been one of progressive concessions of successive Viceroys to the convenience either of the Cantonment or of the public. Lord Lytton lent the Viceregal Band Barracks as a Library and Reading Room to the Barrackpore Club in 1878, and this loan was continued by each of his successors. At a later date the members of the Club were permitted to make, and to keep up, lawn-tennis courts in the Viceregal grounds. In 1891 Lord Lansdowne gave leave to the Barrackpore Golf Club to establish links and play in the Park, with certain reservations as to hours when the Viceroy was in residence at the week-end; and one of the bungalows in the Grounds was always lent to the Club members during the summer months. Picnic parties were also freely admitted to the Park, where a bandstand was erected, and leave was readily given to fish in the tanks. In the summer months, when the Viceroy was away, both Gardens and Park were open without restriction to the public, this being in practice a reversion to the old custom. It gave me pleasure, as it had done

[1] Vol. II, p. 156.

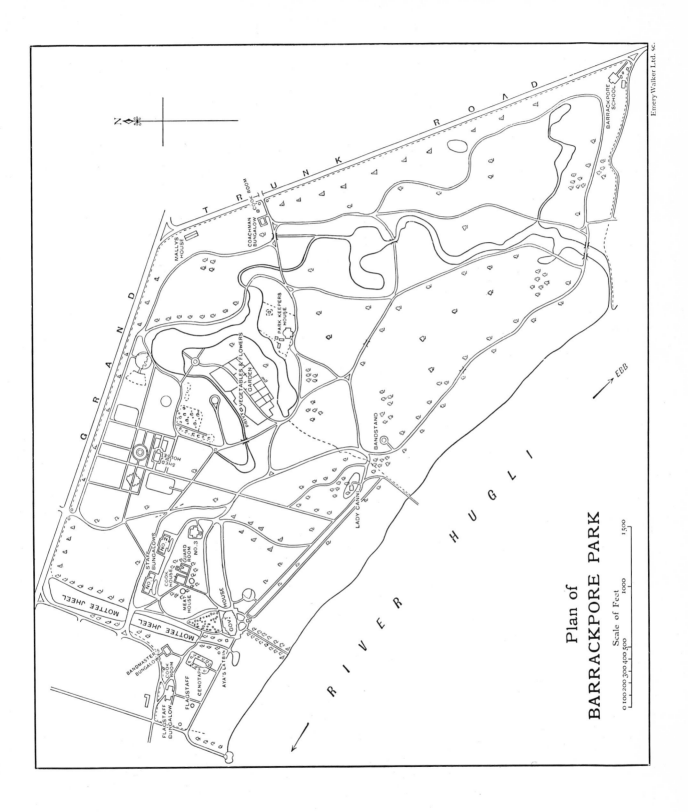

Plan of
BARRACKPORE PARK
Scale of Feet

0 100 200 300 400 500   1000   1,500

Emery Walker Ltd. sc.

to my predecessors, to extend the privileges already in existence. On the other hand, owing to the great increase in motor traffic, Lord Minto was obliged rigorously to exclude the public from the Inner Park when he was in residence. At Barrackpore, as elsewhere, there were occasionally some who, from ignorance of the above conditions, would advance public pretensions to what was clearly established to be private property, and in old files I came across heated correspondence between the Cantonment Magistrate, who generally posed as the local Tribune of the People, and the Military Secretary to the Viceroy or the Public Works official of the time. The rights of Government had, however, not merely been laid down by the highest legal authority, but were effectually demonstrated by the closing of the gates at night and whenever the Viceroy ordered, and by other regulations as to riding, driving, landing from the river, and the admission of dogs. The public in general were very sensible of the advantages conceded to them and very considerate in their use, and with tactful administration no difficulties need ever be encountered.

I have said nothing about the trees in the Park and Grounds, because it would require a knowledge that I do not possess to describe the many varieties. An attempt was made in the Park to give the appearance of an English landscape, and a good many English trees were planted. But the staple trees are the mahogany and the mango, the abundant fruit of which was sold annually by auction, the tamarind, the india-rubber, and the teak. Cattle were grazed here and a dairy established, as far back as 1869, for the convenience of Government House, Calcutta.

Certainly the Park is very beautiful, and with its broad stretches of grass and its bold clumps of timber and occasional lakes is unlike anything else in India, or indeed in Asia. But the Gardens with their profusion of indigenous verdure and trees with blossom of every hue are more beautiful still, and resemble a tropical Kew. Beautiful too is the view down the river to the fantastic pinnacles of Tittaghur, or across the water to the ruined pagoda of the inspired Henry Martyn—which I had pleasure in restoring—and the white houses of the old Danish settlement of Serampore, embosomed in verdure and crowned by the spire of the Church to which Lord Wellesley contributed Rs. 10,000—though it was then the property of a foreign Government, and the shrine of a non-Anglican creed—because, as he is reported to have said, " nothing was wanting to Barrackpore Park but the distant view of a steeple."

I cannot help regarding it as a pity that, in the change of circumstances brought about by the transfer of the capital to Delhi, Barrackpore has not been retained as a residence for the Viceroy, to which he could come from time to time, on the occasion of his visits to Calcutta, and where he could reside in his own house and entertain Calcutta society at his own expense. Such an idea was contemplated for a time ; but a little later the house and park were handed over to the Government of Bengal, by whom the cost of upkeep is now borne, and who regard it technically as a Circuit House for their chief officials, though in practice it is treated as a Government House which is reserved for the Governor alone. The Viceroy, as has been seen during his winter visits to Calcutta, is now accommodated in the former residence of the Lieutenant Governor of Bengal at Belvedere.

During its century and more of official existence, Barrackpore has witnessed many scenes, apart from those already described, which deserve a passing notice in these recollections. Hither, from Serampore opposite, used to come the Baptist missionaries, Carey and Marshman and Ward, to enjoy the hospitality of the Governor General's table. Here on 3rd January, 1812, the first Lord Minto, separated from his wife throughout the seven years of his Governor Generalship, and destined never to see her again, gave a ball and supper on the anniversary of his wedding day to seven hundred guests. Here on 27th December, 1823, Bishop Heber preached in the large saloon or centre room of Government House, because at that date there was no church at Barrackpore, and in this apartment services were constantly held until the church was completed and consecrated in 1847.[1] Here, in the Journal of the Frenchman Jacquemont, we get a pretty picture of the domestic life of Lord and Lady William Bentinck—work in the morning, lunch at 2, a talk or drive or an elephant ride afterwards, music after dinner, and bed at 10.30 p.m.

But undoubtedly its most dramatic moment was in 1824, when three native regiments were ordered from Barrackpore Cantonment to the war in Burma, and mutinied from dread of the Burmese climate, and caste prejudice against crossing the sea. On this occasion the

[1] More than one Governor General have been among its benefactors. Lord Ellenborough presented the font, and Lord Dalhousie contributed half the cost of the organ, which was afterwards removed.

BARRACKPORE HOUSE, NORTH FRONT (1903)

Governor General and his wife (Lord and Lady Amherst) and the Commander-in-Chief, Sir E. Paget, who had hurried up from Calcutta to quell the revolt (and was much censured at the time for his management of the affair),[1] were within an ace of being captured by the mutineers, and might easily have experienced this fate had the latter known their strength. I need say nothing here about the incidents of the mutiny, which was crushed by the firing of the artillery (brought to Barrackpore Park from Dum Dum) upon the rebellious troops, who scattered and fled, and whose ringleaders were forthwith arrested and hanged ; but will confine myself to the experience of the Governor General and his wife, narrated by the latter in a letter which was afterwards published.[2]

" Before the troops arrived on the 1st (November) at Barrackpore, we were for twenty-four hours in great danger and entirely at the mercy of the mutineers. Had they had any clever head among them, and seized the Governor General and the Commander-in-Chief, they might probably have made their own terms. There was not a single European or person to be depended upon, and our situation was awfully alarming. Lord Amherst resolved not to leave the house, and I determined not to quit him. Sarah behaved heroically, and, though ill, declared she would remain, and kept up her spirits, as we all did as well as we could.

" The Commander-in-Chief returned his thanks to us both for not quitting the house ; but it was a frightful scene—English soldiers firing on British uniforms, pursuing them in all directions ; some of our servants were wounded. We fortunately did not know at the moment that the night the mutiny broke out all the sentries in and about the house belonged to the 47th. The scene of action was not a quarter of a mile from the house. Many shots entered the cook-house, and many fell into the water under our windows, and we saw great numbers trying to swim the Ganges.[3] Few reached the opposite shore from the strength of the current.

" Twenty or thirty dead bodies were seen floating down of these unhappy people. The different regiments of British troops remained at Barrackpore about a week, after which the native regiments marched quietly to the Eastern frontier, and the British troops returned to their destination. The English regiments encamped in the Park, as also the artillery and the bodyguard. Had any cause brought them there but the actual one, we should have enjoyed this beautiful encampment and scenery exceedingly."

---

[1] *Vide* " Life of Sir Henry Lawrence," by Sir H. Edwards and H. Merivale, Vol. I, p. 59.
[2] " Lord Amherst " (Rulers of India Series), pp. 150-153.
[3] The Hugli is, of course, one of the mouths of the Ganges, though the main stream has now shifted far to the East.

To Lord and Lady Amherst Barrackpore was the scene of a tragedy greater than that of the abortive mutiny, even though the latter as nearly as possible brought about the recall of the Governor General, in consequence of the angry suspicions of the Court of Directors at home. For here their eldest son, Jeffry, always referred to in his mother's letters as Jeff, a young officer of the utmost promise, who had acted as Military Secretary to his father, and had borne an honourable part in the siege and capture of the great fortress at Bhurtpore, was taken ill and died. From Lady Amherst's Diary for July 1826 we cull the following :

" On the 25th, Lord Amherst, Jeff, and Mr. Hale all ill from what is called epidemic fever, which in general only lasts three days. Jeff recovered for a day, but had a relapse ; he was able to come to Barrackpur. How can I express all our bitter pangs ! Another severe relapse seized our beloved boy on the evening of the 30th, although I had seen him an hour before apparently in high health and spirits. We had all gone on board his pinnace and sat an hour or two with him at Barrackpur. Not long after we landed I received two notes from him, pressing me to send him medicine as his fever was coming on again. We got him ashore as soon as possible, violently and dangerously ill, which illness continued with little or no intermission until a quarter past nine in the morning of August 2nd, when his pulse which had been sinking for the last twelve hours stopped, and he expired with the same placid heavenly smile on his countenance I had been used to see. . . . During his illness he never once complained, and his answer to enquiries was, ' I am very comfortable, I am quite well.' . . . His calm and sweet temper and very warm heart had endeared him to every member of society. . . . Had it pleased God to have spared his life till the 29th, he would have completed his twenty-fourth year. On August 3rd at break of day our dearly beloved son was interred in the burial-ground at Barrackpur with military honours." [1]

There he rests in the Station Cemetery, one more item in the heavy toll which has to be paid by those who give their lives to service in India, that land of sacrifice no less than of glory.

Mutiny would seem to have been indigenous in the atmosphere of Barrackpore, for in 1852, when preparations were being made by Lord Dalhousie for the Burmese Expedition, it was only by a hair's breadth, and that by a display of misplaced lenience, that a similar outbreak was prevented on the part of a Native Regiment that declined to proceed by sea. Five years later it was the men of the same Regiment

[1] " Lord Amherst " (Rulers of India Series), pp. 161-2.

BARRACKPORE HOUSE, SOUTH FRONT (1903)

(the 38th Infantry) who refused to fire on the mutineers at the Kashmir Gate of Delhi. [1]

Barrackpore was also the first scene in the Mutiny of 1857, the famous incident of Mungul Pandy and the heroic conduct of General Hearsey having been enacted on the Parade Ground in the Cantonment. But as these are narrated in every history of that great tragedy, and as they do not concern Government House or its inmates, except in so far as the weakness of Lord Canning contributed to the dénouement, I shall not describe them here.

Since that date peace has settled down upon the scene, and I am not aware of any storm that afterwards ruffled the tranquil surface of Viceregal existence at Barrackpore.

In later days the charm of the place to an overworked man lay not merely in the enjoyment of its restful beauties—though rest there was little, my sojourns at Barrackpore being days of accumulated arrears and unending files—but in the journeys up and down the river in the twilight of a Saturday evening, or in the dewy radiance of a Monday morning. Motors had not yet invaded Calcutta, and a small steam launch was the means of transport. [2] To leave the city in the late afternoon and, after tea on the deck, to lie in a lounge chair and watch the changing panorama of the river banks as they flew by—the thick fringe of the vegetation and the feathery palm-tops ; the smoke of the native villages ; the white-clad figures moving up and down the dilapidated ghats ; the glare of the electric light suddenly switched on in some great jute mill, from which the throb of the engines hurtled across the water ; the vast bulk of some huge flat, laden with tea or jute from the interior, sliding noiselessly down the full current ; the peeping white fronts of villas, once the garden houses of Europeans, but now deserted by them ; the rows of crumbling Hindu shrines on the river's edge, or the fantastic towers of some pagoda silhouetted against the sky ; on the one side the gathering dusk, on the other the red sun sinking in blood on his funeral pyre ; and then, when light had vanished and all was swathed in shadow, to land by the glimmering tomb of Lady Canning, and to walk up the gravelled terrace to Barrackpore House, the hand-borne lanterns twinkling in the darkness ahead— these were sensations that can never be forgotten. They are no longer

---

[1] " Life of Lord Dalhousie," by Sir W. Lee Warner, Vol. I, pp. 425-6.
[2] *Vide* Chapter VIII.

enjoyed by the official who rushes in a panting motor amid whirlwinds of dust along the narrow metalled riband in the centre of the Great Trunk Road. But perhaps Lord Wellesley in his pinnace, or Bishop Heber in his budgerow, would have equally deplored my steam-launch ; and perhaps the rider in the motor of to-day may similarly disparage the aerial vehicle of the future.

CHAPTER XI

PART I

Some Notes on the Viceroyalty and Governor Generalship of India

" It is with the Governor General that the supreme power resides, and on him that the whole responsibility rests. This system, which was introduced by Mr. Pitt and Mr. Dundas, in spite of the strenuous opposition of Mr. Burke, we conceive to be on the whole the best that was ever devised for the Government of a country where no material can be found for a representative Constitution."— Lord Macaulay.

" I repeat, as I have often said before, that a Governor General is unlike any other Minister under heaven—he is the beginning, middle, and end of all."—Lord Dalhousie.

BETWEEN the year 1700 and the siege and capture of Fort William by Siraj-ud-Dowleh in 1757, there were seventeen Governors of the Bengal Presidency, the names of some of whom have been mentioned in this narrative. From Clive, who was the first Governor after the recovery of the town, to Warren Hastings, there were six holders of the office, namely Clive himself, Holwell, Vansittart, Spencer, Verelst, and Cartier. Warren Hastings was the first of this line to be appointed Governor General of Fort William in Bengal. He had already been Governor for more than two years, when the higher title was created by Act of Parliament, and was conferred upon him as the first incumbent.

The same official designation was borne by ten of his successors, and by three officiating Governors General:

NAME	ASSUMED CHARGE OF OFFICE
Warren Hastings	20th October, 1774
Sir John Macpherson	8th February, 1785
Earl (afterwards Marquis) Cornwallis	12th September, 1786
Sir John Shore (afterwards Lord Teignmouth)	28th October, 1793
Sir Alured Clarke	17th March, 1798
Earl of Mornington (afterwards Marquis Wellesley)	18th May, 1798
Marquis Cornwallis	30th July, 1805

47

NAME	ASSUMED CHARGE OF OFFICE
Sir George Barlow	10th October, 1805
Lord (afterwards 1st Earl of) Minto	31st July, 1807
Earl of Moira (afterwards Marquis of Hastings)	4th October, 1813
John Adam	13th January, 1823
Lord (afterwards Earl) Amherst ...	1st August, 1823
W. B. Bayley	13th March, 1828
Lord William Bentinck	4th July, 1828

(The names in italics are those of Acting Governors General.)

In 1834, under another Act of Parliament, which reflected the increasing spread and importance of the Indian Dominions of Great Britain, the head of the Government became Governor General of India as well as Governor of the Presidency of Fort William in Bengal ; and, including Lord W. Bentinck, who was the first to receive the expanded title, six actual, and two officiating Governors General bore the twofold designation. They were—

NAME	ASSUMED CHARGE OF OFFICE
Lord W. Bentinck	16th June, 1834
Sir C. (afterwards Lord) Metcalfe ...	20th March, 1835
Lord (afterwards Earl of) Auckland	4th March, 1836
Lord (afterwards Earl of) Ellenborough	28th February, 1842
W. B. Bird	15th June, 1844
Sir H. (afterwards Viscount) Hardinge	23rd July, 1844
Earl (afterwards Marquis of) Dalhousie	12th January, 1848
Viscount (afterwards Earl) Canning	29th February, 1856

(The names in italics are those of Acting Governors General.)

Before the end of the above period the Governor General ceased to be Governor of Bengal, the first Lieutenant Governor of that Presidency being appointed in 1854. After the suppression of the Mutiny the Government of India was taken over from the East India Company by the Crown, and for the first time the Governor General was designated Viceroy and Governor General—the twofold title which he has ever since borne.

The use of this double appellation has been a source of some bewilderment, and the question has sometimes been asked, When is the head of the Government of India one and when is he the other ; and why, since he is always called Viceroy, should he not be so designated in all official instruments ? The practice adopted for the use of the two titles will in reality provide an explanation of the distinction. The term Governor General alone is always employed in Acts both of the British Parliament and the Indian Legislature, in the Warrant of Appointment of the Governor General, and in the Notification of Appointment in the "London Gazette." On the other hand, the double title " Viceroy and Governor General " or " Governor General and Viceroy," which was first employed by Queen Victoria in the Royal Proclamation of 1st November, 1858, announcing the assumption of Government by the Crown, is used in the Warrants of Precedence and in the Statutes of the Knightly Orders. The distinction therefore is held to be that where the Governor General is referred to as the statutory head of the Government of India he is designated Governor General : where he is regarded as the representative of the Sovereign he is spoken of as Viceroy. The latter title however has no statutory sanction, and is the result merely of usage and convention.

Until the capital of Government was removed from Calcutta in 1912—the period with which this book is concerned—the list of actual and officiating Viceroys and Governors General was as follows :—

NAME	ASSUMED CHARGE OF OFFICE
Viscount (afterwards Earl) Canning	1st November, 1858
1st Earl of Elgin	12th March, 1862
Sir Robert Napier (afterwards Lord Napier of Magdala) [1]	21st November, 1863
Sir W. Denison	2nd December, 1863
Sir John (afterwards Lord) Lawrence	12th January, 1864
Earl of Mayo	12th January, 1869
Mr. (afterwards Sir John) Strachey [2] ...	9th February, 1872
Lord Napier of Merchistoun (afterwards Lord Napier of Ettrick) ...	23rd February, 1872

[1] He only officiated for a few days as senior Member of Council, upon the death of Lord Elgin, until the Governor of Madras, Sir W. Denison, arrived.

[2] He only officiated as senior Member of Council, upon the assassination of Lord Mayo, until the Governor of Madras, Lord Napier, arrived.

NAME	ASSUMED CHARGE OF OFFICE
Lord (afterwards Earl of) Northbrook	3rd May, 1872
Lord (afterwards Earl of) Lytton ...	12th April, 1876
Marquis of Ripon	8th June, 1880
Earl (afterwards Marquis of) Dufferin	13th December, 1884
Marquis of Lansdowne	10th December, 1888
2nd Earl of Elgin	27th January, 1894
Lord Curzon of Kedleston	6th January, 1899
Lord Ampthill	30th April, 1904
Lord (afterwards Marquis) Curzon of Kedleston	13th December, 1904
4th Earl of Minto	18th November, 1905
Lord Hardinge of Penshurst ...	23rd November, 1910

(The names in italics are those of Acting Viceroys.)

These lists have been given in some fullness, since they will enable the reader to apprehend with greater ease much of what follows. It will be observed that during the 140 years from the date when Warren Hastings first assumed office in 1772 to the date when the Government of India left Calcutta in 1912, 27 Governors General and 9 Acting Governors General—the latter by the accident of death or resignation, and as a rule for quite short periods—ruled at that place. Excluding these *interregna* the term of office of the 27 substantive Governors General works out at an average of five years—the exact period for which, not by law but by custom, the post is supposed to be filled.[1]

The longest terms for which any individuals have served have been Warren Hastings, nearly 13 years (including his first term as Governor), Lord Cornwallis 7 years, Lord Wellesley 7 years, Lord Hastings over 9 years, Lord Dalhousie 8 years, Lord Canning 6 years, the writer $6\frac{1}{4}$ years. The normal tenure in modern times has been from 4 to 5 years.

Three of the long list given above have died in India—Lord Cornwallis (after little more than two months of his second term of office) in October 1805, at Ghazipur, where he was buried and where his monument is preserved by the State ; the first Lord Elgin at Dharm-

---

[1] The five years' prescription is a legacy from the first Regulating Act of 1773, which appointed the first Governor General (Warren Hastings) for a term of five years. This was only a temporary enactment, and Hastings' appointment was continued thereafter, for a year at a time, by successive Acts of Parliament.

MARQUIS WELLESLEY,
GOVERNOR GENERAL OF INDIA,
FROM 1798 TO 1805.

ERECTED BY THE
BRITISH INHABITANTS OF BENGAL,
IN TESTIMONY OF THEIR HIGH SENSE
OF THE
WISDOM, ENERGY, AND RECTITUDE,
OF HIS ADMINISTRATION.

STATUE OF LORD WELLESLEY

Sculpt.: John Bacon.

sala in November 1863, where he lies buried ; Lord Mayo, by assassination in the Andamans, in February 1872. His body was taken back for interment in Ireland.

Three only (including the Governors before Warren Hastings) have been reappointed for a second term, viz. Lord Clive, Lord Cornwallis (who was actually appointed three times, though he only went out twice) and the writer.

Lord Clive's double appointment cannot however be regarded as a lengthy tenure of office, since his two terms in combination amounted to less than five years.   On the other hand, the prolonged service, without a break, of Warren Hastings, Lord Wellesley, Lord Hastings and Lord Dalhousie was tantamount to a double term.   Perhaps either a protracted stay or a renewed appointment is on the whole to be deprecated, since too high a price may have to be paid for the honour, although, as I shall show later on, the permission now accorded to the Viceroy to return to England during his term of office may operate to extend the average term of office in India.   Lord Granville wrote in a letter to Lord Canning on 26th July, 1861 :

" I hear Dalhousie attributes his whole breakdown to the extra time he served.   Pray consider all this, and do not be led away by the natural temptation of seeing everything you have undertaken brought more or less to a close." [1]

This is a temptation to which others beside Dalhousie have succumbed ; and it rests upon the pardonable illusion, to which politicians are particularly prone, that the keystone alone is missing from the arch and that there is only one mason who can place it in position ; whereas in fact other hands may be equally capable of the task, and in some cases the keystone will only be fixed in order to be dislodged by the next builder who comes along.

The great change that has come over the Government of India in the last century, converting the problem of Government from the management of the affairs of a mercantile company and the military defence of a scattered and precarious dominion, to the civil administration of a vast and powerful Empire, is indicated by the fact that, whereas among the earlier Governors General several were also Commanders-in-Chief and were appointed in some cases not without reference to

[1] " Life of Earl Granville," by Lord Edmond Fitzmaurice, 1903, Vol. I, p. 386.

their military career or capacities—namely Lord Cornwallis, Lord Hastings (who only accepted the office on condition that he was also made Commander-in-Chief), and Lord W. Bentinck—since 1835 no soldier has been appointed to the office, and it is well known that Lord Kitchener, who greatly desired it, was passed over in 1910, in the main for that reason. One other Governor General, the first Lord Hardinge, was also a great soldier, and actually insisted while Governor General on serving under Sir Hugh Gough in the first Sikh War. This was an error that has fortunately never been repeated. But Lord Hardinge was not Commander-in-Chief in India, though he subsequently became Commander-in-Chief (in succession to the Duke of Wellington) in England.

Another great soldier, Sir Henry Norman, who had been Commander-in-Chief in Madras, only accepted the Viceroyalty in 1893, to throw it up immediately afterwards, recognising his unsuitability for the post.

It will not be without interest to consider the categories of persons from whom the heads of the Government of India have, as a rule, been drawn.

Generally speaking, it will be found that they have been chosen either from those who have already held office or been prominent in public life in England, or from those who have already had governing experience in other parts of the Empire. I have been at some pains to explore and collate the previous records of the Governors General of India—a subject which has been very generally passed over in the summaries of their careers.

No small fraction of their number have sat previously in the British House of Commons. Before the time of the first Governor General, Warren Hastings—Lord Clive, who was an Irish Peer, had sat there, both in the interval between his first and second Governorships, and again after his final return to England. Sir John Macpherson was also an M.P. while at home in 1779-1782, and again after his final return in 1796-1802. Of the remaining Governors General the following had also sat in the House of Commons before going out to India—Lord Cornwallis, Sir John Shore, the first Lord Minto (who had twice aspired but failed to become Speaker of that House),[1] Lord Auckland, Lord

---

[1] He was beaten in January 1789 by Grenville, and in June of the same year by Addington.

Ellenborough, the first Lord Hardinge, Lord Dalhousie, Lord Canning, the first Lord Elgin, Lord Mayo, Lord Northbrook, Lord Ripon, and the writer.

The following had, previously to going out to India, sat in the House of Lords—Lord Cornwallis, Lord Wellesley (as Baron Wellesley 1797), the first Lord Minto (as Baron Minto 1798), Lord Hastings (as Baron Rawdon 1783), Lord Auckland, Lord Ellenborough, Lord Dalhousie, Lord Canning, the first Lord Elgin, Lord Northbrook, Lord Ripon, Lord Dufferin, Lord Lansdowne, the second Lord Elgin, the fourth Lord Minto.

It would appear therefore that no fewer than nineteen, or more than two-thirds of the entire list, had already had experience in one or other of the two Houses of Parliament, many of them in both.

But their experience was in reality much greater and wider ; for of the above list no fewer than sixteen had held office, and no fewer than nine had been Cabinet Ministers. I will give the roll of the latter : the first Lord Minto as President of the Board of Control (1806) ; Lord Hastings, as Master of Ordnance in the Ministry of All the Talents (1806) ; Lord Auckland as President of the Board of Trade (1830-1833) and First Lord of the Admiralty (1834-1835) ; Lord Ellenborough as Lord Privy Seal (1828) and President of the Board of Control (1828-1830, 1834-1835, and 1841) ; Sir H. Hardinge as Secretary of State for War (1828-1830 and 1841-1844) ;[1] Lord Dalhousie as President of the Board of Trade (1845) ; the first Lord Elgin as Postmaster-General (1859) ; Lord Mayo as Chief Secretary for Ireland (1866) ;[2] Lord Ripon as Secretary of State for War (1863-1866) and for India (1866), and as Lord President of the Council (1868-1873).

Some of the above list had also held subordinate offices in the Administration ; and no fewer than five had been Under-Secretaries for India. These were Lord Northbrook (1859-1861 and 1861-1864), Lord Ripon (1861-1863), Lord Dufferin (1864-1866), Lord Lansdowne (1880), and the writer (1891-1892). Two—Lord Canning (1841-1846) and the writer (1895-1898)—had been Under-Secretaries for Foreign Affairs.

---

[1] Sir H. Hardinge, when Secretary for War the first time (1828-1830), was not a member of the Cabinet.

[2] Lord Mayo had twice before been Irish Secretary, in 1852 and 1858, but without a seat in the Cabinet.

It will have been observed that a small number, three in fact, had been the heads of the Indian Government in London. Two had been Presidents of the Board of Control (the equivalent to Secretary of State before the Government of India was taken over by the Crown). These were the first Lord Minto, for a few months only (February-July, 1806); Lord Ellenborough three times—for over two years (1828-1830), for four months (1834-1835), and for one month (1841); one, Lord Ripon, had been Secretary of State for India for four months (1866).

One Governor General only, Lord Ellenborough, after returning from India, from which office he had been recalled in 1844, was actually made President of the Board of Control for the fourth time for four months in 1858—an experiment which was attended with disastrous results both to himself and to the State, seeing that in consequence of his insolent Despatch to Lord Canning about the latter's Oudh Proclamation, he was disavowed by the Cabinet and was compelled to resign.

The cases that have been named in the last two categories have a more than personal interest, since they raise a question of some constitutional importance, and are concerned with a precedent which, with the above exceptions, has been consistently acted upon for a century and a quarter, until it has come to be regarded as a fundamental principle of Indian Government. This is the principle that it is not right or expedient either that one who has been head of the Indian Government in England should become head of the Government of India in India; or alternatively that a returned Viceroy should become Secretary of State for India in London.

This principle rests, in my judgment, upon a sound foundation. In the former case it might be difficult for an ex-Secretary of State for India who has been the official superior of the Viceroy, and may have been called upon to overrule him on many occasions, to defer, as Viceroy, to the authority which he had once wielded himself in England: and further he might be tempted to use his power in India to enforce projects which he had initiated and perhaps failed to carry, in London, thereby enjoying, so to speak, a double spell of office.

Conversely the returned Viceroy, if appointed at a later date to the India Office, might be inclined to pursue at home, whether wisely or unwisely, the policy with which he had been identified in India; he might even not be averse from applying to his successor the curb under which he had fretted himself. If on the other hand he were to look at cases too exclusively through the glasses of " the man on the spot," he might fail in his duty as Secretary of State.

The relations between Secretary of State and Viceroy are in any case too delicate and sometimes difficult to allow of their being hampered by any such possible complications. I have known cases in which it has been sought to break through this prescription, and in which Secretaries for India have aspired to become, or have been considered as possible, Viceroys. I hope however that in the interests of good Government, and the avoidance of almost certain friction, the rule, which I am convinced is sound, may continue to be observed.

To revert to the previous Parliamentary or official experience of Governors General and Viceroys, it needs but little imagination to realise how valuable in practice this has been, and must continue to be. Apart from strength of character, courage, and sympathy with the people committed to his care, the principal desiderata in a Viceroy are undoubtedly some familiarity with public affairs, some experience in administration, and some power of speech. The first of these is pre-eminently necessary for one who is called upon to deal with so wide a range of policy as is the head of the Government of India. Otherwise he is apt to find himself at sea, and can neither give a lead to his colleagues in India nor adjust his actions to those of the Cabinet at home. As to administrative experience, the importance of this can scarcely be exaggerated. Without it the Viceroy falls into the grip of the most highly organised and powerful departmental machine that exists in the world, which he is impotent either to correct or control : and he is liable to become a cypher in the administration instead of its head. Cases are well known in which the absence of this knowledge has led to vacillation and worse. On the other hand, those who have come out to India with administrative experience, like that, for instance, of Lord Mayo or Lord Northbrook, have been able to address themselves at once to the problem with which they were faced, instead of spending the first half of their term of office in the endeavour to understand it, and the second half in capitulating to its demands. Lastly as to power of speech, while the Viceroy no longer (unless on rare occasions he decides to the contrary) presides, as he did in my time, over the Legislative Council, where he was formerly called upon to sum up the debates, yet the occasions when he has to speak in public are so frequent that even though the majority of his deliveries are in reply to Addresses and are prepared in advance, readiness of speech is an invaluable adjunct of success : and those heads of the Government, who have had no previous training in this respect, have been severely handicapped in their tasks.

For all these reasons it may be held that a Parliamentary and administrative training is on the whole the most valuable that a Viceroy can receive. I will add a further consideration. It is the tendency of all Departments, whether in India or in England, to regard the matters that come before them almost exclusively from the departmental point of view, and not only to ignore but even to be unaware of the manner in which the departmental solution will strike either public opinion or the House of Commons or the Cabinet. All persons who have been engaged in public life in England will be thoroughly aware of this idiosyncrasy. Much more is it likely to prevail in India ; and the service that a Viceroy who has been in Parliament, and still more in a Government at home, is capable of rendering in establishing contact between the Indian and the English points of view, is almost incalculable.

There is a further class of experience which has been enjoyed by some heads of the Government of India, namely administrative experience in some other Dominion or Dependency of the Crown, or diplomatic experience, either in the regular Diplomatic Service or as Special Envoy. Only one Governor of an Indian Presidency has been promoted to Calcutta, although many have hoped for and even been promised the elevation. This was Lord William Bentinck, who had been Governor of Madras (1805-1807), and had actually been recalled from that post 21 years before being appointed Governor General of India. Four Viceroys have previously been Governors General of Canada, namely the first Lord Elgin (1846-1854),[1] Lord Dufferin (1872-1878), Lord Lansdowne (1883-1888), and the fourth Lord Minto (1898-1904). Two Governors General before going to India had been charged with Special Missions to China, Lord Amherst (1816) and the first Lord Elgin (1857 and 1860) ; and it was largely as a consolation for his lack of success at Peking that Lord Amherst received the Indian appointment.

[1] He had also been Governor of Jamaica (1842).

The first Lord Minto had also been Governor of Corsica during the British occupation (1794-1796), and Envoy and Minister Plenipotentiary at Vienna (1799). Lord Dufferin had been charged with special Missions to Vienna (1855), Syria (1860) and Egypt (1882-3), and had also been Ambassador at Petersburg (1879) and Constantinople (1881). Lord Lytton was Minister at Lisbon (1872-1876) when he was appointed by Disraeli Viceroy of India. Lord Hardinge of Penshurst had also been Ambassador at Petersburg (1904-1906).

And here we come to the rather remarkable fact that, with scarcely an exception, no member of the Indian Civil Service has, since the beginning of the 19th century, been elevated to the supreme position of head of the Government of India. While the rule of the Company was still supreme, Warren Hastings was succeeded by Sir John Macpherson (1785-1786), who had on one occasion been dismissed from the Service in Madras. Sir John Shore (1793-1798) had also been a Writer in the service of the Company ; and it is noteworthy that when appointed Governor General, he did not want the post and asked leave to decline it.[1]

Another Civilian, Sir George Barlow, was Governor General for nearly two years (1805-1807) in rather peculiar circumstances, which will be referred to later on. Other Civil Servants, such as John Adam (January-July 1823), W. B. Bayley (March-July 1828), Sir Charles (afterwards Lord) Metcalfe (March 1835-March 1836), and some others for shorter periods, have held the office for a while in an officiating or provisional capacity pending the appointment or arrival of a successor. It is not till 1864 that we find, in the person of Sir John Lawrence, the first and only Viceroy who, being a member of the Indian Civil Service, has in the past century become its official head, and it is generally conceded that his experience was not such as to encourage a repetition of the experiment. Sir Henry Norman, who spent a large part of his life in the Indian Army (having originally joined the East India Company's Military Service in 1844) and had risen to be Military Member of Council, was indeed nominated Viceroy in succession to Lord Lansdowne in 1893 (being at that time Governor of Queensland), and his appointment was announced in the Press. Very shortly however, realising that his 67 years were a fatal impediment to an adequate discharge of the duties, he asked that his name

[1] " Life," Vol. I, pp. 221-4.

should be withdrawn. Lord Lawrence therefore retains his unique position.

The question will here not unnaturally be asked, whether this bar of disqualification has been deliberate, and, if so, to what considerations it has been due. Perhaps the answer may best be given in the recorded opinions of the highest authorities. Lord Cornwallis, when a Civilian in the person of Sir John Shore was nominated provisionally as his successor in 1793 and eventually succeeded to the office, while welcoming the appointment on personal grounds, deprecated the precedent and wrote :

" It is very difficult for a man to divest himself of the prejudices which the habits of twenty years have confirmed and to govern people who have lived with him so long on a footing of equality." [1]

The first Lord Minto expressed the same sentiment with even greater emphasis when he wrote :

" A Company's servant, raised to the commanding height above his fellows which the Governor General holds here, excites envy rather than respect or love. They are all comparing themselves with him and their own pretensions with his." [2]

But the *locus classicus* on the subject is contained in a letter from George Canning to the Court of Directors when resigning the post of President of the Board of Control, on 25th December, 1820, in which he wrote that :

" I can hardly conceive the case in which it would be expedient that the *highest* office of the Government in India should be filled otherwise than from England. That one main link, at least, between the systems of the Indian and British Governments ought, for the' advantage of both, in my judgment, to be invariably maintained." [3]

For a century this rule of guidance has, except in the single case of Lawrence, been observed, and it seems to me desirable that it should be maintained. I do not say that no occasion can ever arise in which the considerations that have been cited should not be overborne in the public interest. But as time has passed, the case has grown stronger rather than weaker, especially in its relation to the home position. The

[1] " Lives of Indian Officers," by Sir John Kaye, Vol. I, p. 158.
[2] " Lord Minto in India," p. 28.
[3] " Letters from the Board " (India Office), Vol. V, p. 282.

difficulties in India—arising from the jealousy caused by preference accorded to a single member of the Civil Service, however eminent, from the *parti pris* which on many matters he must almost inevitably have taken, from his presumed exclusive fidelity to the traditions of the Service, and from the necessarily circumscribed range of his administrative experience, will still be found to apply. But in their bearing upon home politics they have increased with time. No member of the Civil Service can possibly have acquired that knowledge of public affairs in England, or that personal acquaintance with the governing class in this country and notably with the Government which he is serving, that is so indispensable to a Viceroy. Further, the trend of Indian public opinion is undoubtedly in the direction of attaching an increasing value to the appointment of Provincial Governors, and *a fortiori* still more of the Governor General, from the outside. The appointment of a Civilian Viceroy would probably now be assailed with a chorus of condemnation by the Native Press. I think therefore it will be found that the principle, supported by such valid reasoning and hallowed by so long an observance, will continue to apply.

The idea of a Royal Viceroy has sometimes been mooted, and the suggestion has been made that a Prince of the Royal House, or even a son of the Sovereign, might be sent out to Government House in India. Undoubtedly there is some fascination in the hope expressed by the Court Poet of the Hebrew King, that " instead of thy fathers (*i.e.* elder statesmen) thou shalt have children (*i.e.* sons) whom thou mayest make princes (*i.e.* satraps) in all lands " ; and the Overseas Dominions of the British Crown may be cited as having furnished more than one example of the signal success of such appointments. It has even been said that the scheme of a new Imperial Capital, with a magnificent Government House, at Delhi, was not wholly disconnected with such ideas ; and the theory of a British Prince as the centre of a constellation, the principal satellites of which are themselves Princes and Rulers of States, and as the head of a society which is still penetrated with the monarchical idea, presents many attractions. I have even heard of a British Secretary of State who aspired to merge the Viceroyalty in the Royal House, and himself to go out as Prime Minister to a Princely Viceroy.

Personally I have never favoured this idea, and I am disposed to favour it still less now. The head of the Government in India, as is apparent from almost every page of these Volumes, is regarded by the Indian peoples as the executive head of the administration, and as directly and personally responsible for the acts of Government. If these are popular he is applauded ; if they excite animadversion or hostility he is attacked and condemned. It may be said that the hostile shafts would be aimed at the future Prime Minister of India, assuming such an office to be created, as would doubtless be necessary, and would glance off the person of the Royal Viceroy or never touch him at all. In practice it is to be feared that this would not be the case. He would be identified by the native mind, inured to the conception of personal rule, with the policy of his Government, would receive the credit if it were praised, and would be included in the censure if it were assailed. When I desired, at the Delhi Durbar of January 1903, to intimate in my speech that in honour of the occasion (*i.e.* the Coronation of King Edward VII) the Government of India hoped to be able to announce a remission of taxation in the ensuing Budget—as we had decided to do—I was solemnly informed from home that such a proposal was open to the most serious objection, because if the remission of taxation was even remotely connected with the name of the Sovereign, he could not fail to be blamed if it were at any time reimposed. If, however, these pleas were valid in the case of an occasion like the Durbar, so closely associated in the Oriental mind with ideas of Royal clemency and favour, how much more would they apply in the daily conduct of Indian administration, where the Government is continually called upon to take steps that excite the liveliest criticism, and where the finger, if not the figure, of the Viceroy is always discerned in the background.

A further point may be noted. In the Dominions a British Prince, when appointed Governor General, goes out as the titular head of a community composed entirely or almost entirely of his own countrymen, whose principles and ideas are in general harmony with his own, and who treat him as the august representative of the Imperial Throne. In India, where there seems to be increasing friction, often racial in its origin, between the ruling minority and the ruled, who can guarantee that in moments of excitement the position of a Royal Viceroy might not be involved in the conflict, and things might be said or done which would impair the prestige of the King-Emperor, at present elevated by common consent far above the brawl of political controversy ?

It is conceivable that a day may arise when Provincial autonomy may have reached a stage of development in which the nexus between the various Local Governments might be supplied by a Royal Head of the State, wholly dissociated from politics, and charged with social and ceremonial duties alone. But such a situation, quite apart from its acceptability or the reverse to the holder of the office, would involve the complete transformation of the Imperial Government in India as it has hitherto existed : and it is not, in my view, a consummation that is either to be encouraged or desired.

I have spoken of the classes from which the heads of the Government of India have hitherto been drawn. A word may be added as to the age at which they have been appointed. Warren Hastings left India for the last time at the age of fifty-two, and that or thereabouts is the average age at which his successors have gone out. There have, however, been notable exceptions at both extremes. Warren Hastings himself was thirty-nine when he became Governor, and nearly forty-two when he became Governor General ; Lord Wellesley was nearly thirty-eight ; Lord Dalhousie, the youngest of all, was not yet thirty-six ; the writer of these pages was thirty-nine. It was perhaps a curious coincidence that, while the last-named had long aspired to the post, he had frequently expressed the opinion that he would not care to cut short his Parliamentary career in England unless it came to him before the age of forty. He was six months short of that age when the offer was made, and he assumed charge at Calcutta five days before his fortieth birthday.

At the other end of the scale, Lord Hastings and Lord Dufferin were fifty-eight, and the first Lord Hardinge was fifty-nine, when they were severally appointed. It was perhaps because of his years that Lord Dufferin, in a letter of 10th February, 1888, wrote to a friend : " Four years of such constant labour and anxiety as a Viceroy is called upon to bear are almost as much as is good for anyone." Lord Cornwallis, when he came out for the second time, was sixty-six, and undoubtedly owed his speedy demise to his already declining years. The conditions of life in India have, however, so much changed, and are so much more conducive to physical energy and strength, that there is now much less reason than formerly why a man in middle life should be unequal to the strain. And this position will be enhanced if, as has now been finally enacted, the Viceroy is permitted in the future to come home—under strictly defined conditions—during his tenure of office.

I have often been asked the question by whom and in what circumstances the appointment to the Viceroyalty is made. In the 18th and early 19th centuries it would have been difficult to give a precise answer to this question, because of the conflict that raged between the Court of Directors, the Board of Control (corresponding to the present India Office), and the Cabinet ; and also because of the occasional and independent intervention of the Sovereign.

The story of contested or abortive appointments to the Governor Generalship, which I shall presently relate, and which has never before been consecutively told, will sufficiently demonstrate the truth of this proposition. In more modern times, while the appointment is vested as a matter of course in the Sovereign, the respective parts that are played in the selection by the Prime Minister, the Secretary of State for India, and the Cabinet, depend not upon any law, written or unwritten, but upon the Prime Minister for the time being. I have known cases, and others are recorded in published Memoirs, where prolonged discussions took place in Cabinet upon the merits of a suggested candidate or candidates. I have known other cases where the Prime Minister consulted a few of his colleagues before making his submission to the Sovereign. Ordinarily the Secretary of State for India would be the first to be asked to offer suggestions. But I have known one case where he was not even informed until after the appointment had been made by the Prime Minister and the Sovereign in combination. The tendency, as Cabinets have grown in size to their recent unwieldy dimensions, is unquestionably to treat important appointments less and less as matters for Cabinet discussion, and more and more as falling within the province of the Prime Minister, relying upon such advice as he may choose to seek.

I have been struck in my studies with the persistence with which the Irish Peerage has been associated with the Government of India. In former days appointment to it or promotion in it was regarded as a less exalted form of honour than corresponding steps in the English or British Peerage. Further, an Irish Peerage was compatible with a subsequent seat in the House of Commons. Clive was made an Irish Peer (Baron Clive of Plassey) in 1762, in the interval between his first and second terms of office ; and as such he sat in the House of Commons.   Sir John Shore was created an Irish Peer (Baron Teignmouth) in 1798, without even being consulted, and his title was selected behind his back.[1]   If consulted, it had been his intention to refuse.   He never took his seat in the Irish House of Lords, nor sought to be elected an Irish Representative Peer to the Upper Chamber in Great Britain. Lord Macartney, who had been created an Irish Peer in 1776 and was Governor of Madras (1781-1785), was offered but declined the Governor Generalship in 1785.   In the course of the negotiations he asked for a British Peerage, but was refused by Pitt, on the advice of Dundas.   At a later date he was made an Irish Earl, in 1792, but he did not receive an English Barony till 1796.   Lord Wellesley, who had succeeded his father in the Irish Earldom of Mornington in 1781, and as such had sat in the House of Commons, only received a British Peerage (Baron Wellesley) in 1797, and was indignant when his services in India were merely rewarded by an Irish Marquisate in 1799. In a foolish letter of 28th April, 1800, to Pitt he described this title as " a double-gilt potato," while he denounced it as an outrage in his correspondence with his friends.

Lord Hastings, who had sat both in the Irish House of Commons and in the Irish House of Lords, received an English Peerage in 1783, and succeeded through his mother to four other English Baronies in 1808.   But he went out to India as the bearer of an Irish title (Earl of Moira), and only received a British Marquisate in 1817.   Lord Dufferin entered public life as an Irish Peer, but was advanced to the British Peerage at the age of twenty-four.   The writer of these pages was made an Irish Peer by Queen Victoria in 1898, at the suggestion of Lord Salisbury.   The latter disinterred this device from a long oblivion in order to enable the bearer of the title (who had asked leave to decline a British Peerage) to re-enter the House of Commons on his return from India.   It was to the possession of an Irish Peerage that he owed his subsequent admission to the House of Lords in 1908, when he was elected a Representative Peer of Ireland, the Liberal Government having declined, on party grounds, to call him up to that House in the lifetime of his father, who was already a Peer.

In an age when the hereditary tenure of office is subject to much rather hypocritical depreciation, it is amusing to note how often in India, where the hereditary principle is greatly esteemed, and is the basis of

[1] " Life," Vol. I, pp. 455, 519.

most professions, the son or grandson of a British ruler has been selected to fill, and has filled to the general satisfaction, either the same office or an office akin to that which his father or grandfather had occupied at an earlier stage. The second Lord Clive, while he bore the same title as his illustrious father (he was afterwards created Earl of Powis), was for four years Governor of Madras. In quite recent times it was thought eminently right that another Lord Minto should follow his great-grandfather, the first Lord Minto, as Governor General, after the lapse of nearly a century. George Canning having first accepted and then declined the same office, it was conferred rather more than a quarter of a century later on his third son. The first Lord Elgin, whose Viceroyalty was so short, bequeathed a longer tenure to his son, who forty years later served for the full term. Sir Henry Hardinge, the soldier ruler, was succeeded after an interval of sixty years by his grandson, the diplomatist Viceroy, Lord Hardinge of Penshurst. More recently, Lord Lytton, who reigned as Viceroy in Government House, Calcutta, from 1876 to 1880, has been followed in the same residence by his son, the present Lord Lytton (who was born there), as Governor of Bengal. We may observe similar illustrations of the family tradition in the Presidency Governorships. Two Lords Hobart, uncle and great-nephew, were Governors of Madras respectively in 1794-1798 and 1872-1875 ; Lord Harris, Governor of Madras (1854-1859), was followed by his son as Governor of Bombay (1890-1895) ; Lord Mayo, Viceroy (1869-1872), had a brother, Lord Connemara, who was Governor of Madras (1886-1890). Lord Wenlock, Governor of Madras (1891-1896), was followed in the same office by a brother, Sir A. Lawley (1906-1911). The father of the Governor General Lord Dalhousie had been Commander-in-Chief in India ; Sir William Mansfield, who filled the same position, and became the first Lord Sandhurst, bequeathed a son as Governor to Bombay (1895-1900). Thus in India, in happy disregard of the prejudice that declares in England that a son ought not to be allowed to inherit governing responsibilities from his parent, the opposite system obtains much favour ; and, while no one is the worse for the anomaly, a great many people will frankly acknowledge that it has proved to be a very serviceable and a very successful practice.

Perhaps, having heard the history of the various heads of the Government of India before they assumed that office, my readers may be interested to know what became of them officially after they had laid it down.   The majority returned to the political life in which they had already won their spurs, and in which they commonly achieved higher office and earned greater distinction.   Lord Cornwallis became Master General of Ordnance (then a political office of the highest importance) in 1795, and Special Ambassador to conclude the Peace of Amiens in 1802.   Lord Wellesley filled a long succession of offices, as Ambassador Extraordinary to Spain (1809), Foreign Secretary (1809-1812), Lord Lieutenant of Ireland (1821-1828 and 1833-1834), Lord Steward (1832-1833), and Lord Chamberlain (1835)—the two latter posts surely a tragic descent.   Lord Hastings became Governor and Commander-in-Chief in Malta in 1824, and died at sea in the Mediterranean in 1826 ; Lord Auckland was made First Lord of the Admiralty for the second time in 1846 ; Lord Ellenborough filled the same office in the same year, but came to final grief, as already narrated, when he became President of the Board of Control for the fourth time in 1858.   The first Lord Hardinge was Master General of Ordnance in 1852 and Commander-in-Chief (1852-1856) ; Lord Northbrook became First Lord of the Admiralty (1880-1885) and was charged with a Special Mission to Cairo.   Lord Ripon was First Lord of the Admiralty (1886) and Colonial Secretary (1892-1895), Lord Lansdowne was Secretary of State for War (1895-1900) and Foreign Affairs (1900-1905) ; the second Lord Elgin was Colonial Secretary (1905-1908).   Three ex-Viceroys reverted to a diplomatic career—Lord Lytton as Ambassador at Paris (1887-1891), Lord Dufferin at Rome (1888-1891) and Paris (1891-1896), and Lord Hardinge of Penshurst at Paris (1920-1922). The writer became successively Lord Privy Seal, Lord President of the Council, and Foreign Secretary.

It will have been seen that three retired Viceroys have filled the last-named office, viz. Lord Wellesley, Lord Lansdowne, and the writer. Lord Canning had declined it when offered to him by Lord Derby in 1851, before he went out to India.   Three also have become Leaders of the House of Lords, Lord Lansdowne, Lord Ripon, and the writer. Three have received the distinguished office of Lord Warden of the Cinque Ports, with Walmer Castle as a habitation, namely Lord Dalhousie, who was too ill ever to go into residence, Lord Dufferin, who occupied the post (1891-1895), and the writer (1905-1907).   The first and the last of this trio received the office while still in India.

No Governor General or Viceroy has ever yet become Prime Minister. Lord Wellesley in 1812, when Foreign Secretary, and after him Lord Moira, before he went out to India, endeavoured successively to form an Administration. Where they jointly failed, Lord Liverpool presently succeeded. Another ex-Viceroy in later times is believed to have narrowly missed the appointment.

Only one ex-Governor General (unless we include Sir John Macpherson, M.P. for Horsham 1796-1802) has entered the House of Commons after his return from India. This was Lord William Bentinck, who declined a Peerage and was returned for Glasgow in 1837. When the writer came back from India after his second term of office in 1906, and was anxious to re-enter that House, having indeed been made an Irish Peer by Queen Victoria on the suggestion of Lord Salisbury in 1898 for that purpose, King Edward VII, in conversation with him, expressed the strongest objection to an ex-Viceroy sitting in the Commons Chamber, and was only willing to modify his attitude if the individual in question were to obtain an uncontested seat, either for the City of London (which had been offered to him but which he could not at that moment for other reasons accept), or for the University of Oxford, which was not then vacant. He was therefore driven to seek entrance to the House of Lords.

The great majority of Governors General and Viceroys have upon their retirement, if not during their term of office, received official recognition of their services either by a step in the Peerage, or by the Knighthood of the Garter, or otherwise. There have been notable exceptions. Lord Clive, upon his return from his second Governorship, was made the victim of a Parliamentary Enquiry into his conduct in India, the worry and anxiety of which drove him ultimately to take his own life. Warren Hastings, the greatest man who ever filled the office, returned after a glorious thirteen years to endure the long agony of an Impeachment that remains one of the scandals of history. Only thirty years later, in 1814, was he made a Privy Councillor, and he never received the Peerage, which his wife coveted, but which he declined even to consider unless the accusations against him were erased from the Records of the House of Commons. Lord Wellesley narrowly escaped a similar impeachment. Lord Hastings was censured by a vote of the Court of Proprietors two years after his retirement from India. An attempt was made to recall Canning in the height of his struggle during the Mutiny, and it was not till after his death, worn out by grief and suffering, that he received the full meed of his labours. Other Viceroys have met with similar obloquy or injustice, and have had to wait for a belated, sometimes only a posthumous, recognition of their service.

I said a little earlier that I would explore the extraordinary vicissitudes that have attended the nomination of Governors General and Viceroys of the past, and reveal some of the bitter animosities and disappointments to which it has given rise. But in order to understand these, it is necessary to say something about the amazing and almost incredible system under which these appointments were made and the Government of India was conducted. By a seeming fatality that Government has never been able to divest itself—nor can it now—of a dualism that has been inseparable from its being and has at times almost ruined its strength. This dualism has arisen not merely from the simultaneous existence of one half of the Government in England, and the other half in India—for that is a feature of the administration from a sovereign centre of all dependencies or dominions—but from the subdivision of that authority both in England and in India. In England for nearly three-quarters of a century there were Homeric contests between the Court of Directors and the Government as represented by the Board of Control. When both the Court and the Board had disappeared the rival antagonists were sometimes the Secretary of State for India and his Council. As between England and India the Secretary of State in Council has at times been in active disagreement with the Governor General in Council, or the Secretary of State with the Viceroy. In India, British administration started with an almost inconceivable division of the attributes of sovereignty between the East India Company and the Mohammedan representative in Bengal of the shadowy phantom at Delhi. Later on the contest was waged sometimes between the Governor General and his Council and sometimes between the Governor General and the Commander-in-Chief. More recently a fresh source of dispute has arisen from the creation in India of two branches of the administration, the one in Indian and the other in Government hands. But never was the dual system more productive of mischief or more pernicious in its effects than when it was applied to the selection of the man at home who was to be the head of the Government at Calcutta.

Before the Regulating Act of 1773 the English in India were merely the representatives of a Trading concern, the East India Company, whose object was to make money, and which had no statutory warrant either to annex territory or to exercise sovereign rule. Under the Charter of 1698 the Company was administered by a Court of 24 Directors possessing £2,000 worth of stock, and a Court of Proprietors possessing £500 worth of stock (raised by the Act of 1773 to £1,000). The foundation of British rule in the stricter sense of the term was laid by that Act, and upon it has been reared the entire superstructure of subsequent British statutes, which have converted India into the most powerful possession of the British Crown. This legislation may be viewed in its effect upon the Government of India (*a*) in England and (*b*) in India ; and a few words may here be said about both. We will begin with the former.

Lord North's Act of 1773 left the control in London in the hands of the two Courts of Directors and Proprietors, with the slight modification above referred to. Pitt's Act of 1784 made the first real and drastic change in the position of the Company, for there was now instituted a Board of Control, to represent the Government, consisting of a President and five other Privy Councillors (to include the Chancellor of the Exchequer and one Secretary of State). This unpaid body was invested with great powers, for it had access to all records, papers and correspondence of the Court of Directors, it could approve, modify or amend the latter's Despatches, and issue independent orders of its own. In practice this was done through a Secret Committee of the Court, consisting of three Directors chosen by the Court, who were empowered to transmit to India any orders from the Board of Control, requiring secrecy, without informing the other Directors. As time passed, this Secret Committee was always composed of the Chairman and Deputy Chairman of the Court, who were popularly known as The Chairs. At the same time that the new and extraneous authority of the Board of Control, as representing His Majesty's Government, was set up, the Court of Proprietors (who had recently shown their independence by overruling a resolution of the Court of Directors to recall Warren Hastings, in 1781) was deprived of its powers to modify or veto the proceedings of the latter. Nevertheless, while the Court of Proprietors was thus extinguished, and while the Court of Directors was reduced to a position of deliberate subordination to the Government, as representing the Crown, the Court was allowed to retain its right of patronage and considerable powers of revision. In other words, it could still appoint the Governor General[1] and all the principal functionaries in India ; but the power of removal might in future be exercised, not merely by the Court, but also by the Crown. In practice the powers of the Board of Control came to be exercised exclusively by the President, who was not at first, though he later became, a Cabinet Minister, and who gradually took the position that was afterwards filled by the Secretary of State.

Such was the form of Government that was invented by the wisdom of our ancestors for the regulation of the affairs of India. Had a Committee been assembled from the padded chambers of Bedlam, they could hardly have devised anything more extravagant in its madness, or more mischievous in its operation. To it must be attributed many of the astounding errors and contradictions that characterised our Indian policy at that time.

An account has been left by Sir John Kaye of the manner in which this dual form of administration worked in practice. He describes how the Despatches to India were originally prepared by the Directors, and sent over to the Board of Control; how the latter acted in dealing with them, very often substituting something entirely different; how the Secret Committee gradually became " a mystery and a mockery "; how the Board of Control also dwindled into a single and often ignorant man, and how in all questions of peace and war, and foreign affairs, the Court of Directors ended by " having no more power than the Mayor and Aldermen of any Corporation Town."[2] We have ourselves seen in the first volume of this work the astounding fatuity of this system in the long controversy between the Court of Directors and Lord Wellesley.

Sir John Kaye's picture was true enough in one aspect, but it underrated the power that was still left to the Court of Directors both by the prerogative of patronage and by the right of initiation. Though the Government could decline to accept the nomination of the Court, it could not actually enforce its own, and was on several occasions driven to compromise. Further, the Governor General, who had been appointed by the Court of Directors, had, if he were wise, to live on

[1] By the Act of 1786 the assent of the King to the choice of a Governor General by the Company was not required. It only became obligatory under a subsequent Act of 1813.
[2] " The Administration of the East India Company," 1853.

friendly terms with them. Lord Wellesley suffered in the long run for his persistent insubordination. Lord Dalhousie, who was scarcely less imperious, always prided himself upon having maintained good relations with the Court, and wrote regularly by every mail to the Chairman, as well as to the President of the Board of Control—a prudent but indefensible duplication of labour. In the last resort the Governor General possessed the immense advantage that, owing to the enormous distance of time—very often from a year to a year and a half—that separated the issue of a Despatch at Calcutta from the arrival of the reply, he could count upon forcing the hand either of the Court or of the Home Government by a *fait accompli* (though he might have to pay the penalty afterwards) ; and Lord Wellesley made ample use of this advantage. On the other hand, the Governor General could never be quite sure—unless he had the President of the Board of Control and His Majesty's Government behind him—that he might not in the end find himself suddenly recalled. The Court of Directors enjoyed the further advantage that, as the Despatches to the Government of India were drawn up in the first place at their office in Leadenhall Street, and as the experts were stationed there, and not in those days in Whitehall, it was not very easy for the President of the Board— except in matters of peace or war and the drawing up of treaties, in which he was supreme—to exercise his authority or even to criticise what the experts had written. Thus in the last resort he was frequently obliged to sanction what the Court with its superior knowledge, or the Governor General with his superior independence, had already half carried out. But this is only a further illustration of the anomalous nature of the entire proceedings.

By the Charter Act of 1833 the Company was required to close its commercial business in India, and its trading power now came to an end. The Court of Directors, however, was still so firmly entrenched that its administrative and political powers were left undisturbed, and it continued to enjoy the right of Indian patronage, the appointment of the Governor General being subject to the approval of the Crown. But the numbers of the Court were now reduced in 1853 from 24 to 18, one-third of whom were in future to be nominated by the Crown.

While I was in India there appeared in the " Life of Lord Dalhousie," by Sir W. Lee Warner, who, after service in India, had a long official career in the India Office in London, an account of the above system, based upon the official records of the Office, which throws so valuable a light upon its almost incredible features that I do not hesitate to transcribe a portion of it :

" The system by which the President of the Board controlled the Indian Governments from its office in Cannon Row through the Court of Directors in Leadenhall Street, affords an interesting study in the methods of compromise.   The law gave to the Commissioners for the affairs of India authority to control, direct, and superintend all acts, operations and concerns which in anywise related to civil or military government or revenues of India.   And yet there was no direct official correspondence between these Commissioners and the Governments in India.   In order, then, to ensure to the Board the full knowledge of what was going on, the Directors were bound by law to send to that body copies of all their proceedings, and of all the letters which they received.   The Directors were similarly required to obey the orders and instructions of the Board touching the civil or military government or revenues of India.   Thus the Court of Directors was tied hand and foot by the Board, which signified the President, while he in turn signified the Government or Crown.

" But a Government, even in the United Kingdom, does not like to share its secrets with twenty-four gentlemen not in the Cabinet.   Therefore ' secret ' arrangements had to be made for confidential communication between the Board and the Indian Governments.   The statutes of Parliament conferred upon two authorities the power of making a despatch or order ' secret.' The Board at home had a wide, but not an unlimited, range of discretion in dealing with a matter of business in the secret department.   It might issue orders as ' secret ' on matters concerning war or peace, negotiations with the Native States, and foreign affairs.   But the Governments of India might go further.   They might mark their letters ' secret,' if they treated of the subjects just mentioned, and also if they concerned the civil government of India. The effect of a letter being marked ' secret ' was to exclude it from the general cognisance of the Court of Directors, and yet the letter had to proceed from that body.   The procedure adopted to this end was as follows :—If the President of the Board prepared a despatch to the Governor General and marked it ' secret,' he caused it to be sent by his secretary to a Secret Committee of the Court of Directors, with the following endorsement on the draft : ' The Commissioners for the affairs of India direct that a letter be sent by the Secret Committee according to the tenor of the foregoing draft.'   Thereon the Secret Committee, who were a small section of the Directors, and were under a sworn obligation not to divulge its contents, issued under their own signature, and as from themselves, the letter sent down to them for communication to the Governor General or to the Governor of the Presidency concerned.   When the Governor General, or a Governor, in his turn either wrote a ' secret ' letter or replied to a secret letter, he addressed it to the Secret Committee and not to the Court of Directors, and the Secret Committee were bound by law to send it on to the Board of Control. The records of the India Office show how jealous the Board of Control was of its rights. It frequently censured a Government of India for writing to the Court on matters which, in its opinion, ought to have been made secret, and addressed to the Secret Committee. On the other hand, if the Government of India marked a letter ' secret ' on a subject in which the Board did not wish to concern itself, the letter was handed over by the Board to the Court for disposal.

" The wonder is that such a system ever worked without intolerable friction. There were, however, three checks which operated to prevent any grave misuse of the arbitrary authority which, through the signature of two or three members of the Court, the President exercised in the name of a body of Commissioners. In the first place he was acting with the knowledge of his colleagues in the Government, or at any rate his acts involved them in a common responsibility. Secondly, the Court of Directors had its representatives in Parliament. When Hobhouse, afterwards Lord Broughton, was President of the Board, Hogg, the Chairman of the Court and member of the Secret Committee, his political opponent, was also a member of the House of Commons. On rare occasions Hogg protested against the issue of a despatch from the Board, and carried his opposition so far as to demand an interview with the Prime Minister. At other times he would threaten opposition in Parliament, and so secure a compromise. The Company had other champions of its rights besides the Directors, and even in the House of Lords it arranged matters so as to secure a hearing. Thus indirect checks were brought to bear on the Board in Parliament ; and outside the Chambers the press was freely used. Thirdly, the Governor General and the Governors could make their voices heard, and they maintained a constant ' private ' correspondence by the fortnightly mails with the President of the Board. It must be admitted that, even with these checks, the system of dual government led to mistakes which might have been avoided if the Board could have acted in closer consultation with members of the Court of Directors, who knew the feelings of the Indian peoples, and possessed an expert acquaintance with problems of Indian administration."

It will, I think, be generally recognised that Sir W. Lee Warner's apologia is in no sense an exculpation. The system over whose nakedness he sought to throw the garb of official decency *did* lead to mistakes that were gross and calamitous. The friction which it generated *was* intolerable, as the evidence recorded in other parts of this work will have abundantly shown ; and it brought the career of more than one Governor General to an inglorious end.

In 1858 the final act of decapitation of the Company took place :

LORD CORNWALLIS AS GOVERNOR GENERAL (1793)

From the painting by A. W. Devis.

the system of dual government, after lasting, with all its incongruities and misadventures, for over 80 years, was terminated ; the two rival fictions of the Court of Directors and the Board of Control both disappeared ; and the Government was transferred from the East India Company to the Crown.   The Home Government of India was reconstituted on its present basis, a Secretary of State for India, assisted by an India Council, being set up ; and this is the constitution, responsible to Parliament and subject to its final authority, by which India has ever since been, and still is, governed.

Next let us see the manner in which the same series of statutes, dealing as they did with both aspects of Indian Government, affected the position of that Government and its head in India.   By the Act of 1773 the former Trading Council in Calcutta was replaced by the appointment of a Governor General with a Council of four for the Presidency of Bengal.   These were to hold office for five years, at the end of which time the patronage became vested in the Company. Decisions were to be made in Council by the majority of those present, the Governor General having a casting vote in the case of an equal decision.   This was the fatal system of dualism in its worst and most pernicious form, under which the administration of Warren Hastings was held up for nearly two years, and that great man was subject to a weekly and almost daily obstruction that would have broken the heart of anyone less prescient and indomitable.   It was because of the scandal thus created that Lord Cornwallis, before he went out for the first time to India, insisted as a condition of his acceptance that he should be given the constitutional power to overrule his Council. Accordingly the Act of 1786 was passed, which clothed the Governor General with that power " in cases of high importance, and essentially affecting the public interest and welfare "—a provision which was repeated in the Act of 1793, and slightly expanded in the Act of 1870, where the words " the safety, tranquillity or interests of the British possessions in India " are cited as the determining test.   In such cases both parties, the overruler and the overruled, were originally required and are now authorised to record their opinion in formal Minutes to be sent to the Secretary of State.   Since 1870 this overruling power has only twice been taken advantage of by the head of the Government of India, viz. by Lord Lytton in 1879, when he partially abolished the Indian import duties on English cotton goods ; and by Lord Ripon in 1881, when he insisted upon the evacuation of Kandahar.[1] I never had occasion to make use of it, and would have shrunk greatly from doing so. Under the political system that has grown up within the last few years the Viceroy is much more likely to have to overrule the Legislative Council or Assembly than the colleagues with whom he sits in the Executive Council.

By the Charter Act of 1833 the Governor General in Council of Bengal became the Governor General of India in Council, and Lord William Bentinck, as we have seen, became the first Governor General under the new system. In 1861 the Governor General was given the power, when visiting any part of India without his Council—as he was increasingly obliged to do—to nominate one of his Council to be President of the Council in his absence. But the poison of dualism was still rioting in the veins of Indian Administration, for the two parties were both invested with semi-dictatorial powers. The Governor General, many hundreds of miles away from his colleagues, could exercise the full powers of the Governor General in Council, except that he could not legislate ; the Council, left behind at Calcutta, could exercise the same powers, except that it could not give assent to laws. By this astonishing system or lack of system were the affairs of India carried on. Under the Act of 1833 the Governor General had also been constituted the Governor of Bengal, though when absent from Calcutta he could delegate his functions to the senior Member of his Council. Eight such appointments, with the title of President of the Council of India and Deputy Governor of Fort William and the Town of Calcutta, were made between the years 1837 and 1855. In 1855, the Governor General having ceased to be Governor of Bengal, and a Lieutenant Governorship having been created for that Presidency instead, the title was changed to Deputy Governor of the Fort and Garrison of Fort William, and four such appointments were made in the succeeding decade. It is interesting to recall that the Deputy Governor in the period before 1855 used to reside, in the absence of the Governor General, either in Government House, Calcutta, or at Barrackpore. Mr. W. B. Bird was in occupation of the former in 1843, Sir H. Maddock and Sir John Littler of the latter in 1849 and 1851.

In 1861 a new arrangement was made by statute for filling a vacancy

---

[1] " Life of Lord Ripon," by Lucien Wolf, 1921, Vol. II, p. 164.

caused by the retirement of the Viceroy.   Hitherto, as has been seen, the senior Member of Council officiated pending the arrival of a successor.   But now, in order to escape the situation in which a man might be called upon to act as head of the Government without possessing a first-hand knowledge of Indian administration—*e.g.* a Law or Finance Member, who might happen at the moment to be the senior Member of Council—it was decided that the senior of the two Governors of Madras and Bombay should fill the place, the senior Member of Council only occupying it (as he did after the deaths of Lord Elgin and Lord Mayo) for the few days that might elapse before the Governor could arrive.   It was as Governor of Madras that Lord Ampthill acted for me in the interval between my first and second terms of office from May to December 1904.   The Governor of Bengal has, since the creation of that office, been added to the qualifying list.

It will be seen from this narrative to what chances and vicissitudes the appointment of the head of the Government of India was exposed, until it was finally taken over by the Crown.   Nominally the Court of Directors were the appointing Power ; but their prerogative was continually being modified or restricted, partly by legislation, partly by the growing power of the Government.   The general practice was for the President of the Board of Control, after his right had been established by law, to intimate to the Court of Directors that such or such an appointment would receive the sanction of the Crown.   Sometimes, on the other hand, the Court of Directors would be first in the field by submitting their preference to the Government ; sometimes again they acted on their own account.   Neither party was, however, in the position to ensure the acquiescence of the other, and the question was quite likely to resolve itself into a ding-dong battle between the two, in which in the last resort the Government possessed the superiority.   The same conflict of interest, leading to undignified quarrels and unsatisfactory compromises, existed in the relations of both Powers with the Governor General.   If the Court of Directors supported him, the Board of Control was likely to go into opposition.   If he was a Government man, the Directors were not inclined to make things easy.   On the whole it was to the interest of the Governor General to have the President of the Board behind him ; and if they stood together, they were tolerably certain to prevail.   But again can anything more incongruous be imagined than a system which provided a man with two masters shouting, or rather posting, defiance to each other, at a distance of 6,000 miles from their victim? In only a very ambiguous sense could he be described as *tertius gaudens*.

I will now show how this extraordinary system operated in the selection and treatment of individual men. It is a tale, collected from many often obscure sources, which has never before been told, and if it leaves us with a feeling of consternation at the methods, it also leaves us with a profound sympathy for the sufferers. It will further reveal that the appointment was the subject of much more systematic and at times reprehensible political intrigue in England than is fortunately now the case.

During Warren Hastings' prolonged tenure of the office of Governor General, in the course of which he more than once resigned or nearly resigned, or was recalled or nearly recalled (*vide* the next chapter of this work), there were plenty of aspirants for the soon-to-be-empty post. Foremost among these was Sir Philip Francis, whose bitter animosity in India was inflamed by the hope of succeeding his formidable rival. Indeed he was firmly convinced that if only Hastings could be got rid of, he would become Governor General, and he continued to cherish this vain ambition from 1777 to 1780.[1] He wrote from India to a friend in London : " I am now, I think, on the road to the Government of Bengal, which I believe is the first situation in the world attainable by a subject. I will not baulk my future." [2] We shall see how at a later date this hope was again revived.

As a matter of fact the Ministry at home had made up their minds that Lord Cornwallis was to be the man ; and as far back as May 1782 Lord Shelburne, during his brief tenure of office as Prime Minister, had approached him on the subject, offering him the combined posts of Governor General and Commander-in-Chief. Cornwallis had some doubts on the subject, considering the powers of the Governor General, as shown in the case of Warren Hastings, to be unduly restricted, and regarding himself as not yet released from his parole after the surrender at York Town. These objections, however, had been overcome when Shelburne fell and was succeeded by the brief coalition of North and Fox. They also considered the suggestion ; but it would appear to have advanced so little that in September 1783 the Duke of Portland

---

[1] " Memoirs of Sir Philip Francis," by J. Parker and Herman Merivale, Vol. II, pp. 79, 192.
[2] " Private Life of Warren Hastings," by Sir Ch. Lawson, 1895, p. 75.

wrote to the Duke of Manchester to sound him as to his willingness to succeed Warren Hastings. The Duke was not anxious to go to India unless it was necessary in the public interest.[1] Almost immediately afterwards the Coalition fell and Pitt came in (December 1783). He at once sounded Cornwallis, but offered him the Indian Command-in-Chief alone. The worthy soldier was torn between considerations of personal convenience—for he had no desire to go out—and public duty, but replied that, as he had previously been offered the two offices in combination, he must either have both or neither. In February 1785 Cornwallis positively refused the offer. But the negotiations continued fitfully throughout the year after Hastings had already left India, and finally culminated in a reluctant acceptance by Cornwallis and his appointment by a unanimous resolution of the Court of Directors of 24th February, 1786, the condition which he had laid down, that the powers of the Governor General should be extended so as to admit of his overruling his Council, having been acceded to by Pitt, and embodied in an Act that year.

Meanwhile Sir John Macpherson had already, on the departure of Hastings from India in February 1785, become Acting Governor General under the Acts of 1773 and 1781, by which the senior Member of Council filled the vacancy until an appointment was made from home. Macpherson, who was cordially detested by Cornwallis and by a good many others, was reappointed to Council, when the latter arrived in September 1786 (he resigned four months later); but had the impertinence to claim that, having been appointed, he had a right to the post for five years and that Cornwallis' appointment was illegal[2]—a contention which was warmly repudiated by Pitt. He subsequently endeavoured, but without success, to obtain a promise of the reversion to Cornwallis. This was the first of the bickerings to which the appointment of the Governor General was henceforward to be so freely and continuously exposed.

Whether Macpherson was or was not substantive Governor General is a question that admits of dispute. The view has been generally held in India that he was only acting. The India Office incline to the opposite opinion, which is supported by the terms of the preamble to the Commission given to Lord Cornwallis, which ran as follows :

[1] " Eighth Report of the Historical MSS. Commission," App. II, pp. 132-7.
[2] " Correspondence of Marquis Cornwallis " (ed. Ch. Ross), 1859, Vol. I, p. 326.

. . . " Whereas on or about the 12th day of February 1785 John Macpherson Esq. as our senior Civil Counsellor of the Presidency of Fort William in Bengal succeeded to the office and place of Governor General of the said Presidency upon the resignation of Warren Hastings Esq. our late Governor General of the said Presidency and hath ever since held and now doth hold the said office. Now know ye that we the said United Company do remove and displace the said John Macpherson Esq. from the said office of Governor General of the said Presidency . . ."

Had he been merely acting, such formal removal would hardly have been necessary.

Meanwhile another tentative Governor General had also arrived upon the scene. This was Lord Macartney, whose meteoric appearance and exit are among the most extraordinary episodes of that disordered time. Macartney, who was a man of considerable distinction— he had already been Chief Secretary for Ireland (1767-72), had been made an Irish Peer (1776), and had become Governor of Madras (1781) with a half-promise of the reversion of Bengal—was actually appointed Governor General by a Resolution of the Court of Directors of 17th February, 1785. The votes on this occasion are said to have been equal, and the final decision in favour of Macartney over the rival candidate (Vansittart) was arrived at by the casting of lots.[1] The British Government, however, who were angling for Cornwallis, did not approve.

While these events were passing in England, Macartney, who had resigned the Governorship of Madras, when his policy towards Tippu was not approved in England, turned up at Calcutta in June 1785, being anxious to secure the support of the Bengal Government for his views. While there he received a Despatch from the Board of Control offering him the post of Governor General in succession to Hastings. Learning however that Macpherson claimed to be acting under the Act of 1774, which laid down that the senior Member of Council should succeed on the occurrence of a vacancy, and that the Supreme Court would support this contention, even to the point of ordering his deportation from the country, should he persist, he declared with commendable prudence that the offer from England was one which, in the circumstances of the case, he could not accept. The anecdotal William Hickey, who

---

[1] Sir N. Wraxall ("Posthumous Memoirs," Vol. II, pp. 1-4) says that he was appointed by a majority of one in the Court.

was living in Calcutta at the time, says that Macartney's visit was chiefly remarkable for the penalty that he was called upon to pay for too openly avowed a prejudice against the use either of carriages, punkahs or palanquins. He insisted on walking about Calcutta in the height of the summer carrying a small umbrella in his hand which he disdained to open. The result was that he was assailed with violent headaches and then with fever, after which he adopted a more rational procedure, and speedily recovered his health.[1]

Macartney, however, though he had declined the rather precarious nomination that had reached him at Calcutta, resumed active negotiations for the post, which had not yet been filled, when he returned to England. Here he pitched his claims too high, demanding *inter alia* a British Peerage. At the same time his candidature was not acceptable to many of the Directors and Proprietors of the East India Company and was vigorously opposed by the partisans of Sir John Macpherson, who was already in the saddle at Calcutta, and of Warren Hastings. Pitt is said to have been persuaded at one stage by Dundas to concur in this appointment. But there was a growing feeling that another choice was required ; and it soon became apparent that Macartney had lost his tide. He took this in very good part and is even said to have expressed delight.[2] He was granted a life annuity of £1,500 and was presented with a valuable piece of plate by the Court of Directors, and was plentifully consoled at a later date by being made an Irish Earl (1792), Ambassador Extraordinary to Peking (1792-1794), Confidential Envoy to Louis XVIII at Verona (1795), a British Peer, and Governor of the Cape (1796-1798). Thus disappears one more transitory phantom from the scene.

At this point another figure passes with even greater rapidity across the stage. This was Lord Walsingham, who was actually offered the appointment by Pitt. The arrangement fell through because Walsingham made conditions, in the event of his dying while in India, which the Minister declined to accept.[3]

Cornwallis was now left in undisputed possession of the scene : and his appointment was made, amid general consent, in the manner already described. During his long tenure of the office, the question of a

[1] " Memoirs of Wm. Hickey," Vol. III, p. 268.
[2] Compare Sir John Kaye's " Lives of Indian Officers " and Barron's " Life of Lord Macartney."
[3] Sir N. Wraxall, " Posthumous Memoirs," Vol. II, p. 62.

successor did not become urgent for some time, although at an early date Cornwallis himself expressed a desire that General, afterwards Sir William Medows, a capable soldier, of whom he had formed a high opinion and who became Governor and Commander-in-Chief—first in Bombay, and afterwards in Madras—should be the man. In July 1787 Dundas wrote to Cornwallis that such also was the intention of the Home Government. Later, in April 1790, Pitt informed the Chairman of the Court of Directors that he thought no better choice could be made ; and the Court on the same day passed a Resolution approving the appointment, when Cornwallis, who was talking of coming back, should retire. Medows, however, declined the offer, which reached him in camp before Seringapatam, and, being dissatisfied with his own conduct in the campaign against Tippu, tried to take his life, an attempt in which he fortunately failed. In 1792 he returned to England, and afterwards became Governor of the Isle of Wight, and Commander-in-Chief in Ireland.

Cornwallis finally retired in October 1793.

Pitt would appear for some time to have been casting about for a successor, and we hear, on the authority of Lord Malmesbury, that in July 1792 he " offered the Governor Generalship of India to be disposed of by opposition ; he had mentioned Lord North, Mr. Wyndham and Tom Grenville as three of the properest men to be chosen from—the Duke of Portland wished for Sir Gilbert Elliot " [1] (the future Lord Minto). A little later Fox told Lord Malmesbury that Lord North (who was soon to become the third Earl of Guilford) had actually been offered the post, but had declined it. The way in which the Governor Generalship was hawked about at this period—the Prime Minister, the President of the Board of Control, and the Court of Directors making offers, usually for political reasons, and even proceeding to appointments, quite independently of each other, and with bewildering rapidity—being one of the marvels of that topsy-turvy age. Meanwhile the Court of Directors, apprehensive of a political appointment, had already provisionally appointed as Cornwallis' successor Sir John Shore (afterwards Lord Teignmouth), who had been a Member of Council for three years but had returned to England in 1790, on the understanding that if the Government decided to send

<hr />

[1] " Diaries and Correspondence " of the 1st Earl of Malmesbury, 1844, Vol. II, pp. 468-9, 472.

out a statesman from England he would take second place.   Shore was in rather a delicate position, having arrived in Calcutta in March 1793 in the expectation of taking over at once.   For seven months he resided, without a seat in Council, in a Garden House in Garden Reach ; and it says much for his tact and good sense that his nomination was warmly welcomed by Cornwallis, although the latter was strongly opposed to a Civil Service appointment.   Like his predecessors in the same category, Shore does not seem to have coveted the promotion, and would have preferred not to take it.   There was further a doubt as to the legality of his position, since the Act of 1784 forbade the appointment of a Covenanted Servant as Governor General.   This point however was slurred over or ignored, and Shore remained as substantive Governor General for close upon the full term of five years.

We now come again to a period of some confusion, and Madras once more holds the key to the situation.   It would seem to have been the regular thing in England at that time to appoint a man to the Governorship of Madras—which ranked next in estimation to Calcutta —with the reversion to Bengal in his pocket.   We have already seen two instances of this practice : and we are here presented with a third. Lord Hobart, afterwards fourth Earl of Buckinghamshire, had expected to become Governor General in place of Sir John Shore, and is even said to have been officially nominated by the Court on 24th December, 1793.[1]   This appointment however was not ratified, as Shore was maintained in office.   Hobart was consoled with Madras, to which he went as Governor in September 1794 with a clear promise of the succession in Bengal.   Unfortunately for himself he had a violent quarrel with Sir John Shore, over the affairs of the Nawab of the Carnatic.[2] The Court of Directors took the side of the Governor General, and recalled Hobart in 1798, consoling him with a pension of £1,500 per annum and a summons, during his father's lifetime, to the House of Lords.   He did not fare badly in the future, for he became in succession Secretary of State for War and the Colonies (1801-1804), Chancellor of the Duchy of Lancaster (1805 and 1812), Postmaster General (1806-7), and President of the Board of Control (1812-1816).

Meanwhile, as Sir John Shore's term of office was drawing to a close, Pitt in England, casting about for a successor, decided upon his own

---

[1] R. R. Pearce, " Memoirs and Correspondence of the Marquis Wellesley," Vol. I, p. 132.
[2] The story is told in the " Life of Lord Teignmouth," Vol. I, pp. 247, 297, 353, 393.

brother-in-law, Edward Eliot, eldest son of Lord Eliot of St. Germans. Dundas, who was President of the Board of Control, forwarded the recommendation to the Court of Directors, who acquiesced. This was in February 1797. Eliot however, who suffered from ill-health, was forbidden by his doctors to accept, and a few weeks later died. He was a popular person, but without achievement.[1]

Either before or immediately after this abortive nomination, a further attempt was made to secure once more the services of the veteran Cornwallis. The Government had been made very anxious by the mutiny of the officers of the Bengal Army, which it was thought that a soldier of the prestige of Cornwallis could alone compose. Dundas urged him most strongly to go : and matters proceeded so far that he was actually " sworn into office " as Governor General and Commander-in-Chief on 1st February, 1797, and began to make his preparations for a twelve months' residence in India. Shortly afterwards however the Court of Directors and the Board of Control decided upon concessions which quieted the officers, but which Cornwallis did not at all approve ; so he gave up the appointment in August, although at a later date (April 1799) he repented the decision.[2]

Madras now again came to the rescue. When it was anticipated that Lord Hobart would proceed to Calcutta, Lord Mornington had been offered the Governorship of that Presidency with the familiar reversion of Bengal. He had not made up his mind to accept the post, when the scenery was suddenly shifted by the incident which I have described, and the larger prize was open to the young man, whose ambition would never have been satisfied with so humble a stage as Madras. His achievements in Bengal are told in many other parts of this book.

Three-quarters of a century later, the same experience was repeated in the case of Lord Lytton, who, having been offered and having declined the Governorship of Madras in 1875, was greatly astonished, as was everyone else, when, a year after, Disraeli insisted on sending him to Calcutta.

Pending the arrival of Mornington in Calcutta, Sir Alured Clarke, who was Provisional Commander-in-Chief in Bengal and senior Member

---

[1] The story may be found in Lord Stanhope's "Life of Pitt," Vol. III, p. 63, and in Torrens' "Marquis Wellesley," p. 120.
[2] *Vide* "Cornwallis" (Rulers of India Series), by W. S. Seton Karr, p. 162, and "Lives of Indian Officers," by Sir John Kaye, Vol. I, p. 168.

of Council, acted as Governor General from March to May 1798, having been provisionally nominated to that office by the Court of Directors in the previous year. He did not however vacate his seat in Council, and reverted to it when Lord Mornington assumed office.

It must have been between 1800 and 1802, if a story in the recently published Diary of the Royal Academician, Joseph Farington, is true, that on one or other of the occasions when Lord Wellesley was either on the verge of being recalled or was threatening resignation, Pitt tried to persuade Lord Castlereagh to go out to India. The following is the reference, which, so far as I know, is not confirmed by any other source :

"July 27, 1811. Lord Castlereagh sat to Lawrence this morning. He told Lawrence that, after the measure of the Union had been effected, an offer was made to Him by the Ministry (Mr. Pitt, etc.) of the Governor General-ship of Bengal, which He declined."

When it was known that Lord Wellesley (the previous Lord Morn-ington) was finally to retire in 1805, the reaction in England against his spirited but costly policy, with its ruinous financial entailments, was so strong, both in Whitehall and in Leadenhall Street, that, by common agreement, it was decided once again to appeal to the indis-pensable Cornwallis. The claims of Sir George Barlow, who was destined to act a few months later, had indeed been canvassed. But the Court of Directors was alarmed at the succession of a member of Wellesley's Government, and the Home Government (Lord Castle-reagh was now at the Board of Control) also shared the view that some-one possessing greater authority and independence than an Indian Civilian was required. Lord Powis, till lately Governor of Madras as Lord Clive (he was the son of the great Robert Clive), declared that he had been promised the succession to Bengal by Lord Melville (Dundas) when he went out to Madras, and was very angry at being passed over.[1] But the Government and the Court would have no one but Cornwallis.

The old war-horse responded to the call with an alacrity and a loyalty that cannot be sufficiently praised. He was already sixty-six years of age, and his strength was greatly, and as it soon appeared fatally, impaired. Nevertheless for the third time he shouldered the burden, and for the second time went out to India as Governor General

[1] " Diaries and Correspondence of Rt. Hon. Geo. Rose," Vol. II, p. 158.

and Commander-in-Chief. Within little more than two months of his resumption of office he was a dead man.

With the death of Cornwallis, the floodgates of intrigue in England were at once opened, and for the best part of a year a turbid torrent poured through. Sir George Barlow, a Civilian, at once took over at Calcutta (October 1805) as senior Member of Council under the Act of 1793, without a special appointment being required for the purpose. The Court of Directors however, who as far back as 1802 had nominated Barlow as the successor to Wellesley, when the latter was expected to retire in that year, were now anxious that he should continue in the office, having confidence in his cautious and economical policy. Accordingly they confirmed his appointment on 25th February, 1806, and Lord Minto, who was President of the Board of Control, is said to have concurred.[1] But the succeeding Whig Government refused their assent, Lord Grenville, who was now President and who was a personal friend of Wellesley, being afraid that the latter's policy might be sharply reversed. The King accordingly was induced to vacate the appointment of Barlow (whom the Directors refused to recall) by the exercise of an extraordinary power vested in the Crown by the Act of 1784, and this in spite of the declaration in the Act of 1786 that the King's approval of the Company's choice of a Governor General was not required. It was not indeed till the Act of 1813 that it became necessary. Barlow may claim therefore to have been a real Governor General, and he discharged the duties of that office for the unexpected period of nearly two years. At the end of that time, inverting the familiar process, he was translated to Madras, where he served as Governor from December 1807 to May 1813, being eventually recalled, in connection with a military mutiny which his policy was thought to have provoked.

The scene now changes to London, and the malignant personality of Francis reappears upon the stage. Pitt died in January 1806, and upon the friendship of Fox, who became Foreign Secretary in the ensuing Administration, as well as upon the favour of the Prince of Wales,[2] Francis confidently relied. The old antagonist of Hastings had been active in Parliament, where he had made an elaborate speech on India in April of the previous year, and he now triumphantly antici-

---

[1] Thornton's " History of India," Vol. IV, p. 87.
[2] The Prince of Wales told Francis that " he had always designated me, particularly to Mr. Fox, as the person whom he meant to appoint to the Office of Governor General, and that he had signified the same expressly to Lord Moira, who heartily concurred in it."

pated that the dream of his life would be fulfilled.[1] It was a forlorn and foolish hope.   He had been absent from India for twenty-six years, and he was close upon sixty-six years of age, the age that had just driven Cornwallis to the grave.   As Lord Brougham caustically remarked : " The new Ministers could no more have obtained the East India Company's consent, than they could have transported the Himalaya Mountains to Leadenhall Street."[2]   Fox's friendship was unequal to the strain ; the appointment was refused ; and Francis quarrelled finally with his former patron, against whom he indulged in almost insane abuse, but who in a few months' time himself passed away.

Lord Brougham goes on to say that so lost to decency was Francis in the pursuit of the ambition of his life, that " a proposition was made to Lord Wellesley by him, through a common friend, with the view of obtaining his influence with Lord Grenville, supposed erroneously to be the cause of his rejection as Governor General " ; but that this was " at once and peremptorily rejected by that noble person, at a moment when Sir P. Francis was in the adjoining room, ready to conclude the projected treaty."[3]   A little more detail is furnished by Lord Colchester (Speaker Abbot), who says in his Diary for 30th June, 1806, that the emissary to Wellesley was Lady Devonshire, and that the proposed bargain was that if Wellesley would not oppose the appointment of Francis, the latter would extinguish Paull, who was threatening Wellesley with impeachment in the House of Commons.[4]

To revert to our narrative, Lord Minto, who had become President of the Board of Control in February 1806, but without a seat in the Cabinet, supported the Directors in their confirmation of Sir G. Barlow. But the Cabinet were determined to appoint the Earl of Lauderdale, in spite of a character of no great repute either in public[5] or in private life, and Minto was instructed to inform Barlow that it was intended to supersede him.   Two months later he was told to send out the news of the intended nomination of Lauderdale.   Writing on the same day to Lord W. Bentinck at Madras he thus unburdened himself :—

" The arrangements with regard to the Government of Bengal are always

[1] " Memoirs of Sir P. Francis," Vol. II, p. 350.
[2] " Statesmen of the Time of George III."
[3] Lord Brougham's sketch of Sir Philip Francis in his well-known Series of Statesmen is as pungent, though friendly, as that of Lord Wellesley is colourless and vapid.
[4] " Diary and Correspondence of Lord Colchester," 1861, Vol. II, p. 74.
[5] Farington in Volume III of his Diary says that during the French Revolution Lauderdale had avowed the strongest democratic principles and called himself " Citizen Lauderdale."

considered as belonging to the Cabinet, in which I have not a seat. But in fact this particular measure has been settled and conducted, I may say, with the entire exclusion of my voice or judgment in the affair. It was determined upon some weeks before it reached my ears, and it was only communicated to me on the day on which I was desired to communicate it to the Chairs."[1]

The Court of Directors were indignant at this treatment, regarding the appointment of Lord Lauderdale as an approval of Lord Wellesley's policy, which they had openly condemned. Accordingly they declined absolutely to consider his nomination, and, were it persisted in, had resolved to petition the King; to which the Government retorted by cancelling the Commission of Sir G. Barlow in the exercise of a power conferred by the Act of 1793,[2] by an instrument under the Sign Manual of the King.

" Both parties being equally resolved, the quarrel grew hot and bitter. Mr. Fox supported the pretensions of Lord Lauderdale with that passionate carelessness of consequences where his feelings were concerned which made him so beloved as a friend and so distrusted as a Statesman. He positively refused to listen to any other name, and somewhat autocratically desired that the Ministry should abandon the right of nomination altogether, rather than withdraw the one they had made in compliance with the objections of the Court of Directors. The discussions in the Cabinet were so prolonged and warm that Lord Minto appears to have had misgivings as to the extent to which the divergence of opinion manifested there might ultimately be carried. In the course of the summer he wrote to Lady Minto that, while believing Lord Lauderdale to have many qualifications for the Office of Governor General which would justify the appointment, he should himself resign if the Government persisted in forcing on the Company an individual obnoxious to them. A rupture between the Directors and the controlling power was imminent, when Lord Lauderdale suddenly withdrew his pretensions, induced by the serious illness of Mr. Fox to spare him further agitation on the subject."[3]

Lord Holland remarked that Lord Lauderdale's action,[4] designed out of regard for Fox's health, had the further advantage of " preserving his own, then recently recovered from a liver complaint, from the severe trial of an Indian climate."[5]

---

[1] " Lord Minto in India," p. 3. "The Chairs," as previously mentioned (*cf.* p. 68), was a synonym for the Secret Committee of the Court of Directors.

[2] *Vide* a letter from Lord Grenville to King George III, dated 27th May, 1806. (" Dropmore Papers," Historical MSS. Commission, Vol. VIII, p. 160.)

[3] " Lord Minto in India," p. 4.

[4] How certain Lord Lauderdale had been of his appointment may be seen from some passages in the " Farington Diary" for 27th and 29th May, and 8th and 19th June, 1806.

[5] " Memoirs of the Whig Party," by Lord Holland, Vol. I, p. 225.

This is the only occasion on which, to the best of my knowledge, the Court of Directors, in a stand-up fight with the Government over an appointment to India, won the day.   Even so it was only a qualified triumph, for they could not secure the appointment of their own nominee ; and the struggle left the two parties so exhausted that, after an interval in which the Directors sought to appease Fox by telling him of their willingness to appoint either Lord Howick, Lord H. Petty, or Lord Holland,[1] if he so desired, both parties acquiesced without more ado in the compromise appointment of Lord Minto himself. The latter was far from desirous, for private and domestic as well as public reasons, to accept the post, which, as he wrote, " I thought a week before no human persuasion could have led me to undertake." But that he did so from a sense of public duty is certain, although, as Fox remarked, " I suppose he can hardly expect that anyone will give him credit for having done his utmost to crush an opposition which, when successful, ends in his own appointment, nomination and acceptance of the office."[2]   Anyhow, Minto's nomination was accepted with equal grace by both sides. He did not however start for his new office till February 1807, or take over till July in that year.

The next succeeding appointment, that of Lord Moira (afterwards Lord Hastings), was happily devoid of the stormy accompaniments of its predecessor.   But, on the other hand, it illustrated the occasional and powerful intervention of the Court, for he is said to have received the offer direct from the Regent (George IV), of whom he was a personal friend, without any previous consultation with the Prime Minister, Lord Liverpool.[3]   Moira was, however, so important a personage that no objection was raised in any quarter.

When Lord Hastings sent in his resignation in the course of 1821, the Directors in January 1822 offered the post to the Right Hon. George Canning, who had been President of the Board of Control from June 1816 to January 1821.   Canning, who had withdrawn from the Ministry because of his unwillingness to share the responsibility for the trial of Queen Caroline, and who saw no immediate prospect of high office at home, accepted the offer, and made his preparations for departure.   Then came the news of the suicide of Castlereagh (who had

[1] "Farington Diary," Vol. III, p. 282.
[2] "Memoirs of the Whig Party," Vol. I, p. 227.
[3] "Glenbervie Journals," p. 204.

become Marquis of Londonderry) in August 1822. This opened up the prospect of the Foreign Office, if the King's illwill towards Canning could be overcome. The latter however thought it prudent to make no sign, and continued his preparations for departure. On 30th August he was entertained at a great banquet at Liverpool, and made a farewell speech to his constituents. However, the Prime Minister, Lord Liverpool, was determined to have Canning back at the Foreign Office, and succeeded eventually in obtaining the consent of the King. Therewith disappeared the chance of obtaining for India one of the most powerful intellects that would ever have administered its Government. His son, who was a very different type of man, made a great and deserved reputation in very different conditions. But would not the father have made a much greater?

Canning having been compelled to withdraw, the post of Governor General was again thrown open to the Tapers and Tadpoles, and they proceeded to gather around. Lord W. Bentinck, who had been once recalled from Madras in 1807 and had refused that Governorship when offered to him again in 1819, asked for the succession to Hastings, but was refused.[1] He was to obtain it six years later. Canning, who was anxious to create a vacancy in the Speakership for his friend Wynn, and to bring Huskisson into the latter's place in the Cabinet, then made the offer to the Speaker, Manners Sutton, who took a fortnight to consider the proposal, but finally declined. The post was finally offered to and accepted by Lord Amherst, under circumstances already detailed (see p. 56).

Amherst had his full share of troubles with the Court of Directors and the Government, and trembled for long on the verge both of resignation and recall. During this time Madras was once more on the brink of reappearing as the *deus ex machina*; for Sir Thomas Munro, who had made a great reputation as its Governor and had been made a Baronet in June 1825, heard that the home authorities were considering his translation to the higher sphere. He thereupon begged that the idea should be dropped, as he needed rest and was apprehensive that if he went to Bengal he could hardly hold out for two years.[2] He was right : for, before Lord Amherst had retired, Munro had himself paid the penalty of a career of devoted exertion with his life.

[1] Greville's " Journals of the Reigns of George IV and William IV," Vol. I, pp. 59, 60.
[2] " Sir Thomas Munro " (Rulers of India Series), by J. Bradshaw, pp. 204-5.

Canning, having become Prime Minister in April 1827, at once set about filling the prospective vacancy in India, and in the same month offered the Governor Generalship to Sir Charles Bagot, who had been Minister Plenipotentiary to France in 1814, the United States 1815–1820, St. Petersburg 1820, and The Hague 1824. On the next day the offer was withdrawn, but not before Bagot had declined it on the ground of a liver complaint, of which fourteen years later, when he was Governor General of Canada, he died.[1]

There now ensued a curious interlude in which the great name of Wellesley startles us by its reappearance. Canning had heard that Lord Wellesley, who was at that time Viceroy of Ireland, might wish to resign that office and might even be disposed to go out again to the scene of his former greatness twenty years before. He accordingly sounded the Court of Directors and wrote to Wellesley himself. Before the reply came from the East India House, Wellesley answered Canning, declining the offer, which indeed it is scarcely conceivable that, after his previous career and at the age of sixty-seven, he should have been willing for a moment to consider.[2] Canning then enquired (22nd May, 1827) whether Wellesley would take the Vienna Embassy, if a vacancy were created there by appointing as Governor General his brother, Sir Henry Wellesley, who had been Private Secretary to him in India over a quarter of a century before and had afterwards been Lieutenant Governor of Oudh. Lord Wellesley however refused to leave Ireland. Canning pressed him again about Vienna (7th June, 1827); but this suggestion also he declined. Lord Colchester says that the Indian appointment was actually offered to but declined by Sir Henry Wellesley, and that the Duke of Buckingham wanted to go.[3] But this is not confirmed by the Wellesley Papers; and I am disposed to think that when the elder brother refused, the idea of sending out the second (afterwards Lord Cowley) was abandoned.[4]

By a process of exhaustion therefore all parties arrived at the selection of Lord William Bentinck, whose perseverance was thus rewarded and his previous misfortunes wiped out.

When in due course the time came for Bentinck to retire, the era of controversy was once more revived, and the clash of competing claims

[1] " George Canning and his Friends," by Sir J. Bagot, Vol. II, pp. 484-5.
[2] But if Lord Colchester (" Diary," Vol. II, p. 122) is to be believed, he had been willing to consider a second term of office twenty years earlier.
[3] *Ibid.*, Vol. III, p. 468.
[4] " Wellesley Papers," Vol. II, pp. 153, 163, 192, 198.

was loud and prolonged. On this occasion no fewer than nine candidates appeared upon the scene. There were two names, either of which would have been accepted by the Court of Directors. These were Mountstuart Elphinstone and Sir Charles Metcalfe. Elphinstone, one of the most eminent administrators whom the Indian Civil Service has ever produced, had returned from the Governorship of Bombay in 1827, and was living in retirement in England. In 1834 the Chairman of the Court wrote and asked him to allow his name to be put forward as a candidate ; but Elphinstone declined on the score of health, and, though pressed to reconsider his refusal, persisted in it. Therein he was probably wise, for the Whig Government then in office held strongly to Canning's opinion that a Company's servant should not in any circumstances be made Governor General. Before the end of the year there was a change of Government, Sir Robert Peel becoming Prime Minister, and Lord Ellenborough President of the Board of Control. Again the Chairman proposed to His Majesty's Government that Elphinstone should be nominated, and Ellenborough approved. But again Elphinstone declined.[1] Had he accepted, it is not unreasonable to conjecture, from his earlier experience, that the war with Afghanistan would never have occurred.

The Company then put forward Metcalfe as their candidate. This distinguished man (afterwards Lord Metcalfe, known as the Liberator of the Indian Press) had been a Member of Council in India since 1827 and became Governor of Agra in 1834. Prior to that the Court of Directors, anticipating Lord W. Bentinck's retirement, had nominated Metcalfe Provisional Governor General by a letter of 27th December, 1833. They would gladly have followed this up by his permanent appointment ; but it was pointed out that this would be in contravention of the Act of 1784, which prohibited the selection of a Covenanted Servant, and was also contrary to the views of His Majesty's Government, who held to the Canning precept. Accordingly the Directors had to be content with a vigorous protest ; and Metcalfe, though he actually officiated as Governor General for a year, dropped out as a candidate for the substantive succession.[2] The contest was henceforward confined to home politicians.

---

[1] Kaye's " Lives of Indian Officers," pp. 431, 433.

[2] His subsequent career was remarkable, for the very Directors who had done their best to make him Governor General declined to make him Governor of Madras a few years later (being incensed at his action about the Press). He then became a Colonial Governor—Jamaica (1839-1842) and Canada (1843-1845).

The Melbourne Ministry, while it was still in office, proposed Charles Grant, then President of the Board of Control and afterwards Lord Glenelg ; but to this the Directors, still sore over the Charter Act of the previous year, which Grant had piloted through the House of Commons, refused to agree. They would have accepted Lord Auckland, but he, having received a pension of £2,000 per annum for life, was not inclined to go to India then. Lord Palmerston, who was Foreign Secretary, was then talked of, at which the Company manifested some reluctance, as also Lord Minto, son of the former Governor General. The name of Sir James Graham was next mentioned by the Directors with an intimation that they were unanimous in favouring his selection. Graham decided not to take action unless he received a formal proposal from Lord Melbourne. When the latter fell and was succeeded by Peel, Graham was again sounded, but, after declining to join Peel at home, was unwilling to accept from him a highly paid appointment abroad. Melbourne having returned to power, and the fifth Duke of Richmond having refused the post, Graham was once more offered it, but again declined. Once again, in June 1847, before the appointment of Dalhousie, Sir James Graham was approached by Lord John Russell, but on the advice of Peel again declined. At a later date he regretted his refusal.[1]

Among other names which are mentioned in the chronicles of the period as possible candidates were those of Lord Durham, Lord Mulgrave, and Lord Munster.

During Peel's short-lived Administration, the board having been swept clear by the numerous failures or refusals that I have recorded, the Directors and the Government agreed upon the nomination of Lord Heytesbury, a diplomatist of fair repute, who accepted and was duly sworn in. Then came the Dissolution of Parliament, as the result of which Peel was replaced by Melbourne (April 1835).

The new Ministers revoked Lord Heytesbury's appointment, although he had made all his preparations and was about to start. This unexpected development created a great stir, as indicating a determination to treat the Viceroyalty as a party question. Melbourne then made the offers to the Duke of Richmond and Sir James Graham, to which I have referred ; and, when they were refused, desisted for a

[1] " Life and Letters of Sir James Graham," by C. S. Parker, 1907, Vol. I, pp. 210, 225, 237 ; Vol. II, pp. 57, 439.

while from filling up the post, which was accepted somewhat later by one of his own colleagues, Lord Auckland.[1]

From this point we pass into a more tranquil zone. The appointment of Lord Ellenborough, unfortunate as it turned out to be, does not appear to have been contested—a man who had been three times President of the Board of Control might be thought to have overwhelming claims. Similarly the military position in India when he retired was such as to produce general acquiescence in the selection of an eminent soldier, Sir Henry Hardinge, to succeed him.

When Lord Hardinge's short term of office came to an end, there were several who desired or were mentioned for the post. The Court of Directors sent a list of names to Lord John Russell, including those of Lord Clarendon, Sir James Graham, and Lord Dalhousie. The offer was actually made for the fourth time to Graham with the approval of the Duke of Wellington, who was always consulted about Indian appointments. But Graham would take nothing from Russell, though the latter was so anxious to secure him that he left the offer open for a while.[2] The " Dictionary of National Biography " says that Lord Clarendon, at that time Lord Lieutenant of Ireland and afterwards Foreign Secretary, twice refused the office, and, if this be true, the present must have been one of those occasions.

We learn from Lord Dalhousie's Life that, Sir George, Arthur having resigned the Governorship of Bombay, the Chairman of the Directors (Sir J. Hogg) proposed to Hobhouse (President of the Board of Control) that the appointment, whether of Clarendon or Dalhousie, should be first made to Bombay, with the reversion of the Governor Generalship beyond.

At one moment the extraordinary idea was actually entertained by Hobhouse, the Duke of Wellington, and Lord John Russell, of sending out Sir Charles Napier, the conqueror of Sind, to succeed in a dual capacity both Sir Hugh Gough (Commander-in-Chief) and Lord Hardinge. Happily this aberration was not persisted in ; but it encouraged Napier, when he had been made Commander-in-Chief after Gough's recall, to put forward a claim to the reversion of the Governor Generalship, and in this pretension he was characteristically

---

[1] For the above narrative *vide*, in addition to the authorities already quoted, Thornton's " History of India," Vol. VI, pp. 22-50, Kaye's " Life of Metcalfe," Vol. II, pp. 233, 237, and Cotton's " Life of Elphinstone," p. 210.

[2] Greville's " Memoirs of Reign of Queen Victoria " (1837-1852), Vol. III, p. 87.

STATUE OF LORD DALHOUSIE

Sculpt. : Sir J. Steell.

supported by Lord Ellenborough.[1]   Napier seems actually to have proposed himself to Sir John Hobhouse, at a moment when the Government were believed to be dissatisfied with Dalhousie.[2]

Lord Normanby (the previous Lord Mulgrave), who had been Lord Lieutenant of Ireland (1835-1839), Colonial Secretary (1839), and Governor of Jamaica, also coveted Lord Hardinge's post.   But Russell would not agree, and sent him as Ambassador to Paris, finally offering the Governor Generalship to the junior of all the candidates, Lord Dalhousie, who, in a happy hour for India, accepted it.

When Lord Dalhousie in 1855 was drawing near to the end of his long term, it seems to have been confidently anticipated by him as well as by Indian public opinion in general that Lord Elgin, who afterwards followed Lord Canning, would be his successor.   But the Home Government had other ideas ; and Elgin was thought to have compromised his chances by previously refusing Madras.

Finally, after the Viceroyalty of Lord Canning, when the Company disappeared and the Government of India became an exclusive appanage of the Crown, the long reign of controversy and discord, one phase of which I have here traced, came to an end ; and henceforward any difference of opinion that might arise as to the selection of this or that individual for the supreme position in India was not a struggle between two rival powers, but only an incident of Governmental patronage.   A few interesting figures still pass across the stage.   It was always thought that Sir Henry Lawrence might, if his life had been spared, have been elevated to the office to which his brother afterwards succeeded ; and early in 1857, when Canning's health was believed to be breaking down, a provisional Commission had been sent to Henry, which however had not reached him when he died.   Indeed he had already been dead for three weeks (the news not having yet reached England) when the Commission was drawn up.   It was then sent on to his brother John.[3]   When the latter retired in 1869, the name of Sir Stafford Northcote was suggested, and he appears to have been willing to go.   But Disraeli chose Lord Mayo.   Doubt was felt in some quarters, including Lord Mayo himself, whether, after the Tory Ministry had fallen and Mr. Gladstone had succeeded in December

[1] " Life of Lord Dalhousie," by Sir W. Lee Warner, Vol. I, pp. 306-7.
[2] Greville, " Reign of Queen Victoria " (1837-1852), Vol. III, p. 280.
[3] " Private Letters of Lord Dalhousie," p. 392.

1868, the appointment would be persisted in ; and Lord Granville suggested to Mr. Gladstone the name of Lord Salisbury, who had been Secretary of State for India less than two years before. But the opposition of Queen Victoria was fatal to this proposal, and Lord Mayo, who had already started, was not interfered with.[1]

At a later date, when Lord Northbrook resigned in 1872, Disraeli offered the post to the third Earl of Powis, a nobleman of no great fame but with a solid reputation for sound sense, who declined it on the score of health. He then offered it to his lifelong colleague and friend, Lord John Manners, afterwards Duke of Rutland, who declined it for similar reasons. The names of Lord Dufferin and Lord Derby were both suggested to the Queen, but the Prime Minister preferred Lord Lytton, who was duly appointed.[2]

After the resignation of the latter and the formation of the Liberal Ministry in April 1880, Mr. Gladstone offered the Indian Viceroyalty to Mr. Goschen, who declined it.[3] He told me that among the reasons that influenced his refusal was the statutory inability of the Viceroy to return to England, for however brief a period, during his tenure of office.

Lord Lytton in a letter to the Queen of 4th May, 1880, stated that upon his own resignation, the post was also offered for a second time to Lord Northbrook.[4] But I have ascertained from the present Lord Northbrook that there was no foundation for this report. Indeed it was most unlikely that a Viceroy, who had resigned from India only four years before after a four years' term of office, should either be invited or be willing to resume the office.

I have already narrated the circumstances in which, on the retirement of Lord Lansdowne in 1893, Sir Henry Norman was offered, accepted, and then almost immediately declined the appointment, being replaced by Lord Elgin. The first choice of the Government had been Lord Cromer, and the appointment was pressed upon him by Lord Rosebery, at that time his chief as Secretary of State for Foreign Affairs. It would have been an ideal choice. But Lord Cromer told me personally that, like Lord Goschen, he could not consent to a five years' exile : and that he regarded the good health which he had

[1] Buckle's " Life of Lord Beaconsfield," Vol.V, p. 75.
[2] Ibid., Vol. V, p. 435.
[3] " Life of Lord Goschen," by Hon. A. D. Elliot, Vol. I, p. 196.
[4] " Personal and Literary Letters " (ed. Lady B. Balfour), Vol. II, p. 211.

enjoyed during his long service in Egypt as almost exclusively due to his annual holiday on the Scotch moors.

The biographer of that eminent Indian Administrator and charming man, Sir Alfred Lyall, says that the latter hoped to obtain the post on this occasion and was deeply disappointed at his failure.[1] I can hardly think that, at the age of nearly sixty, his candidature can have been seriously contemplated, though it is within my knowledge that at a later date, when he was already sixty-four, he desired to be considered for the Governorship of Bombay.

When the later Lord Minto retired in 1911, it is well known and has already been mentioned that Lord Kitchener desired greatly to fill the vacancy. His appointment was said to be favoured in the highest quarters, and not to be looked upon unfavourably by the head of the then Government. But the opposition of the Secretary of State, Lord Morley, based not on personal grounds but on the broadest considerations of political expediency, was invincible, and Lord Kitchener was denied his supreme ambition.

The most pleasing reflection that is suggested by the narrative which I have here unfolded is that the Viceroyalty of India—one of the greatest positions to which a subject of the Crown can aspire—has, as time passed, become less and less a subject of party or public contention, and is now conferred, not without the most anxious deliberation, upon the person believed to possess the highest qualifications for the office. It is also a matter for congratulation that, whereas in earlier times, and indeed as recently as the days of Lord Northbrook and Lord Lytton, a Governor General was apt to resign when a Government of different political complexion from that by which he had been appointed came into power, we are now familiar with the spectacle of the Viceroy, as a great public servant, superior to the political passions of the hour, remaining at his post and serving faithfully the Home Government, from whichever party it may be drawn.[2] But this is a tribute, not so much to the loyalty of the individual, still less to any flexibility of conscience on his part, as it is to the principle by which the Government of India has been increasingly lifted above the plane of political controversy at home, and is in process of becoming a tradition. May there be no rupture in its continuity.

[1] "Life of Sir Alfred Lyall," by Sir M. Durand, p. 358.
[2] For instance, the present Viceroy, Lord Reading, though he has only been in India four years, has already served under five British Administrations.

CHAPTER XI

PART II

SOME NOTES ON THE VICEROYALTY AND GOVERNOR GENERALSHIP OF INDIA

FROM the historical and constitutional questions which have occupied the greater portion of Part I of this chapter, I pass on to say something about the position, powers and prerogatives of the Viceroy and Governor General, and about the conditions which regulate his work in India, and his relations both with his colleagues and the Indian public and with the Government at home.

This is a subject that is rarely dealt with, if at all, in text-books, and that can perhaps only be adequately explored by one who speaks from personal experience.

On the material side, questions have often been put to me as to the cost of the Viceregal establishment in India, and as to the emoluments and allowances that are or have been paid to the Governor General. The subject has some historical interest, in relation both to the social and economic conditions of official life in Calcutta at different times, to the standards of remuneration laid down by the British Government for its public servants, and to the moral obligations imposed upon the latter. I will therefore give such details as my studies of the matter have enabled me to ascertain.

We may, I think, in this context distinguish broadly between three epochs in the history of our relations with India. There was the short-lived period before the second Administration of Clive, which has been depicted in letters of fire in Macaulay's Essays, when the pagoda tree was shaken recklessly into the lap of every Civil Servant from the head of the Government downwards, and when the immense fortunes secured by illicit trading, bribery and the like rendered the so-called Indian Nabob an object of well-merited loathing and scorn in this country. After Clive's reforms (although they had not applied to himself), reinforced towards the close of the century by those of Cornwallis, a higher and purer standard prevailed, and peculation or dishonesty gradually disappeared. The emoluments, however, of Indian service during this era, which lasted until India was taken over by the Crown, were very considerable ; and those persons who went out to India from England to serve either as Governors, as Members of Council, or as High Court Judges not only expected to make but did make in a few years what would now be regarded as ample fortunes. Finally came the period, still unterminated, in which the great increase in the cost and standards of living and in the scale of obligatory entertainment, together with the simultaneous fall in the exchange value of the rupee, have rendered it impossible to regard Indian service any longer as a means of fortune and have in many cases made it a source of embarrassment.

How lavish was the scale of Government House expenditure, even in the relatively primitive days of Clive, when the Government of India could hardly be called a Government, and when society was insignificant, may be seen from an account sent home by him to the Company (Bengal Public Proceedings of 20th January, 1767) of the expenses which he had incurred between May 1764 and December 1766.

To travelling expenses from Europe, over and above the sum of £3,000 paid to me for that purpose by the Hon. Company   Rs. 73,489. 15. 4

To amount general expenses from time of arrival until the 31st December, 1766   Rs. 99,624. 12. 0

To amount of expenses of my table from Ditto to Ditto ... ...   Rs. 16,987. 14. 7

For allowances to my Secretary, Assistants, Steward and others employed under me from Ditto to Ditto ... ...   Rs. 19,722. 11. 4

Other charges ... ...   Rs. 11,674. 10. 7

To balance of this account of expenses general, now given to Mr. Edward Philpot for his good and faithful services to me ... ...   Rs. 14,928. 15. 8

_____

Current Rupees 333,895. 7. 2

To this was appended a Note that these charges were almost wholly met by the sale of the costly presents made to the Governor by the Native Princes.

Clive, as is well known, came away from his first administration in India with an immense fortune, estimated at £40,000 per annum, the profuse display of which was one of the main sources of his unpopularity in England.   His own defence—and so far as it went a valid one —was that, but for his moderation, he might have come away with far more.   Richard Barwell, who was not a friendly witness, said that Clive cleared about £200,000 more from his second administration, although it lasted little more than a year and a half.[1]   But Clive declared that he was poorer at the end of his second term of office than at the beginning.   Barwell himself returned to England with a fortune that was estimated by popular gossip at £800,000, and which was in any case so large that he was able to purchase the estate and house of Stanstead from Lord Halifax for £102,500, and to live in a style of great ostentation, being generally known as Nabob Barwell.   He was said to have covers for 18 laid every day at his dinner table for any friends who might turn up.[2]   Barwell was in fact the typical Nabob of whom Cowper wrote in " The Task " :

> " It is not seemly nor of good report
>   That thieves at home must hang, but he that puts
>   Into his overgorged and bloated purse
>   The wealth of Indian provinces, escapes."

The Regulation Act of 1773 fixed the salary of the Governor General at £25,000 per annum (commonly described as 2½ lacs) : and in the year before his retirement (*i.e.* 1784) Warren Hastings, drawing this at the then rate of 1s. 9d. to 1s. 10d., received Rupees 283,250 or £25,646.   This was a handsome salary admitting of considerable savings ; and indeed it was afterwards publicly stated that Hastings, after his return to England, was possessed of a fortune of £80,000. This may even have been an under-statement, for he declared himself that at no time of his life had he had a fortune of more than £100,000—a figure which would probably apply to the end of his Indian career.   Although this sum may be thought large in relation to modern standards, it was in reality a very moderate return for a total service of nearly thirty-five years in India and a thirteen years' tenure of office as head of the Government, in an age when the latter had but to lift his little finger to have thousands poured into his palm.

[1] " Bengal Past and Present," Vol. **X**, p. 19.
[2] " Letters of Mrs. Montague " (ed. R. Blunt), Vol. II, pp. 204-5.

As Macaulay remarked, it would not have been difficult for Warren Hastings, had he chosen, to return to England with a fortune of three millions sterling.

Mrs. Hastings, who seems to have accepted presents on a very liberal scale, and probably with insufficient scruple, brought home considerably larger means of her own, bringing her in an independent income of some £2,000 per annum,[1] and enabling her to bequeath at a later date a large sum to her son.

In addition to his official salary, Hastings while in India received the following allowances :

For Garden House ... ... Sicca Rs.	6,000
(i.e. Belvedere or Alipore)	
For Town House ... ... ,, ,,	19,500
(i.e. Buckingham House)	
For Family House ... ... ,, ,,	14,400
(i.e. Hastings Street)	
,, ,,	39,900
Batta of 16 p.c. ... ... ,, ,,	6,384
,, ,,	46,284

Later on, when the present Government House and Barrackpore were built by Wellesley, the above House allowances disappeared, and were replaced by the Durbar and Furniture Funds, as they are now called, from which the charges for keeping up the official residences of the Viceroy and the native establishment are now met.

The successors of Warren Hastings drew the same salary, but were paid in Sicca Rupees 2.44.180 down to Lord W. Bentinck. The Charter Act of 1833 fixed the scale at Sicca Rs. 2.40.000 or current Rs. 2.56.000. In Lord Auckland's day the equivalent sum in Company Rupees was fixed at 2.50.800, and this has been the payment that has been made ever since. Hence the popular illusion, repeated *ad nauseam* in the native Press, that the Viceroy draws from an impoverished

---

[1] This statement was made by Mr. W. Lushington, when pleading the cause of Hastings at the Court of Proprietors on 29th May, 1795. He also declared that at that time Hastings had not more than £1,000 per annum, which was probably true, seeing that he had, since his return from India, spent nearly £12,000 in the purchase of Daylesford House and estate, and a further £48,000 in rebuilding and restoring it. This would have made a considerable hole in the £80,000 (or £100,000) with which he was believed to have returned from India.

country a personal stipend of £25,000 per annum. As a matter of fact, deducting Income tax which he is called upon to pay, but including an allowance of Rs. 6,000 per annum which was paid towards the cost of State entertainments, the Viceroy received in my day—at the exchange rate of 1s. 4d.—a total salary of £16,684, and from this he was called upon to bear the entire expenses of his own family and household, a very heavy subscription list, and the cost of all entertainment, public or private, at the various Government Houses.

An outfit allowance (for voyage and equipment) has always been made to an outgoing Governor General. Clive, as we have seen, received £3,000 for the purpose. In 1833 this was fixed at £3,500, and at this figure it stood in my day. With it the new Viceroy had to purchase all the carriages and horses of his predecessor (there must now be a great reduction in this item), to pay for the outward journey of himself and family, and, assuming him to go out in the winter, to provide all the stores from Europe for his first Calcutta season. In my day the allowance did not cover much more than one-third of the total liability. The allowance has since been increased to £5,000.

The allowances for the official journeys of the Governor General, the wages and pensions of the huge native establishment, the Private and Military Secretaries' Offices, and the maintenance of the Viceregal palaces, have always been a charge upon public funds.

The amount which was found from the public purse for all these purposes was in my time about £56,000 per annum, so that the total annual cost of the Viceroyalty of India, run as it was upon a scale of great but by no means extravagant splendour, only amounted to some £73,000, in my opinion a very remarkable feat of good management.

In earlier days the Company bore the expense of the public entertainments that were given on such occasions as the King's and Queen's Birthdays at Calcutta, and in Lord Wellesley's time this amounted to Rs. 8,000 or £1,000 per annum. A later statement in 1841 says that the Governor General was allowed Rs. 20,000 per annum for the State Balls. Lord Dalhousie[1] said that a Government allowance was made for the fête on the Queen's Birthday. Gradually all these allowances disappeared, and, with the exception of the small grant of Rs. 500 per month or £400 a year towards State entertainment, the Viceroy bore the entire charge of all these functions himself. While the Govern-

[1] " Private Letters," p. 186.

ment remained in Calcutta, where I have given the figures of society in an earlier chapter, this amounted to a very heavy annual charge. Now that the seat of Government has been moved to Delhi, where the society is almost exclusively official, and entertainment on the Calcutta scale is out of the question, the economy to the Viceroy must be very great.

That the Governor General and his colleagues had it in their power to make very substantial savings in what I have described above as the middle period, is evident from the admissions in published works. Francis, an obscure dismissed War Office clerk, who avowedly only went out to India in order to line his pockets, from a salary of £10,000 per annum began by expecting only to carry home £15,000 as the result of five years.[1]   But he soon found that these expectations were much below the mark.   In 1777 alone he sent back £10,000.[2]   After six years' service he finally returned with a fortune that yielded him £3,000 per annum for life ;[3] and yet he received the enthusiastic encomiums of Lord Brougham for his financial purity and extreme moderation.   His earnings were greatly enhanced by the reckless gambling in which Calcutta society then indulged, and in which he appears to have been singularly fortunate.   Francis recorded on one occasion that his colleague, Richard Barwell, had lost £30,000 at the table, of which he had annexed from £12,000 to £14,000.[4]

Lord Cornwallis during his first term of office wrote :

" Any person with a good constitution, not much above 35, might reasonably expect to be able to hold the office (*i.e.* of Governor General) long enough to save from his salary a very ample fortune."[5]

Lord Wellesley, who, when he was expecting to go to Madras (1797), stated that the salary and emoluments of that Governorship were £18,000-£20,000 per annum, and the expenses £10,000 at the outside,[6] found, after proceeding to Calcutta, that the Governor General was even better provided for.

" Although my household is magnificent, and my table open to every

[1] " Memoirs," Vol. II, p. 31.
[2] *Ibid.*, Vol. II, p. 122.
[3] " Private Life of Warren Hastings," by Sir Ch. Lawson, p. 83.
[4] " Memoirs," Vol. II, p. 70.
[5] " Correspondence " (ed. Ch. Ross), Vol. I, p. 378.
[6] " Wellesley Papers," Vol. I, p. 32.

respectable person in the Settlement, and to all new comers, I find my savings far greater than I expected." [1]

Thirty years later Macaulay went out to India as Law Member, with a similar object to Francis, *viz.*, to use his own words, " to make a competency."   His salary was £10,000 per annum, and he expected to save half of this annually and, " by the time I am thirty-nine or forty, to return to England with a fortune of £30,000."   This was in 1833.   But before he had been in India three months, he wrote to his sister that his expenses would be much smaller than he anticipated, and that he hoped " to lay up on an average about £7,000 per annum while I remain in India." [2]

Macaulay's estimate of the savings of a Civilian in his day, 90 years ago, may also be deduced from a passage in his " Essay on Clive " : " A Writer is fortunate if at forty-five he can return to his country with an annuity of £1,000 per annum and with savings amounting to £30,000."   At the thought of such figures a modern civilian would grow pale with envy.

Dalhousie, in whose case the impoverishment of a Scottish laird was a similar inducement to accept the honourable exile of India, wrote on 26th August, 1852, that one of the reasons why he could not re-enter public life upon his return to England was that he would only have £6,000 per annum.   At the same time he revealed what it was then in the power of the Governor General to save, by the statement: " At the outside I shall make £9,000 additional by a year's stay." [3]

Since then, for the reasons that I have given, India has become less and less the fabled mine of wealth either to the Civilian or the Councillor or the Governor General.   I have known one of the latter during the last half-century who in his tenure of office confessed to having saved £30,000.   But I think that this was the exception, and that it has only been the departure from Calcutta to Delhi which has arrested a swing of the balance in the contrary direction.   Generally speaking the salaries given by the British Government to its officers in distant parts compare very favourably with those that are conferred by other foreign Governments.   But the entertainment so freely dispensed by the British official, particularly in India, which is increasingly overrun

[1] "Wellesley Papers," Vol. I, p. 82.
[2] " Life and Letters," by Sir G. Trevelyan, Vol. I, pp. 345, 374.
[3] " Private Letters," pp. 220, 240.

by cold weather visitors, is much greater than in the dominions of any other Power, and it is not unreasonable that the occupant of high and responsible office should be able to return to his country, after years of laborious and often trying exile, with a provision that will not merely constitute some remuneration for his services, but will enable him to maintain a style of living at home that does not present too glaring a contrast with his recent surroundings in India.

One means of financial support is for obvious reasons denied to the modern Governor General. He no longer has the purse of the East India Company to fall back upon. The Directors were often niggardly and captious towards their principal servants while serving them at the distance of several thousand miles. But they more than once atoned at a later date for this churlishness by a generous recognition of deserts which at the moment they had disparaged or ignored.

To Warren Hastings, the most deeply injured, but also the noblest of their servants, they made ample amends. After his acquittal at Westminster, the Court of Proprietors on 3rd June, 1795, voted him an annuity of £5,000 for twenty-eight and a half years (the unexpired term of the Company's privileges) from 24th June, 1785, the date of his return to England ; but, owing to the opposition of the Board of Control, this amount was cut down to £4,000 per annum. The legal expenses of his defence had further amounted to the ruinous total of £71,080 ; and to meet this charge the Company in March 1796 advanced him £50,000, to be repaid in instalments of £2,000 per annum free from interest. He repaid £16,000 of this sum, but in July 1804 was excused from further reimbursements as from 30th June, 1803, so that from that date he received the annuity of £4,000 in full. At a General Court held on 12th January, 1820, it was stated that the Company had presented him in all with upwards of £168,000.

Sir John Macpherson, who was Governor General for a year and a half, and who always contended that he had been very badly used in being superseded by Lord Cornwallis, after infinite badgering at home, secured £15,000 as pecuniary compensation from the Company, who afterwards granted him an annuity of £1,000 for life. But this was not till June 1809, twenty-three years after he had left India.

Like Warren Hastings, Lord Cornwallis was also most handsomely treated. He was very profuse in his expenditure in India, and in a letter to his brother, the Bishop of Lichfield, of 8th September, 1793, he said that he was much out of pocket by the Mysore war, having spent £27,360 (reckoning the rupee as 2s.) between 1st December, 1790, and 31st July, 1792, outside the wine from England, and his two Arab hunters.[1]   On 26th June, 1793, the Company voted to him and his heirs a pension of £5,000 per annum for 20 years, to commence from the day of his departure from India. On 14th March, 1806, after his death, a further grant of £40,000 was made to his son by the Court of Directors in recognition of his father's services.

We have already seen the rather painful circumstances in which Sir John Shore, sent out to India in 1792 to replace Lord Cornwallis on his expected retirement, had to wait for full seven months after his arrival in Bengal before Cornwallis was prepared to hand over charge. But the Directors did not treat Shore badly, for they voted him " the sum of 10,000 Current Rupees per month from the date he embarks until he succeeds to the Governorship of Bengal," so that the expectant ruler did not suffer at least in purse from the delay.

The Company might have found many reasons for not treating Wellesley with conspicuous generosity. But in this respect they did not err. In January 1801 they voted him an annuity of £5,000, to commence from 1st September, 1798 (in return for his having declined to take his share of the prize money of Seringapatam, said to have been worth £100,000), this payment to continue to Wellesley and his heirs for twenty years ; and in May 1814 it was continued to him for the rest of his life. Further, when they heard that in advanced years he was seriously impoverished, they voted him an additional sum of £20,000, at which the old man was greatly pleased, as well as at the offer to make a wide distribution of his printed Despatches in India.

Sir George Barlow, whom we have seen as a Civilian Governor General for nearly two years from 1805 to 1807, and who was recalled from Madras, where he had quarrelled with everybody, in 1813, received in 1819 a pension of £1,500 per annum, to date from May 1818—as a sort of consolation for his many misfortunes—and continued to enjoy it for another twenty-eight years.

Lord Hastings is the next in the list. In June 1819 a grant of £60,000 was made by the Company for the purchase of an estate for himself and his issue. In September 1827, the year after his death, a further sum of £20,000 was voted for the benefit of his son and heir.

[1] " Correspondence " (ed. Ch. Ross), Vol. II, p. 179.

Sir Henry (Lord) Hardinge was doubly blest ; for in addition to the grant from the nation after the first Sikh war of £3,000 p.a. for his own and two succeeding lives, he also received from the East India Company a pension of £5,000 p.a.

His successor, Lord Dalhousie, was similarly and even more deservedly honoured, for on the morrow of his return to England, bruised in spirit and broken in health, the Directors voted him a similar pension of £5,000 p.a. commencing from the date of his vacation of office.

Sir John (Lord) Lawrence, whose means as an Indian Civilian were small, received an annuity of £2,000 from the expiring Court of Directors on his return from India after the Mutiny in 1859. When he retired from the Viceroyalty and was made a Peer, this pension was extended for the life of his successor in the title.

I am not aware of any subsequent pecuniary grant to a Governor General. On several occasions, however, sums have been voted by Parliament to victorious Generals, whose triumphs had been won in Indian warfare.

Among the anomalies attaching in my time to the position of the Viceroy and Governor General, was the statutory prohibition imposed upon him to take leave outside of India during his tenure of office. This disability he shared with the Commander-in-Chief and the Governors of Madras and Bombay. It dated from the Act of 1793, afterwards confirmed by the Act of 1833, which laid down that the departure of any one of the above officials from India " with intent to return to Europe, shall be deemed in law a resignation and avoidance of his office." Ordinary Members of the Councils of the three afore-named high civil officials had been relieved of a similar disability by the Act of 1861, and had been allowed leave of absence for not more than six months during their term of office " under medical certificate " alone. But this relaxation was still denied to their official superiors, in the mistaken belief that the entire machinery of Government would come to a standstill if such important personages were allowed to absent themselves once in five years.

The rigour of this prohibition had on one occasion been evaded by a palpable subterfuge. For when Sir Robert, afterwards Lord Napier of Magdala, who was Commander-in-Chief in Bombay, had been sent from India to command the Abyssinian Expedition in 1867, he was permitted to proceed to England afterwards on the plea that he was still on duty.

On the other hand, when the Duke of Connaught, holding the same position in Bombay, wanted to attend the first Jubilee of Queen Victoria in London in 1887, a special Act of Parliament had to be passed to enable him to do so.

In 1905, when, after more than five years' service as Viceroy, I was offered a second term of office, and accepted only on the condition that I should be permitted to return for a short time to England before taking it up, I had to resign the Viceroyalty on the day that I left Bombay " to return to Europe," and to receive a second Warrant of Appointment when I returned to India seven months later.

The anomaly was rendered the more absurd because, while " return to Europe " was the statutory criterion of disqualification, the Viceroy and the other high officials might, under the law, leave India for any other purpose or any other destination on the globe. Thus the first Lord Minto accompanied a military expedition to Java, Lord Dalhousie went for the sake of his health to Malacca and Singapore (these places being at that time under the administration of the East India Company), while I was allowed to proceed on official duty to the head of the Persian Gulf. These excursions sufficiently demonstrated the hollowness of the plea that the mere absence of the Governor General from headquarters must impair either the continuity or the authority of the administration. Indeed the numerous references in this work to the absence of the old-time Governor General from Bengal when on tour in the Upper Provinces—sometimes for more than a year at a time—will have shown that the Government of India survived the shock of absences far longer in duration than any that could be entailed by leave to England under modern conditions.

Thus it had come about that, alone among the great servants of the Empire, the Viceroy of India and his aforenamed colleagues were not able, on whatever plea of public interest or ill health or private need, to return to England without resigning their offices. Every other Governor General in the Empire and indeed in the world has long enjoyed this modest privilege. It was further enjoyed by the rest of the Viceroy's colleagues in Council. I know of cases myself where this restriction prevented the acceptance of the Viceroyalty by a candidate who might otherwise have taken it, and where it has driven the incumbent of one of the disqualifying offices to stay on in India and die there, because he could not return to England for medical treatment except by vacating his post.   Of course the restriction had originated in days when a journey to Europe and back occupied from a year to a year and a half of time, and when the absence for so long a period of the head of the Government might have seriously shaken the prestige or interrupted the thread of Government.   In process of time it had become an indefensible and even a mischievous anomaly, since, under conditions where the journey to England and back can be accomplished in little more than a month, and may even be accelerated by aviation in the future, the absence of a Viceroy (and the same applies to a Governor or a Commander-in-Chief) for a few months can now be no detriment to any important interest and may, quite apart from personal considerations, be invaluable in the opportunity thus afforded for consultation between the Home Government and its absent representatives.

An attempt had been made by legislation to do away with the restriction on all these officers, as far back as 1891-1892, when I was Under Secretary for India, and a Bill to that effect passed the House of Lords in both those sessions (though the Viceroy was at the last moment unwisely excluded from its operation), but was not proceeded with in the House of Commons.   In 1902 my colleagues and I addressed the Home Government in a Despatch, the argument of which was both unanswerable and unanswered, and was repeated by Lord Chelmsford's Government in 1921.   It was reserved for the Conservative Government of 1923-4 to revive and endorse the proposal, and had not that Government fallen in January 1924, a Bill would certainly have been introduced and carried into law.   While these pages were leaving my hands, a Bill in the same sense, introduced by their successors, passed through Parliament and is now the law of the land. Conditions were introduced that will safeguard the privilege from abuse and will provide for the due replacement of the absentees in each case.   The surest guarantee against abuse will however be found, more particularly in the case of the Viceroy, in his reluctance to take his hand for any length of time from the plough which he is given but five short years to drive through the Indian furrow.   The change in the law was accepted without a dissentient voice, the only wonder being that it had been so long and needlessly delayed.

In the next chapter we shall trace the experience of the several Governors General and Viceroys, and shall see how each of them in turn fared in his tenure of the office, and in his relations with the Government at home. But enough has already been said to show that there is a very wide difference between the conditions now and those that prevailed in the closing years of the 18th and the first half of the 19th centuries. The introduction of the electric telegraph marked the beginning of the change. The substitution of the Crown for the Company was its second stage. The Governor General both lost and gained in the process. On the one hand a very necessary check was placed upon his initiative, and he could no longer wage war or make treaties, or commit his employers in England behind their backs, conscious that even if, a year after the event, they censured the agent, they could not reverse the act. The Governor General ceased henceforward to be a quasi-independent potentate. A Wellesley or a Hastings, perhaps even a Dalhousie, became impossible. On the other hand, though the Viceroy was still exposed to the curb of Whitehall, sometimes pulled in his mouth with quite unnecessary violence, he was freed from the tempestuous caprice of the Court of Directors and the internecine conflict between the rival authorities in London. The loss of concrete power was compensated by the greater security of position. Viceroys may still be obliged or may elect to resign. But we no longer read of the acrimonious exchange of affronts, almost of insults, of abrupt dismissals, and petulant recalls.

Further, although the transference of the Government of India to the Crown has involved an inevitable increase in the power of Parliament, and although this has not always been wisely exercised, there has been a growing tendency to recognise the unfitness of the House of Commons to take the Government of India into its own hands, and the desirability of entrusting a large measure of independence to the man on the spot. India has become in a much less degree the sport of political parties in England, and Ministries here do not rise or fall on Indian issues. Now and then some disturbing and controversial event, such as an Afghan war, a Frontier rebellion, or an internal convulsion, may shake the placid surface of the ocean, and rouse the House of Commons or the electorate in England into a fierce but transient interest in Indian affairs. But ordinarily the speeches on the Indian Budget in that Chamber are delivered to almost empty benches ; and for really valuable and authoritative discussions upon Indian affairs we must look to the House of Lords.   A means of bringing the India Office into touch with expert Indian opinion, so far as it is represented in Parliament, has been devised in the shape of a Joint Committee of both Houses, to which Indian questions are often referred by the Secretary of State.

In India itself the power of the Viceroy has remained on a singularly uniform and impressive level of distinction.   It is recognised that his intimate connection with the Home Government, his Parliamentary or public experience, and his personal detachment from the minor or local controversies of the hour, place him in a quite exceptional position. The Services look or have hitherto looked to him, not merely as the official figurehead of the administrative machine, but as the supreme embodiment of British authority in India.   Indian public opinion is apt to credit him with even greater power than he really possesses, and to identify every act of the Government with his personality or influence.   The degree in which he takes advantage of this double opportunity will depend in part upon his personal relations with the India Office and the Cabinet at home.   But it depends much more upon his own character and individuality.   As the movement towards Provincial autonomy in India develops, and as the Parliamentary analogy is more and more applied to the conduct of affairs at Simla and Delhi, so the prestige of the Viceroy may be diminished and his influence curtailed.   No such diminution had occurred in the time for which I can speak.   Nor has it yet been carried so far as materially to weaken his hands.

Perhaps I can best illustrate the position and prerogatives of the head of the Government in India by comparing them with those of the head of the Government in England.   Having studied the two at close quarters, I am inclined to think that the former wields for a short time, or used to wield, a superior power.   Both, it is true, are Governors in Council, the one as the Chairman of a Cabinet, the other as the Chairman of an Executive Council, and their acts are, in constitutional theory, and to a large extent in fact, the result of decisions for which their colleagues are equally responsible.   I shall presently have something to say about the relations of the Viceroy to his Council, and the measure of their participation in the policy which is ordinarily associated with his name.   But both in England and in India there is a large sphere of action which by convention, as distinct from statute, is regarded as the peculiar province of the head of the Government, and in which his colleagues make little or no attempt to dispute, or even to share, his prerogative. In England this relates more particularly to the special responsibility of the Prime Minister for the highest appointments and honours, and for all that comes under the name of patronage. The fact that he appoints every member of his own Government, some 80 in number, and that they look to him for promotion or reward, is a source of enormous and, as some think, undue influence.

The patronage of the Viceroy of India is on a greatly inferior scale ; and he does not appoint a single one of his immediate colleagues. Indeed, on the solitary occasion on which I pressed for one such appointment, I was informed by the Secretary of State that the duty of advising the King on the choice of a Member of Council rested solely with him, and that no greater violation of the Constitution could be imagined than that this duty should degenerate into a mere formal submission to His Majesty of the views and recommendations of the Viceroy !

On the other hand, a great authority attaches in India to the Viceroy by reason of his almost exclusive responsibility for Foreign and Frontier affairs (he is himself the Member or Minister for the Foreign Department), his sole conduct of relations with the Indian Princes, and his prerogative of correspondence with the Sovereign and with the Government at home.

The Prime Minister of Great Britain enjoys one supreme advantage which is denied to his Indian counterpart, *viz.*, that he yields to no higher authority than that of Parliament, while the Viceroy is directly subordinate to the Secretary of State for India and his Council—a subordination at which many Indian rulers have openly chafed and which by some has been found insupportable. As the narrative contained in these pages will have shown, he may even be recalled by his official superiors in England—a fate which, though less common now than it once was, has befallen no small number of the Governors General of the past.

It is true also that the Prime Minister in England enjoys the advantage of being able, whenever he chooses, to expound or defend his action by speech in Parliament or in the country, a resource which it is much more difficult for the Viceroy to employ, and that he has behind him, until he forfeits it or is defeated, the faithful support of a majority in the House of Commons, and of a great popular following in the country. The Viceroy of India is the leader of no party, though he is the official head of the Indian Civil Service—a very loyal as well as capable body of men ; and he has no personal following but that which he may create by his own character or ability.

On the other hand, he possesses advantages which are denied to the most powerful Prime Minister at home. He is not dependent for his tenure of office upon the vicissitudes or vagaries of a Parliamentary vote. Representing as he does the Sovereign, he enjoys some small measure of the immunity as well as a good deal of the respect that is ungrudgingly conceded to the Throne. Coming as a rule from public life in England, he is acknowledged as bringing to the discharge of his duties in India an experience differing from and larger than that of the officials by whom he is surrounded. He has by law the power of veto, however rarely exercised, over his Council, which technically no English Prime Minister enjoys, and he is not liable to be confronted with the resignations or threatened resignations of his Ministers. The credit or failure of his administration is in popular usage ascribed to him even more than it is to the head of the Government in England ; and while this is sometimes unfair either to his Council or to himself, it tends to invest him with a personal pre-eminence that no one is disposed to challenge. He stands much more apart from the world about him than does any official, however powerful, at home. Moreover, although the Provincial Governments in India are yearly becoming more independent, his authority, if he chooses to exercise it tactfully and wisely, extends, not over a Kingdom, but over a Continent, and can be felt in every corner of the vast Indian Empire.

This comparison of the respective powers and influence of these two great officials is far from exhaustive, and may sometimes relate to matters not exactly in *pari materia*. It is however in the general control of administration that the Viceroy is able to exercise a much superior power. The Prime Minister in England can inaugurate a policy ; but he can only execute it, at least so far as legislation is concerned, by carrying his measure through both Houses of Parliament—a long and anxious process, in the course of which many chances have to be encountered and many reverses sustained. Even in administrative measures there is nothing to prevent a vote of censure upon him from being recorded in the House of Commons in any week of the Parliamentary

Session.   His daily and hourly existence is largely one of compromise. On the other hand, a Viceroy of India, if supported by his Council in India, and not unduly hampered by the Secretary of State in London, can in five years, or could in recent times, leave an enduring mark on Indian Administration.   There is no subject relating to the life of three hundred millions of people that he cannot take up if he chooses.   He is dealing with a community and a nation, or nations, still in the process, and in the majority of cases in the earlier stages, of political and social evolution, and the moulding of this plastic material is to a large extent in his hands.   He has an influence in every branch of Government immeasurably greater than that which is possible in the highly organised departmental system of the home country.   His initiative is unquestioned, his power of translating it into action immense.   When I left India, I sought in my farewell speech at Bombay to summarise some aspects of the Viceroy's work as it existed in my day, which perhaps I may be permitted to quote here in general illustration of my thesis.

" The Viceroy very soon finds out that the purely Viceregal aspect of his duties is the very least portion of them, and the Court life, in which he is commonly depicted by ignorant people as revelling, occupies only the place of a compulsory background in his everyday existence.   He soon discovers that he is the responsible head of what is by far the most perfected and considerable of highly organised Governments in the world ; for the Government of China, which is supposed to rule over a larger number of human beings, can certainly not be accused of a high level of either organisation or perfection.   So much is the Viceroy the head of that Government that almost every act of his subordinates is attributed to him by public opinion, and if he is of an active and enterprising nature, a sparrow can scarcely twitter its tail at Peshawar without a response being detected to masterful orders from Simla or Calcutta.

" You want English Ministries therefore to send you their very best men, and then you want to get out of them, not the correct performance of ceremonial duties, but the very best work of which their energies or experiences or abilities may render them capable.   Anything that can deter them from such a conception of their duties or confine them to the sterile pursuit of routine is, in my view, greatly to be deplored.

" However, I am only at the beginning of my enumeration of the Viceroy's tale of bricks.   He is the head, not merely of the whole Government, but also of the most arduous Department of Government, *viz.*, the Foreign Office. There he is in the exact position of an ordinary Member of Council, with the difference that the work of the Foreign Department is unusually responsible, and that it embraces three spheres of action so entirely different and requiring

such an opposite equipment of principles and knowledge as to the conduct
of relations with the whole of the Native States of India, the management of
the Frontier provinces and handling of the Frontier tribes, and the offering
of advice to His Majesty's Government on practically the entire foreign
policy of Asia, which mainly or wholly concerns Great Britain and its relation to India.

"But the Viceroy, though he is directly responsible for this one Department, is scarcely less responsible for the remainder. He exercises over them
a control which is, in my judgment, the secret of efficient administration. It
is the counterpart of what used to exist in England, but has died out since
the days of Sir Robert Peel—with consequences which cannot be too greatly
deplored. I earnestly hope that the Viceroy in India may never cease to be
head of the Government in the fullest sense of the term. It is not one-man
rule, which may or may not be a good thing—that depends on the man. But
it is one-man supervision, which is the very best form of Government, pre-
suming the man to be competent. The alternative in India is a bureaucracy,
which is the most mechanical and lifeless of all forms of administration.

"To continue, the Viceroy is also the President of the Legislative Council,
where he has to defend the policy of Government in speeches which are apt
to be denounced as empty if they indulge in platitudes, and as undignified
if they do not. He must have a financial policy, an agricultural policy,
a famine policy, a plague policy, a railway policy, an educational policy,
an industrial policy, a military policy. Everybody in the country who has
a fad or a grievance—and how many are there without either ?—hunts him
out. Every public servant who wants an increase of pay, allowance or
pension—a not inconsiderable band—appeals to him as the eye of justice ;
everyone who thinks he deserves recognition, appeals to him as the fountain
of honour. When he goes on tour he has to try to know nearly as much
about local needs as the people who have lived there all their lives, and he
has to refuse vain requests in a manner to make the people who asked
them feel happier than they were before. When he meets the merchants
he must know all about tea, sugar, indigo, jute, cotton, salt and oil. He is
not thought much of unless he can throw in some knowledge of shipping and
customs. In some places electricity, steel and iron, and coal are required.
For telegraphs he is supposed to have a special partiality ; and he is liable
to be attacked about the metric system. He must be equally prepared to discourse about labour in South Africa or labour in Assam. The connecting
link between him and the Municipalities is supplied by water and drains. He
must be prepared to speak about everything and often about nothing. He
is expected to preserve temples, to keep the currency steady, to satisfy 3rd
class passengers, to patronise race meetings, to make Bombay and Calcutta
each think that it is the capital city of India, and to purify the Police. He
corresponds with all his Lieutenants in every province, and it is his duty to
keep in touch with every Local Administration. If he does not reform every-

thing that is wrong, he is told that he is doing too little; if he reforms anything at all, that he is doing too much.

"And yet I desire to say on this parting occasion that I regard the office of Viceroy of India, inconceivably laborious as it is, as the noblest office in the gift of the British Crown.   I think the man who does not thrill on receiving it with a sense not of foolish pride but of grave responsibility, is not fit to be an Englishman.   I believe that the man who holds it with devotion, and knows how to wield the power wisely and well, as so many great men in India have done, can for a few years exercise a greater influence upon the destinies of a larger number of his fellow creatures than any head of an administration in the universe.   I hold that England ought to send out to India to fill this great post the pick of her statesmen, and that it should be regarded as one of the supreme prizes of an Englishman's career.   I deprecate any attempt, should it ever be made, to attenuate its influence, to diminish its privileges, or to lower its prestige.   Should the day ever come when the Viceroy of India is treated as a mere puppet or mouthpiece of the Home Government, who is required only to carry out whatever orders it may be thought desirable to transmit, I think the justification for the post would have ceased to exist. But I cannot believe that the administrative wisdom of my countrymen, which is very great, would ever tolerate so great a blunder."

It is only fair to add that the conditions which I have here described have, I believe, been considerably modified since my day.   The Viceroy no longer presides, except on rare occasions, over the Imperial Legislative Council, now known as the Legislative Assembly.   That body is permitted, in the enjoyment of its new Parliamentary powers, to carry Resolutions hostile to his policy or his Government, to defeat his measures, and to refuse his budget.   It is true that under the new Constitution he enjoys overruling powers of no mean order.   But it is obvious that they cannot be constantly in use ; and in these respects the head of the Indian Government must walk much more warily than of yore.   Like Agag he has to move delicately ; and even so there are plenty of wrathful Samuels to hew him down.   Such rebuffs must tend to diminish the prestige of Government and of its chief ; their ultimate consequence may indeed prove disastrous to both.   Upon the future, however, it would be beyond the scope of this work to speculate ; and I am excused from prediction by the fact that I am only concerned to deal with matters as I knew them.   Nevertheless, my information leads me to think that the position of the Viceroy is not at present so far impaired as to preclude him from still exerting the full weight of his authority ; and that, perhaps more than before, rather than less, in consequence of the altered situation, is there a call for the highest qualities both of character and intellect in the occupant of that great post.

My frequent reference to Council and Council Houses will have familiarised my readers with a fundamental feature of the Government of India as it has existed since the earliest days of the East India Company, namely, that great as has always been the power of the Governor General—at least since the sufferings of Warren Hastings brought the change in the law upon which Cornwallis insisted—that Government has always been, as in my judgment it ought to continue to be, a Government in Council. Only so can the almost inevitable Indian ignorance of a ruler fresh from England be guided and controlled by Indian experience ; only so can the precipitate or arbitrary exercise of irresponsible power be prevented. In the long annals of Indian history in the last century and three-quarters, I have found that the majority of Governors General were punctilious in the observance of this fundamental principle of Indian Government ; wherever it has been departed from or slurred in practice, trouble, if not disaster, has ensued. The old records speak of meetings of Council (I need not here describe its composition or numbers, for these can be found in all the text books) very often two and three times in the week. As Government has become more systematised and as devolution has advanced, this is no longer necessary ; and, just as Cabinets in England usually meet once a week (although in the Great War the War Cabinet, of which I was a member, sat every day and often in the night also), so was the Council of the Governor General, as I knew it, except when the Viceroy was on tour, always so convened. I do not think a weekly meeting was missed (unless there was absolutely nothing on the Agenda) more than six times in six years, and even when there was little or nothing to do, I found it a convenient and acceptable practice to make a statement to my colleagues about Foreign Affairs, such as is frequently made by the Foreign Secretary at Cabinet Meetings in Downing Street in London.

Lord Wellesley, as may be imagined, was the first and most determined offender against this salutary prescription. The frequent meetings of Council, with the fussy intrusion of colleagues whom he despised, did not at all harmonise with his conception of a single and self-centred rule. The remedy he adopted was to allow his Council to meet, but to refrain from attending the meetings himself : 9 times in 1801,

28 times in 1802, and 24 times in 1803, he sent a haughty message in the morning to his colleagues that—

" His Excellency the Most Noble the Governor General signifies that it is not his intention to attend the meeting of Council, and desires that the proceedings which may be held at the meeting be communicated to him for affirmation."

He went even further, for he was in the habit of issuing Government orders in his own name, a proceeding altogether illegal as well as improper. This contemptuous neglect of duty was made one of the chief counts in the indictment brought against Wellesley by the Court of Directors, who wrote in their letter of 26th March, 1805—

" Except in case of illness we know not upon what justifiable grounds the Governor General could absent himself from Council, or upon what authority he required the proceedings being sent to him for his approbation ; "

and the Board of Control, in their substituted draft No. 128 of 4th April, 1805, accepted this charge as proven and endorsed it in language of exceptional severity.

With Wellesley's disappearance the constitutional practice was resumed ; nor, except in the cases already referred to, when the prolonged absence of the Governor General on tour in the Upper Provinces or outside of India rendered it impossible for him to preside over the Council meetings—a contingency which was provided for by law, but led to great anomalies and even abuses in practice—is there evidence to show that, with the rarest exceptions, did any Governor General deliberately ignore or supersede his Council.

One such exception occurred in the case of Lord Ellenborough, whose career, alike in England and in India, was fertile in precedents that as a rule recoiled with well-deserved severity upon himself. In the later stages of the Afghan War, which it fell to him as Governor General to conduct to a conclusion, he kept his entire correspondence with Generals Nott and Pollock from the knowledge of his Council from June 1842 to the capture of Kabul. When this transpired his colleagues were naturally indignant, and the Indian Press was unanimous in censure.

Early in the 20th century a fresh departure from constitutional practice excited a good deal of public attention, and at a later date was made the subject of official investigation and rebuke. Allusion has been made to the practice by which the Viceroy and the Secretary of

State exchange weekly letters which are treated as confidential, although passages are sometimes communicated to their colleagues. This correspondence is supplemented by the interchange of telegrams between them, the bulk of which, relating to public affairs, are circulated to the Members of Council, whether in India or in London. A portion, however, is in the nature of secret correspondence between the two heads of the Government, and need not be divulged to the colleagues of either. These relate more particularly to the conduct of foreign affairs, or the personal relations of the two correspondents. In the time of Lord Morley, however, and Lord Minto, it was found that the private and secret correspondence by wire, between the Secretary of State and the Viceroy, without the knowledge of their respective Councils, and uncommunicated to them, had been carried to a point which amounted to a usurpation of the powers of the latter and was inconsistent with the constitutional basis of Indian Government. Lord Morley combined with an austere but flexible Radicalism and an irresistible personal charm, the most despotic of tempers, and was an impassioned apostle of personal rule. He was apt in Parliament to speak of himself and the Viceroy as though the Government of India was conducted by a sort of private arrangement between these great Twin Brethren, upon whom no sort of check ought to be placed by irresponsible and incompetent outsiders. This tendency was carried to an even further extent in a later régime ; under which it took the form, not merely of an undue use of the private wire between London and Simla, but of the practical supersession of Council in India by the independent action of the Viceroy and the Commander-in-Chief, acting as though they and they alone were the Council—a quite unconstitutional action. This procedure came to a head in the case of the Mesopotamian Campaign of 1915 and succeeding years, and was made the subject of severe animadversion by the Royal Commission appointed under the Chairmanship of an ex-Secretary of State of the highest authority and experience, Lord George Hamilton, to enquire into the charges that had been freely brought against the conduct of the War in that area. The Report of the Commission, published as a Parliamentary Paper in 1917, after describing and laying down the correct relations of the Governor General and his Council, went on to say :

" All the Statutes relating to the Government of India were consolidated in the Acts of 1915 and 1916 ; but in these Acts no mention whatever is made of private communications, nor is authority given either to the Secretary of State or the Governor General to substitute private telegrams for the prescribed methods of communication laid down by the Statute. . . . The substitution of private for public telegrams in recent years has apparently so developed as to become almost the regular channel of official intercommunication. This substitution tends to dispossess the Council of the functions which by Statute they are entitled to exercise. . . . We have been informed by two Members of the Governor General's Council that, according to their recollection, the Council was never consulted as to, nor were they privy to, the campaign in Mesopotamia. Their opinion was not asked as regards the advance to Bagdad, though occasionally from time to time some information was given to them in the shape of conversations at the Council. This statement, though traversed in detail by Lord Hardinge, is in the main, we believe, correct.

" We consider it necessary that the attention both of the Government and Parliament should be called to the change we have thus shown to have taken place in the procedure of the two branches of the Indian Government. If the Government and Parliament are of opinion that these private personal telegrams and letters are in the future to become a recognised channel of authoritative and mandatory communication, then the Act of Parliament should be so altered."

It will be observed that this admonition related to two subjects— (1) the abuse of private telegrams, (2) the failure to consult Council. Upon the first point it is unnecessary to say anything further. As to the second, a provision of the Government of India Act of 1915 (Sec. 39) which laid down that—

" at any meeting of the Council the Governor General or other person presiding and one ordinary member of the Council may exercise all the powers and functions of the Governor General in Council,"

which was itself a textual reproduction of a provision in the Act of 1833, when the Council only consisted of three ordinary members, and frequently met in the absence of the Governor General, who might be hundreds of miles away in the interior—quite clearly only fixed a quorum for the transaction of business, and could not possibly be held to justify the failure to summon Council as a whole, or the usurpation of its powers by a small minority of its members.

It is to be hoped that the above weighty pronouncement may have led to a reversion to constitutional procedure and to the abandonment of a practice which would reduce the Council of the Governor General to a cipher. That its members should ever have consented to acquiesce in such a denegation of their powers as has been described was perhaps the most astonishing feature of the entire transaction.

The Government of India is, however, not the only sphere in which a similar usurpation has taken place. The Secretary of State in London is more independent of his Council than is the Viceroy at Simla or in Delhi, being vested by statute with the power of withdrawing certain matters from them, provided that no charge is entailed on Indian revenues; whereas no such statutory right exists in India. But the cases are not rare in which that independence has been strained to a point quite inconsistent with constitutional propriety.

When the Capital of India was moved from Calcutta to Delhi, a decision which has burdened the Indian finances with a still unterminated charge of many millions, the Council at the India Office were not informed, until the matter had already been decided by the Cabinet, when either advice or protest on their part was useless. At an earlier time, when the events occurred which brought about my resignation in India—emphatically a matter of internal administration, and lying outside the sphere of subjects which the Secretary of State is entitled to withhold from his Council—the latter knew next to nothing of what was going on. Familiar as they were with the earlier history of the struggle between the civil and the military administration in India, their consent could hardly have been obtained to the sacrifice of a principle established by a century of conflict and experience. Nor, in the later phase of the controversy, were they made aware either of my resignation or of the circumstances that led up to it, until after it had taken place. Cabinet authority can indeed always be quoted as an excuse for overriding the Council in the India Office. But it is one thing to overrule them, and another to keep them entirely in the dark.

These modern deviations, either from the letter or the spirit of the Constitution, are to be deplored, and public opinion both in England and in India should insist, in so far as it is informed, upon a due observance of the immemorial rule. And I say this, although I suffered sometimes, as so many of my predecessors had done, from what appeared to me the petty or unreasonable attitude of the Council in Charles Street. Nevertheless I would not see that control abrogated or impaired. The movement, whether in England or in India, to substitute the autocracy of the Secretary of State alone or the Viceroy alone, for the corporate authority of a Council, can only lead, in my opinion, to a wider divorce than sometimes already exists between the English and Indian points of view. The further movement, of which symptoms are apparent, to deprive the Secretary of State of the aid of a Council altogether, will convert him into an undesirable despot.[1]

Though I have described the Indian Council of the Governor General as the equivalent of a Cabinet, it was not till the middle of the last century that the parallelism in its departmental application was for the first time established. Up to that date the theory that the Government of India was a Government by the entire body of the Council, and that though the Governor General might, since 1793, overrule his colleagues, yet in 99 cases out of 100 he could not act without them, was exemplified in the disposal of business. All papers with scarcely an exception were circulated to all the Members of Council, beginning with the Governor General. This had the unfortunate effect of placing an undue burden upon him, and of tempting him to note or to decide before he had heard the views of his expert colleagues. Further, since the papers were circulated in order of seniority, the last to receive them might be the Member best qualified to advise upon the case. The practice also led to interminable delays, as the files pursued their weary way, possibly following the Governor General on a tour of 500 miles or more into the interior. When the papers had completed the round, they came before Council, and it is not surprising to know that sometimes two days in the week and many hours on each occasion were required to dispose of them. Listen to the first Lord Minto's pathetic description of a Council in his time. It is to be found in a letter of 15th September, 1807, to his son :

" The Secretaries attend at Council, each department in turn, with its mountain of bundles. The Secretary reads or often only states shortly the substance of each paper, and the order is given on the spot. The Secretaries scarcely read above their breath. It is a constant strain on the ear to hear them ; the business is often of the heaviest and dullest kind, the voices monotonous, and as one small concern succeeds another, the punkah vibrates gently over my eyes, and in this warm atmosphere the whole operation has been found in the course of five hours somewhat composing. It is often a vehement struggle to avoid a delectable obvious wink. . . . The Secretaries reduce all our orders into Minutes of Council, letters, instructions, etc. . . . We hold two Councils a week, Monday and Friday. We meet at 10, and sit till 3 or 4."[2]

[1] There is a very powerful statement of the case for a Council at the India Office in a letter from Lord Dalhousie of 22nd April, 1858, printed in his " Private Letters," pp. 416-422.
[2] " Lord Minto in India," p. 26.

The first check that I can discover as having been placed on this solemn and dilatory perambulation of the files was the work of Lord Dalhousie, whose temper was impatient of delay, and who instituted the plan of taking papers in Council after one circulation and one writing of Notes—previously they had wandered about in a circuitous movement that might continue for months or even for years.

In a letter to Sir George Couper of 2nd October, 1852, he described his own methods of work. Like other Indian rulers, both before and since, who have been accused of doing too much themselves, and of not leaving enough to their subordinates—a criticism which ignores the fact that only if a man does a thing himself, is it done to his own way of thinking, while, if it fails, he is saved the trouble and annoyance of blaming anyone else for the failure—Dalhousie had been reproached in England for "doing everybody's work"; and to this charge he replied :

"I only would not permit them to do the work that is mine. So far am I from having more work sent to me than is necessary, I have greatly curtailed it, though even thus it is too much for any man. I reckon that not less than 20,000 to 25,000 papers are submitted for the order of the G.G. in the course of each year. Yet by systematising ; by causing an analysis or *précis* of each paper to be made by the officers ; by making *them* dispose of each paper on its progress, not troubling me with it *till it is ripe for my orders* (unless my orders should be indispensable during its progress) ; and by causing all unimportant papers to be submitted, not in bulk but in a register, on which my orders are inserted in the column left for the purpose—by all these rules, I say, which are directed to make the Secretaries lighten my labour, where they do not command my judgment or exercise my functions, I do make every man do his duty ; and the aggregate *work* thus condensed does not fill more than eight despatch-boxes each week. Even thus, I repeat, the labour is incessant, and my performance of it unsatisfactory to myself."[1]

But it was reserved for Lord Canning to make the really vital change in the methods of Government. The following was the representation that he made to the Secretary of State on 26th January, 1861 :

"The fault of the present constitution of Council is the waste of labour and the delays that it entails. This has been mitigated of late, but not so much as it might be. It has arisen chiefly from the fact that the wording of the law and long usage appear to prescribe that every Act of the Governor General in Council beyond those of mere routine (and not always excepting

[1] "Private Letters," p. 227.

these) must be done with the actual consideration and concurrence of all the Members of the Council. This tradition was not long ago broken through ; but not without misgivings on the part of some Members of the Government as to whether they were not unduly divesting themselves of a responsibility fixed upon them. A division of departments has, however, to some extent taken place, and the result has been good.

"I would recognise this division by law, and I would carry it out more distinctly.

"For this purpose the law should declare that it shall be in the power of the Governor General to charge each Member of the Council with the direction of such department of the Government as he may think fit ; and that, subject to any regulations which the Governor General in Council may lay down, the orders of that Member of the Council should in such department be held to be the orders of the Governor General in Council.

"It is not possible, or desirable, to define by law what questions should be submitted to the whole Council. Subjects constantly arise upon which it is quite right that a Member of Council should consult the Governor General, but which it would be a waste of time to bring before every Member of the Council. The practice should be regulated as in the English Cabinet by good understanding and common sense, and by the paramount authority of the head of the Government.

"There is no fear that any important questions would be kept from the consideration of the whole Council by such a change.

"The change would certainly not diminish the dignity and weight which should attach to a seat in the Governor General's Council."

In pursuance of this advice Section 8 of the India Councils Act was drawn up, by which the Governor General was authorised from time to time " to make rules and orders for the more convenient transaction of business." Accordingly Lord Canning divided the Departments of Government between his Councillors, assigning to each Department a Member or to each Member a Department. Thereby were laid the foundations of Cabinet Government in India, as we understand its counterpart in England, each branch of the Administration having its official head and spokesman in the Government, who was responsible for its administration and its defence.

Sir Charles Wood, who was Secretary of State at the time, foresaw that the power conceded to the Governor General by the above section was capable of wide and possibly dangerous interpretation, and in his Despatch of 9th August, 1861, forwarding the Act, he remarked :

" I need hardly impress upon your Lordship the necessity of caution in framing the rules and orders, so as not to exceed the limit of the discretion conferred upon the Governor General by the section of this Act. The object to be kept in view is the *more convenient transaction of business.* There is nothing in the provision of a nature to detract from the authority or responsibility of the Governor General, or of the Council."

That this warning was needed is evident from some of the proceedings half a century later, to which I have already called attention.

The next step—in itself the logical sequel to Lord Canning's change —was taken by Lord Lawrence in 1864, when he solved the difficulty of absence from his Council by taking them with him as a regular practice to Simla. While ignorant critics denounced this move as an Epicurean retirement to a Capua in the hills, Sir Henry Maine grasped its true constitutional significance when he wrote in his Minute of 2nd December, 1867 : " All that Sir John Lawrence did, instead of leaving his Council with a sort of mock independence at Calcutta, was to destroy a costly and mischievous practice by summoning them to accompany him to Simla." Lawrence himself dismissed the sneer with an even curter gesture :

" I did not go to the hills because I was sick. I did not go there to amuse myself or to enjoy myself. I spent five months of the year there, because there I could serve the Company more laboriously and more effectively than if I had been in the plains."

The procedure instituted by Lord Canning has been continued and improved upon since, successive Viceroys having utilised the statutory powers which they enjoy to rearrange the work of the Departments or their representatives in Council in the manner required by the needs of the time. An immense amount of administrative work of the routine type does not go before Council at all, any more than it does before the British Cabinet at home. It is discharged on his own responsibility by the Member of Council who is the head of the Department concerned. If he is convinced of its special importance, he refers it to the Viceroy either personally, or through the Secretary of Government in his Department, who sees the Viceroy once a week and takes his orders. The Viceroy can, if he please, circulate the paper and refer the case to Council, with or without his recorded opinion, and the matter is then brought up at the next meeting. Where two or more Departments differ about a case in which they are all involved, a similar reference is invariably made. Still, as in the first Lord Minto's time, the Secretary attends, states the case, takes the orders of Council, and is responsible for seeing to their execution. In this respect the British system has tended, since the Great War, to approximate more closely to the Indian model. For in London, as for a century and a half in India, Cabinet decisions are now recorded by an official Secretary, who is further charged with the duty of seeing that they are carried out.

In the passage of time the mechanical means adopted for the circulation of Government papers to the Members of Council in India have varied. In the earlier part of the last century they travelled about in mahogany boxes from house to house, or from Calcutta to the Governor General's Camp. Lord Ellenborough, fresh from a ripe departmental experience in England, introduced red and gold Foreign Office boxes. In the middle of the century the boxes were " little brick-shaped monstrosities, the papers being folded into four inside." In Lord Lawrence's day both the red leather despatch boxes and the oblong mahogany boxes were still in use. During my time the papers came in boxes to the Private Secretary's office, and were then placed on the Viceroy's table in bundles, strapped to a strong cardboard with a tape riband, the latest paper, requiring orders, being placed upon the top.

Different heads of the Indian Government have adopted widely different standards and methods of work. Lord Wellesley, who was very proud of his literary accomplishments, spent a great deal of time in composing and polishing his own Despatches. But he did this at the cost of chronic inattention to public business, which was in consequence frequently in arrears, if not neglected altogether.

There is a passage in one of Lord Dalhousie's Private Diaries which sheds a curious light upon these idiosyncrasies, and shows that the imperious energy of Wellesley was spasmodic in character, and was compatible with strange spells of idleness and lethargy.

" He was a man of very fine understanding, but indolent to the last degree unless when compelled ; and then he was wonderful as a man of business. The Duke of Wellington told Mr. Arbuthnot so, and, saying that when Lord Wellesley chose he was the most admirable man for the despatch of business that ever he had seen, he gave him, as an instance, what happened to himself in India : after Assaye he was going home to England, and went to Calcutta to see his brother. While he was there the principal Secretary came to him and implored him to get Lord Wellesley to turn himself to the business, saying that none of their boxes were ever opened, and that the whole business of the country was in such horrible arrears that they were afraid the whole Government would get into disgrace with the Directors and everywhere else. Sir Arthur went to the Governor General and said, ' Now you know, here I am, with nothing to do.   You must have a vast deal to do.   I wish you would make any use of me you think proper.' Lord Wellesley was nettled. He set to work, sate up for several nights together, and got through the whole business in the most perfect manner before ever he stopped." [1]

The story is illustrative of Wellesley's temperament as well as of his methods.

H. Thoby Prinsep, who was Political Secretary to the Governor General in the time of Lord W. Bentinck, wrote of the latter, with whom he did not get on very well :

" I never saw a man who had such a love of work, or such an incessant desire to meddle with everything great or small.   He was incessantly writing minutes on all subjects, and his Private and Military Secretaries were employed all day in copying them and sending them to the Departments to be officially brought before the Council." [2]

The same authority wrote of Lord Ellenborough :

" It was his way in all matters of first-rate importance to make no use of his Official or Private Secretaries, but to prepare his despatches by his own hand. He wished them, when they were likely to be published or laid before Parliament, to go forth in his own peculiar style, of which he was justly proud."

Lord Dalhousie did an immense amount of work with his own hand, and in a handwriting singularly neat and clear. Moreover he was the master of a style of admirable lucidity in exposition, but caustic in its irony, and sometimes withering in its scorn. He wrote all his Minutes with his own hand. But he did not as a rule trouble to compose Despatches to the Home Government, thinking it sufficient to collect the drafts submitted by the Departments. He once said that in the whole of his eight years in India he had not written twenty complete Despatches himself. On the other hand his Minutes were legion.

His successor Canning also wrote a beautiful hand, and was laborious in application. At the same time he was one of the worst men of business who ever filled the Viceroy's chair. Descriptions are extant of him, barely visible behind a vast barricade of boxes, with the

[1] " Life of the Marquis of Dalhousie," by Sir W. Lee Warner, Vol. I, p. 12.
[2] Unpublished.

accumulation of which he was powerless to cope, and on whose contents, when opened, he could not bring himself to decide.

In the second half of the last century Lord Mayo was a man of excellent businesslike habits ; Lord Lytton wrote by far the best Minutes and Despatches, viewed from the literary standpoint, that I came across in the records of the past ; Lord Dufferin, though possessed of great literary gifts, was content to write little, except on great occasions, and had a Private Secretary in Sir D. Mackenzie Wallace who acted for him, and even reproduced with lifelike fidelity the signature of his chief.

The mention of a Private Secretary leads me to say that in my account of the work of the British Rulers of India it would be unfair to ignore, although historians have as a rule passed by, the assistance that has been rendered to them by the men who have filled this singularly onerous and delicate post.

They have been drawn from many classes. Some have been members of the Indian Civil Service ; a few, especially in earlier days, were military officers ; some have been relatives or friends brought by the Governor General from home. The peculiar position and environment of the latter, and the nature of his work, have tended to invest the post of Private Secretary in India with a greater distinction than attaches to any corresponding office in public life in England : for he is the intermediary between his chief and every class of person in India, from the titled Maharaja or the powerful colleague, down to the angry merchant or the pertinacious Babu. Hence the P.S.V., as he has been designated since the days of Lord Canning, is as important and sometimes a more influential personage in the Indian hierarchy than a Member of Council or even a Governor. That the men have been well chosen and that their Secretarial experience has often been the stepping-stone to a public career of the highest eminence may be seen from a brief survey of some of those who have filled the office. The first Private Secretary whose appointment was officially notified was George Nesbitt Thompson, whose correspondence with his chief, Warren Hastings, after the latter had left India, is frequently cited in this work. He became a Resident at more than one Native Court, and rose to the rank of Lieutenant General. Lord Wellesley, during his long tenure of office, was served by his younger brother Henry, who afterwards became Lieutenant Governor of Oudh, and at a later date, as Baron Cowley, Ambassador at Vienna and Paris ; by Colonel, afterwards General, Kirkpatrick ; and by Captain, afterwards Sir John Malcolm, Envoy to and Historian of Persia, and Governor of Bombay. Lord Hastings' Private Secretaries, John Adam and Charles Theophilus Metcalfe (afterwards Lord Metcalfe), both became Acting Governors General. Auckland's Private Secretary, John Russell Colvin, was the well-known Lieutenant Governor of the North-western Provinces in the Mutiny, who died during that terrible time and was buried in the Fort at Agra. Two Durands, both afterwards famous, served as Private Secretaries in their younger days : Sir Henry Durand, subsequently Lieutenant Governor of the Punjab, with Lord Ellenborough ; his son Sir Mortimer Durand, who became Ambassador at Madrid and Washington, with Lord Ripon. General Sir Owen Burne served Lord Mayo and Lord Lytton ; the ill-fated Sir George Colley, who perished at Majuba, was the right-hand man of Lord Lytton, and was succeeded by another very able soldier, afterwards General Sir Henry Brackenbury. Perhaps the most famous of all Private Secretaries was Captain Evelyn Baring, then a young Artillery Officer, but afterwards known to the world as Lord Cromer, who accompanied his relative Lord Northbrook to India in 1872. Lord Lansdowne found a capable coadjutor in Sir John Ardagh ; the later Lord Elgin in his son-in-law, afterwards Sir Henry Babington Smith. Nor can I exaggerate the debt which I owed to my principal Private Secretary for five years, Sir Walter Lawrence, who subsequently filled many posts of distinction in England. When the Governor General is commemorated, let not his right-hand man be forgotten.

Though the change in the distribution and regulation of business introduced by Lord Canning was most beneficial and removed one of the chief blots in the previous system, it was far from purging the Government of India of the double reproach of exorbitant writing and unpardonable delay. Because a Member was made directly responsible for an Office, it did not follow that he discharged its business with promptitude, or that any diminution occurred in the manuscript roaring of the young lions of the Department, or indeed of the old lions either, when once the file had started on its way. Viceroy after Viceroy commenced by bewailing the abuse, and ended by succumbing to its deadly embrace. Some by their own paper loquacity gave it a little needed encouragement. Noting became the recognised means by which the youthful esquire who aspired to knightly honours under the

Government of India showed how deft a blade he wielded, and with what dexterous strokes he could either demolish his opponent or slice the air. Department became involved in internecine and unending conflict with Department ; the fact that all manuscript on the file is almost immediately converted into print being an encouragement to all who aspired to this cheap form of immortality. Similarly in the external branches of Government, vast and ponderous Reports on every conceivable subject came pouring in from the Provincial Governments, and from every Department of the Administration—reports which no one outside the Departments read, which were forgotten as soon as issued, and which involved an inconceivable expenditure of labour and time. It is, I think, well known how fierce a warfare I waged against this twofold incubus. I certainly prevailed against it in my time. How far my efforts have had a permanent or lasting effect it would require a knowledge of the present administration which I do not possess, to enable me to say. Systems are as a rule stronger than men ; and a Viceroy is after all only a fleeting phantom.

Furthermore, the intelligent application of orders may be scarcely less important than the orders themselves. Some years after I had gone there was current an amusing tale of the manner in which an order that I had issued was interpreted in the time of my successor, Lord Minto, who had strong sporting proclivities, and was quite indifferent to style. A scheme having been devised in his day to stay the deterioration of the splendid little ponies of Burma, when the proposals were laid before the Viceroy he wrote on the file, " I agree. The Burma pony is a damned good little piece of stuff."

The clerk in the Government of India Secretariat, drafting on the case, accordingly began—" Sir, I am directed to inform you that in the opinion of the Governor General in Council the Burma pony is a damned good little piece of stuff." When taken to task the defence of the culprit was unanswerable. For he explained that in the time of Lord Curzon an order had been passed that when the Viceroy wrote a note of instructions for a draft, the exact words should be adhered to in the draft. That order had never been rescinded, and he had observed it.

I have said that, unlike the practice of the Departments in England, every note is converted almost immediately into print in India, where the setting up of type is so amazingly cheap and the wages of compositors are so low.   The use of print in every office—the Viceroy, for instance, has his own Printing Press—is a source of the greatest convenience, and in no Government in the world is the work of recording so efficient or so speedily performed.   It is also a great comfort in studying the papers of the past.

The true story of each Viceroyalty is in reality written in the weekly private letters which are exchanged between the Viceroy and the Secretary of State, and in which each unburdens himself in accents of explanation, advice, encouragement, warning, appeal, protest, or indignation, according as the situation may demand.   Were these letters to be given to the world, the history of Viceroys might in some cases require to be entirely rewritten.   The Viceroy is also well advised, even in these times when decentralisation has advanced so far and when Provincial autonomy is in many respects almost unqualified, if he maintains a regular correspondence with the Provincial Governors and heads of administration.   The labour may be great ; but he will be rewarded by their understanding of the policy which he is attempting to pursue, and by their active support in times of crisis.   I have known Viceroys who conscientiously pursued this course with the happiest results ;   I have known others whose neglect of it brought about friction and even disaster.

Queen Victoria instituted the practice of corresponding regularly with her Governors General and Viceroys, writing to them (if I may judge from my own experience) every two or three weeks with her own hand.   The latest letter which I was honoured by receiving from her reached me in the week of her death, and was presented by me to the Victoria Memorial Hall at Calcutta.   The letters of the Viceroy to the Sovereign were written in the third person.   The only exception to this rule was created by Lord Lytton, who, with engaging disregard of the established etiquette, began to write his admirable letters to the Queen in the first person, and was allowed by Her Majesty, who was enchanted with their unconventional and interesting character, to proceed.   King Edward wrote less frequently than his illustrious Mother, but followed Indian affairs with a not inferior interest, reinforced by a personal experience which he never ceased to quote with pleasure. Both Monarchs sought, in every possible way, to support their representative in India, and the Viceroy might always rely upon a sympathetic interest from them in labours which they regarded, in many aspects,

2—J

notably in relation to the Indian Princes, as directly affecting the Crown. Now that a reigning King Emperor and his Queen have visited India and have even been crowned there, the bond that unites India with the Throne has become closer and more personal, and may be found, when other supports crumble, to provide a rock of salvation.

Apart from occasional references in the text, I have not thought it necessary in this work to devote any special space to the relations of the Governor General or Viceroy with the great Civil Service of which he is the temporary head. More than thirty years ago I dedicated my first considerable work—that on Persia—to the Civil and Military Officials in India, in words which I see no reason to alter to-day. I have had frequent opportunities since, in and out of India, in Parliament and in print, of renewing that tribute. It has been paid by every British Ruler of India in turn, conscious that whatever of credit or applause he may have received has been for the most part due to their loyal and efficient labours. That a Service so competent, with such a record, and inspired by such traditions, should become disheartened or should lose its power of appeal to the hearts and brains of young Englishmen would be an unspeakable tragedy, and would be the prelude to the ultimate loss of India itself. May no such crowning error ever be committed.

It may be well however that I should add a few words about a subject not less important—namely the attitude that has been adopted by successive British rulers towards the native populations whose destinies have been committed to their charge. Before the Indian people, or rather a minute fraction of them, became vocal, before they were admitted to high judicial and later to high political office, before they became Members of Council and the like, their association with the work of Government in its higher branches was small and sporadic. The administration of British India after the commencement of the 19th century was a British administration, conducted by British agents, in the main on British lines. But even so, and perhaps even more formerly than now, the intermediaries between the British rulers and native peoples, as well as the entire ministerial and subordinate staff, were Indian : and at no time could the Government of India have been conducted without the faithful collaboration of many thousands of Indian subordinates, while the ranks of the police, and other execu-

STATUE OF WARREN HASTINGS

Sculpt.: Sir R. Westmacott, R.A.

tive and administrative services, have necessarily been recruited almost exclusively from those sources.   Moreover in the background at every stage of historical evolution have stood the patient, silent masses of the Indian agricultural population—the *ryot* or peasant—and in more recent times the artisan, so apt to be overlooked by the mere politician, but whose interests have been the special concern of the British administration.

At the other extreme of society the Governor General has always been thrown into close contact with the Indian Princes, sometimes in olden days as formidable rivals and even antagonists, latterly as powerful but loyal feudatories of the British Crown.   The relations of all Governors General and Viceroys with this class have been characterised by punctilious courtesy and a genuine regard, even though it has sometimes been the duty of the British ruler to rebuke or even to depose a guilty or refractory Chief.   I have not observed any variation in the uniform standard of mutual respect that has prevailed for over a century between the representative of the British Sovereign and these Indian rulers.   Their attitude towards him has commonly been that of the greatest deference.   It has given them pleasure to entertain and to honour him.   Reciprocally he has sought to win their confidence, he has been well advised to sustain their prerogative, and he has profited immensely by their support.

It seems to me that in the future these relations will tend to become closer rather than more distant.   The old era of isolation, not unmingled with distrust, has long ago passed away.   We may date the beginning of the change from the Viceroyalty of Lord Canning, from the abandonment of the doctrine of annexation by lapse, and the transference of the Government of India to the Crown.   Since then there has been a steady growth of mutual confidence, which has been reflected in the progressive improvement in the government of the States.   Guaranteed in the possession of his authority, assured of an ample, and in some cases a royal income, endowed with powers that, if at one end of the scale they are little more than those of a country squire, are at the other end those of an all but independent monarch, the Prince on his part accepts the obligation of maintaining a reasonable (it is sometimes an extremely high) level of conduct and administration.   He is less and less interfered with by the Central Government.   On the other hand, a spirit of emulation and the spur of an ever-increasing publicity take the place of official tutelage. Simultaneously higher standards of education, visits to Europe, acquaintance with the amenities of Western life, and above all contact with our own Royal House, have greatly strengthened the ties that unite the Princes to the Suzerain Power. Scandals sometimes occur in Native States ; extravagance exists ; occasional relapses are reported. But these incidents are not more frequent than those which happen in the corresponding state of society in the most advanced Western countries. Disloyalty to the British Raj may be said to have no existence ; the least symptom of it is severely condemned. The internal administration of the principal Indian States is conducted with creditable efficiency ; and the Princes, emerging from the ancestral entrenchments of their former existence, are tending more and more to take part in the public life of the country, and even on occasions to speak as leaders of the people.

Perhaps the greatest change to be noted is their increasing willingness to operate in combination with each other. Where a spirit of suspicious isolation once held them apart, so that they rarely visited each other and could scarcely be said to have a common aim, they now meet in a Chamber of Princes, and act as a corporate whole. The relaxation of caste and other social restrictions, and a common taste for sport bring them into closer touch with English officials and English society. They not only exchange formal and ceremonial visits with the Viceroy, but they stay with him as his guests, and share the hospitality of his table.

But the change is really much wider and more significant. The growth of India, the development of the modern conception of the British Empire as a great Federation of States, and above all the experiences of the Great War, have swept the Indian Princes into the swirling current of international life. The Princes take their seats by right at meetings of the Imperial Conference in London ; they have even been members of a British Cabinet in the War. They attended at Paris during the Peace negotiations ; their signature has been affixed to European Treaties ; an Indian Prince, once famous as a sportsman, sits as an Imperial representative in the Council Hall and Committee Rooms of the League of Nations at Geneva. Who could be so foolish as to think that these forms of recognition would not be followed by an enhancement of their political stature in their own country ?

The main problem that lies before the Princes in the near future will be the adjustment of their relations to the rising tide of rather crude and sometimes emotional Nationalism, commonly called Swaraj, that is sweeping over India. British India is seething with the commotion produced by the attempt to introduce Parliamentary institutions and modified forms of self-government into the archaic fabric of the Indian Commonwealth.   But the structure of the Native State is far more obdurate and far more archaic ; and the conception of the Indian Prince as an autocratic and almost heaven-sent ruler, though hitherto sustained by the traditional loyalty of his subjects, is hardly consistent with the shibboleths of self-government as preached by the modern tribunes of the people.   If India for the Indians is a plausible cry in British India, a similar propaganda is capable of being set on foot in Native States, where the ruling family is sometimes as much an alien in race, and even in religion, to the majority of the inhabitants as are the British rulers of the entire continent.   Some of the Princes have made tentative advances in the direction of democratic institutions ; some have even expressed an ardent sympathy with desires which the majority secretly mistrust.   In the meantime their own position can hardly remain static : a steady infiltration of ideas across the frontiers between British India and their own States is always going on.

In my view the future stability of India depends largely upon the continued existence and stability of the Native States. They need not and cannot all be organised on the same pattern. Nor will they represent the same degree of progress, independence, or power. But they should remain, both as connecting links with the past, and as representing a standard of life and government which is in harmony with the traditions and the tastes of the people. And if this be a sound induction, then I think it follows that there should be an ever closer association between the British Government, by which in India I mean more particularly the Viceroy, and themselves. Already since my day the Punjab States, the Madras States, and now the Kathiawar States and Cutch, have been formally transferred from the jurisdiction of the Provincial Govern-ments to the Governor of India, i.e. the Viceroy. Further measures to strengthen and vitalise this new form of co-ordination will doubtless be required. It will be one of the main preoccupations of the Viceroy of the future. I was, I think, the first Governor General to describe the Indian Princes as partners in the British administration of India. As time passes they will be less and less sleeping partners, and more and more joint managers of that mighty estate. But, equally with the British Governors, will they have to make up their minds as to their attitude and to take their stand. A number of Philippe Egalités in India might place the Princely structure in India in grave peril.

When people, however, write or talk of the relations between a British ruler and the natives of the country, they are not commonly thinking either of Princes or potentates, or of Indian officials or members of the Services, still less of the purely agricultural population. They mean the Indian community as a whole, and in modern times more particularly the Indians who have taken advantage of the English education, with which they are so liberally provided, to nourish political ambitions and to play an active part in the public life of their country.

So different are the conditions in this respect of the present day from those of half a century ago—and still more, of course, as we go further back—that no standard of comparison can be set up. And yet I can truthfully say that in the thousands of Viceregal Minutes, Memoranda and letters, which I have been called upon to peruse, I cannot recall a single harsh or unfeeling reflection by any of these writers upon any section of the Indian race. Each Governor General, as he has assumed his onerous charge, has been inspired not so much by the magnitude of the task as by the moral obligations which it has entailed. Each has sought to do his duty by the millions of every class and creed ; many have formed the warmest attachment to the people of the country : some have left the most touching tributes to their character. I have never found in the records of any Viceroy any trace of that pride of colour or arrogance of tone which is sometimes charged against younger and less experienced Englishmen in that country.

It is perhaps not unnatural that, in a land where a small minority of one race rules a vast population of another, and where racial prejudice either exists or can easily be called into being, the British rulers who have been most popular have been those who appeared to take the side of the Indians against their own countrymen, who openly espoused the native cause in a controversy, or who made social and, in more recent times, political concessions to Indian aspirations. It is very easy to acquire this sort of popularity in India. A speech here, an appointment there, a yielding to popular clamour in a third case—

and the thing is done.   British Viceroys have as a rule risen superior to this form of temptation.   A few, by a consistent policy of deference to Indian sentiment, particularly where it has brought them the disfavour of their own countrymen, have attained a more enduring reputation.   Such has been the fortune of a Bentinck, a Canning, or a Ripon, in eulogising whom the Indian love for hyperbole has found a fruitful field for exercise.   But the Indian is gifted with extraordinary natural acumen ; and while he invests with a nimbus the brow of the Englishman whom he believes to have taken his side, he regards with scarcely less respect the man who has held the scales even and has set justice before partiality.

Warren Hastings was regarded by the Indian community in Bengal —relatively few and voiceless in those days—as their champion and friend ; Dalhousie they approached with mingled awe and admiration ; they bowed to the splendid presence of Mayo ; they could not fail to be attracted by the courtly charm of Dufferin and Lansdowne.

Some Viceroys have interfered openly to protect the natives from violence or outrage at the hands of the white man.   Lord Lytton essayed the task ; the writer exposed himself at one time to considerable obloquy from his countrymen for a renewal of the effort, and exaggerated accounts were circulated of his alleged partisanship in notorious cases.   The truth of these will perhaps one day be told. The right standard of conduct is surely that there should be the same degree of sanctity attached to Indian as to British life in India, and that acts should not be condoned in one case which would be condemned in the other.

The smaller class of Indian officials was intensely grateful for any interest shown in their welfare ; and one of my proudest possessions is the Address that was spontaneously presented to me when I left India by the subordinate native servants of Government in the public offices at Simla ; while the tenacious affections of the Indian peoples may be illustrated by the fact that, though I have left that country for twenty years, I continue to be addressed by natives from all parts of the land who believe themselves to have been treated with injustice, and who imagine that I am still in a position to give them protection or redress.

But the average Indian politician will probably not deny that he is much more concerned with the opportunities for political advancement than he is with abstract conceptions of justice, or with the security of human life ; and a single concession of the former character will be deemed to outweigh in merit a decade of sacrifice to the cause of the humble and the distressed.   I spent many anxious hours in dealing with cases of racial injustice.   But it counted as dust in the balance when I was unable to make political concessions for which I held— and possibly I was not wrong—that the country was not yet ripe.

None the less, no British ruler has, I believe, ever left India without a greater regard for its inhabitants than that with which he entered it.   There is such an infinite capacity for loyal service among its peoples ; there comes from them, like the breath of a warm wind, so irresistible an appeal for justice and protection : they are so grateful for kindness shown.   As Queen Victoria wrote to me in the last six months of her life : " No people are more alive to kindness or more affectionately attached, if treated with kindness, than the Indians are."

Benevolent despotism, however, as a form of Government is now held in India or anywhere else to be out of date ; and the craving for political autonomy, with only the most imperfect realisation of the responsibilities that it entails, has created a new ideal which will carry India very wide and very far.   But it may be questioned whether the Indian under the new dispensation will be any better off or any happier than the Indian under the old.   The relations between the two races will lose somewhat of that old-fashioned confidence and esteem, which was neither patronising on the one side, nor servile on the other, but sprang from the best qualities of both races ; and the Viceroy of the future will have a harder task, though not an inferior duty, in conciliating native sentiment and winning native affection.

There is one respect in which the Viceroy, if so disposed, can exercise a powerful influence upon the sentiments of the Indian population : I mean by the preservation of their monuments and respect for their shrines.   While I was in India I devoted, as may be known, an immense amount of time and labour to the restoration and conservation of the old mosques, and temples, and palaces, and fortresses, and tombs. These form a collection with which, regarded as a whole, whether for grandeur or for beauty, no other country can vie.   I pursued this policy partly from a feeling of profound respect for the religious sentiments of the people, partly because the buildings in question appealed to me as

STATUE OF LORD CURZON IN GROUNDS OF VICTORIA MEMORIAL HALL

Sculpt.: F. W. Pomeroy, R.A.

among the most beautiful and in some cases historic in the world, and also because I thought it a duty that was owed by the governing power to the peoples of whom they had assumed the rule—a duty all the more binding because it had been consistently neglected by the rulers of their own race and creed. A spirit of emulation in restoring and preserving these priceless relics spread rapidly throughout the country : it affected Native States just as much as British India ; and the splendid work of Sir John Marshall, who came to India as my coadjutor, has left an enduring mark upon Indian archæology and architecture. I am often told by those who have visited the country since my day, that this labour of love has had its reward in the recognition of the people, and that I am much more likely to be remembered for having preserved their monuments from decay than for having sought to remedy abuses or to breathe fresh life into the administration. But the work which I have described, to be permanently successful, must be continuous and un-remitting. In the rush of Indian life it is apt to be forgotten, and in times of financial pressure to be rudely brushed aside ; a few years of neglect may produce a shocking relapse both in the buildings treated and in the official attitude towards them. It is only by the unceasing interest and patronage of the Provincial Governors, and still more of the Viceroy, that the duty can be discharged and a high level of efficiency maintained. Never may the British rulers of India be subject to the reproach of the Latin poet :

> *Delicta majorum immeritus lues,*
> *Romane, donec templa refeceris*
> *Aedesque labentes deorum et*
> *Foeda nigro simulacra fumo.*

And now that I have referred to the way in which it is open to the Viceroy to preserve the memorials of India, let me, in concluding this chapter, relate the manner in which India, and Calcutta in particular, as the Capital City where the Viceroys resided, have commemorated them. The public in India has been very generous in the manner in which it has treated the memory of its Governors General and Viceroys, subscribing large voluntary sums for ordering and erecting statues of those whom it has thus elected to honour, either in public buildings or in close proximity to the Maidan.

2—J*

Indeed these statues, some of which are quite excellent, attain a much higher standard of merit than the corresponding effigies with which the more confined spaces and incongruous surroundings of London have been encumbered and in some cases defiled. On the great open expanse of the Maidan they are as a rule well placed and effective. The Governors General who have been thus honoured are:

Subject.	Sculptor.	Site.
W. Hastings	Sir R. Westmacott, R.A.	Victoria Memorial Hall.
Lord Cornwallis	J. Bacon, Junior, R.A.	do.
Lord Wellesley	J. Bacon, Junior, R.A.	do.
Lord Hastings	J. Flaxman, R.A.	do.
Lord W. Bentinck	Sir R. Westmacott, R.A.	Opposite Town Hall.
Lord Auckland	H. Weekes, R.A.	Near Eden Gardens.
1st Lord Hardinge	J. H. Foley, R.A.	S.E. of Government House.
Lord Dalhousie	Sir J. Steell, R.S.A.	Victoria Memorial Hall.
Lord Canning	J. H. Foley, R.A., and T. Brock, R.A.	S.W. of Government House.
Sir J. Lawrence	T. Woolner, R.A.	Opposite Government House.
Lord Mayo	T. Thornycroft	Maidan.
Lord Northbrook	Sir E. Boehm, R.A.	Opposite High Court.
Lord Dufferin	Sir E. Boehm, R.A.	Red Road.
Lord Lansdowne	H. Bates and E. Onslow Ford	Red Road.
Lord Curzon	Sir H. Thornycroft, R.A.	Maidan.
	F. W. Pomeroy, R.A.	Victoria Memorial Hall.
4th Lord Minto	Sir W. Goscombe John, R.A.	New Road.

The rulers who have failed to obtain this form of recognition are, as will have been seen, Sir John Macpherson, Sir John Shore,

Sir George Barlow, the first Lord Minto, Lord Amherst, Lord Ellenborough, the first and second Lords Elgin, Lord Lytton and Lord Ripon.

The sole representation of the first Lord Minto in Calcutta was a bust in St. John's Church, which had been presented by himself at the request of the Vestry, who were much gratified at his regular attendance in Church, and at his restoration of the building. It was destroyed by an earthquake in 1897, but was replaced by his descendant, the later Viceroy of the same name, in 1910. Minto, however, was accorded the honour of interment in Westminster Abbey —a compliment that must I think have been due less to personal claims, since he had actually been recalled from India, than to the tragic circumstances of his death immediately upon his return to England, which excited the natural commiseration of his countrymen. Among the remainder it has always struck me as an astonishing thing that the enthusiasm of the Bengalis for Lord Ripon, whom they regarded as a People's Viceroy, should never have taken the concrete form of raising the funds to erect a statue in his honour. Even if the chill attitude of the European community had denied to him the hospitality of the Maidan, it might have been thought that some other site would be forthcoming. But the gap remains unfilled.

In England the tribute has been more grudging. The only Governors General, besides Lord Minto, to whom a grave in the Abbey has been given, were Canning and Lawrence. Warren Hastings owed the modest tribute of a bust and tablet on the Abbey walls solely to the faithful devotion of his widow.[1] Till I obtained admission for the portrait-relief of Clive, he too was unrepresented there. Lawrence is the sole Viceroy of whom an effigy has been erected in the streets of London, though Indian Generals abound.

As to the mortal remains of the greatest among the company, Warren Hastings sleeps in the secluded Churchyard of Daylesford.

---

[1] A private admirer of W. Hastings erected in the year 1800 a temple in honour of the ex-Governor General, with a bust of the latter, in the grounds of Melchet Park, Wilts. Both temple and bust have long ago disappeared. In 1912 I was instrumental in securing what will, I hope, prove a more lasting memorial of the great Proconsul. Brass tablets had already been let into the stone floor of Westminster Hall indicating the precise spots on which King Charles I and Lord Strafford had stood for their trial, and the bodies of Mr. Gladstone and King Edward VII had rested prior to their interment. I moved in Parliament and secured that a further tablet should be added, on the spot where Warren Hastings faced his accusers. In the India Office is a full-length marble statue of Hastings by Flaxman, which was executed to the order of the East India Company for the Court Room of the East India House, and was afterwards transferred to its present habitation. A plaster bust of Hastings is in the same office, and a bronze cast from it may be seen in the National Portrait Gallery. But the Nation has never taken any steps to testify its supreme debt to one of its greatest sons.

The body of Cornwallis rests, where he died, at Ghazipur ; but there is a monument to him in St. Paul's Cathedral and a statue by the elder Bacon in the India Office. Wellesley is interred in the Chapel of the great Public School which he loved ; the only statue of him in England is one in the India Office by H. Weekes, who carried out a commission for the East India Company that would have been executed, but for his death, by Sir F. Chantrey. Dalhousie lies in a disused vault in the deserted Kirkyard of Cockpen.

CHAPTER XII

PART I

NOTES ON SOME VICEROYS AND GOVERNORS GENERAL

> Some beneath the further stars
>   Bear the greater burden;
> Set to serve the lands they rule
> (Save he serve no man may rule),
> Serve and love the lands they rule
>   Seeking praise nor guerdon.
>
> Bless and praise we famous men—
>   Men of little showing—
> For their work continueth,
> And their work continueth,
> Broad and deep continueth,
>   Great beyond their knowing.—RUDYARD KIPLING.

Sunt lacrymæ rerum et mentem mortalia tangunt.—VIRGIL, *Æneid I*, 462.

CLIVE TO BENTINCK, 1765-1835

IN the course of this narrative we have, in one context or another, come across every occupant of the Governor General's seat, from Warren Hastings to the last tenant of Government House, Calcutta, before the Hejira to Delhi which severed the thread of a century and a half's connection. We have seen something of their history before they came out to India, their social and ceremonial life there, and of the fate that befell them after their return. But we have not seen very much of the men themselves, or become familiar with their own personality and thoughts and feelings, behind the political façade which their administration presented to the world at the time and to history afterwards. There is no department of historical study that is kept more diligently up to date than that which tells the tale of British Government in India, and the retired Viceroy has not been back in

England for a decade before he can read in the text-books of Indian history the precise and tabulated record of his period of rule. He sees many things attributed to his initiative which would have happened even if he had never gone to India at all, and which were the result either of the labour of his colleagues or of tendencies and movements working to inevitable ends. Thus the Permanent Settlement of Bengal is credited to Cornwallis, the abolition of *suttee* to Bentinck, the institution of the Imperial Service Troops to Dufferin, whereas each of these landmarks in Indian history was the result of causes that owed much less to the personal initiative of any individual than to extraneous causes or to the impulse of others. On the other hand the Proconsul sometimes thinks himself, and, as history testifies, with too frequent truth, the victim of undeserved misrepresentation or reproach. Not, indeed, until a long time has elapsed is it possible to disentangle in India or elsewhere the particular from the general, and to determine what part was played by the individual ruler in the organic evolution of his time, or what was the measure of his success or failure. Some men are unable to survive this sifting, and become phantoms rather than figures in history. A few emerge from the background with startling vividness, and stand forth among the great men of their age. The aim of this chapter will be to survey this historic picture gallery and, as we look at the full-length portraits that hang upon its walls, to arrive at some appreciation of their character and merits.

Perhaps a writer who has himself filled the post of head of the Government of India may possess some qualifications for the task, and that for two reasons. Not only does he know the environment in which his predecessors worked, the kind of difficulties that they encountered and the tools that they had to employ; but in a Government where everything is written and nearly everything printed, he is constantly brought in contact—or may be if he chooses—with the *litera scripta* of his predecessors, and can ascertain—what is much more difficult in England—the exact history of and the reasons for this or that step. Thus, more particularly if he is in India as long as I happened to be, he gets to know the men who preceded him ; they become quite familiar to him, and he lives his life, so to speak, in their company. Consequently he may be better fitted to place them in focus with each other and with the history of their time than the purely scientific student who, so to speak, examines and pins the Viceregal

STATUE OF LORD CLIVE

Sculpt.: John Tweed.

specimens in a glass case in the academic workshop of the British Museum.

I have mentioned elsewhere that I have been so fortunate as to know personally and to correspond with no fewer than ten Viceroys, four of whom are still living. It would ill become me to pass judgment upon the careers of the latter, about which it is still too early for history to pronounce. Of some of the former I may be permitted to speak, but even in their cases I am less concerned with the head of the administration than I am with the man. It is no part of my object to condense the history of India under British rule into a single chapter, or to deal with wars and annexations, with economic or political developments, and internal reforms. Rather do I want to show what manner of person was Hastings or Wellesley or Dalhousie or Canning, how he comported himself during his term of rule, and what were his relations with his countrymen and with the Government which he served. We shall follow the procession of Governors General as they climbed the stairs of Government House and, a few years later, as they stepped down ; and we shall contrast the sentiments with which they came and went, and can count the tale of bricks which they had made in their time.

To some of my readers it may be a revelation to learn how much, behind the external glitter of the pageant, there has been of sacrifice and even of suffering. Amid the fanfare of the trumpets and the thunder of the guns, Government House, Calcutta, has sheltered more than its quota of bruised hearts and broken hopes. I doubt if my countrymen have any appreciation of this side of the shield. It will emerge from my narrative as I proceed.

Generally speaking, I have, where dealing with persons long dead and gone, been less concerned with the verdicts that have been passed upon them by the professional historian, than I have with their own words and confessions, and with the opinions of their contemporaries. These are the best material for a picture of the man, even if they are not an irrefragable basis of history. A good deal of information in this chapter has also been derived from private and confidential sources.

Robert Lord Clive, though he has more than once been mentioned in these pages, stands in reality outside the scope of this work. For though he was twice Governor of Fort William in Bengal, he was never Governor General—neither the office nor the dominion having been created in his time—and it is to that category that I have confined my attention. Still no reference to the history of British rule in India would be complete that did not include the name of that great and dæmonic figure, standing forth like a rock of granite against the tempestuous background of his time. Great as a captain—for good judges of warfare have been heard to say that in military genius he was equal to Marlborough and superior to Turenne—greater still as an administrator and statesman—for he was the real founder of that Civil Service which for more than a century and a half has been the glory of British rule in India—to Clive we owe the fact that there has been an India for Englishmen to serve and for British Viceroys to govern. Forgive him his errors—they were great, but never mean ; remember his achievements—they were transcendent ; shed a tear over the final scene—it was tragic but not ignoble. After all, was not Clive the first of the great Indian Proconsuls to suffer from the ingratitude of his countrymen, and did he not thereby inculcate a lesson and set an example that has taught others to endure ?

Of one injustice, at least, I am proud to have been instrumental in relieving his memory. For a hundred and fifty years after his death Clive was commemorated in the land that gave him birth only by a statue in the Market Place of Shrewsbury, which he once represented in Parliament, and by a little-seen effigy in the India Office, the work of the sculptor Peter Scheemaker, who depicted his subject bareheaded and in a Roman costume, holding a sword in his hand ! No inscription has ever marked the place where his body lies in the Parish Church of Moreton Say. In London no effigy of Clive stood in the streets or squares ; no tablet emblazoned his name on the Abbey walls ; in Bengal no representation of him was to be seen in the city which he saved and where he twice ruled.

This triple reproach I was able to remove by the prompt and liberal response to a public appeal in the Press soon after my return to England ; and with the £5,000 thus raised I had the satisfaction—with the co-operation of that powerful sculptor John Tweed—of placing the noble statue of Clive in bronze which now stands at the head of the steps by the India Office, overlooking St. James's Park in London. A replica of this statue in white marble stands in the Victoria Memorial Hall at Calcutta. With the balance of the fund the same artist undertook to execute a portrait medallion of Clive as a young man, on the lines

WARREN HASTINGS

From the painting by Lemuel Abbott.

of the little-known Gainsborough portrait. The consent of the Dean and Chapter to its erection in the Abbey was readily given ; and so at last Robert Clive takes his place among the silent great ones who yet speak, and will speak for all time, from the walls of the metropolitan temple of our race.

The name of Warren Hastings has already appeared many times in these pages. We have seen him in the Council Chamber, in Calcutta Society, in the company of his dearly-loved wife. Can we now frame for ourselves some portrait of this most remarkable man ? I speak not of his features, which, whether in youth, in middle age, or in advanced years, are well known from a dozen portraits by the most famous artists.[1] Here I reproduce two likenesses of him. One is a portrait by Lemuel Abbott, painted while he was in India, and now hanging in the Victoria Memorial Hall. The other is a portrait which but few of my readers will in all probability have seen. It was executed by that excellent painter of horses, G. Stubbs, R.A., in 1791 (while the trial of Hastings was still proceeding), on a plaque or medallion provided by the famous Josiah Wedgwood,[2] and it represented the Governor General mounted on his favourite Arab. This painting, of which there is a replica on panel executed by the artist in the same year and now in the possession of Lord Rosebery, was sold originally in Stubbs' sale on 27th May, 1807. It afterwards passed into Sir Walter Gilbey's collection, from which I bought it and sent it out to the Victoria Memorial Hall at Calcutta, where it is now one of the chief ornaments on the walls. George Nesbitt Thompson, the former Private Secretary and faithful correspondent of Hastings, must have possessed either this medallion or a facsimile of it, for he spoke of it in one of his letters as " the enamelled picture of the Arabian horse with you riding it," and described it as a poor likeness. But among the portraits of Hastings, which as a rule represent either the pensive vigour of youth or the spare austerity of later years, it is the one which appears to me to depict most faithfully the Governor General as he was when his features had settled into the gravity of middle life, and before they had assumed the emaciation of old age. They show him as he was during the most

---

[1] Warren Hastings was painted at different times by Reynolds, Romney, Lawrence, Abbott, Zoffany, Kettle, Devis, Stubbs, Seton, Masquerier.

[2] As early as 1785 Wedgwood must have contemplated reproducing a likeness of Warren Hastings on his return from India ; for in his Account Book for that year was entered the item of a portrait of Governor Hastings made by Flaxman for him at a cost of £3 3s.

trying tenure of office *in partibus infidelium*—it lasted for thirteen years—that was ever borne by a great servant of the British Crown. This was the Hastings who defied and defeated Francis, who rose like a strong swimmer above the mill-race that would have swept any lesser man to his doom, who consolidated the work that Clive had begun, and who, before he left India, had made the British dominion secure. What sort of a man was he and what was the nature of his achievement?

Hastings, being already a servant of the Company in India when he was appointed first Governor General in 1774, did not undergo that ceremonious arrival and installation which we shall see with all its dramatic variations of scene and surroundings in the case of his successors. He had been for years a member of the Service, with every detail of which he was familiar, speaking the native language, understanding the people, and possessing the confidence of his superiors. At that moment of his life who could have foreseen that this supple and determined man, this type of a strong and patriotic public servant, would stand, before ten years had passed, at the bar in Westminster Hall, to answer for crimes that he had never committed, and to be arraigned by the perverted rhetoric of the greatest orators of the age? Were the slings and arrows of outrageous fortune ever launched with a more wayward or inexplicable caprice?

When Mill wrote his History and Macaulay wrote his Essay no serious attempt had been made to explore the evidence on which the presumed case against Hastings rested, and the echoes of the intoxicated declamations of Burke and Sheridan had not completely died down. To anyone who reads the reports of the trial it is almost inconceivable that men of rectitude and honour can have believed the stories that the Prosecution narrated, or painted the diabolical picture which they drew. Macaulay knew better, and in his Essay we see an often painful effort at the same time to denounce and to defend. He writes as though he were conscious of the triumphant greatness of the man whom, nevertheless, he felt it his duty, as a sound Whig pamphleteer, to flagellate and expose. The result is a composite picture that is now seen to bear but a slender resemblance to the truth.

Since those days the publication of the Indian State Papers and the researches and the more judicial writings of Sir James Fitzjames Stephen, Sir John Strachey, Sir Alfred Lyall, Colonel Malleson, Mr. G. W. Forrest, Miss Monckton Jones, and the school of modern historians

WARREN HASTINGS

From the painting by G. Stubbs, A.R.A.

have demolished the greater part of the case against Hastings.[1] The publication of a part of his correspondence with his wife—now in the British Museum—by Miss Grieg (Sydney C. Grier) has materially assisted the task of rehabilitation ; and Hastings now stands forth, not indeed as a perfect or saintly figure—for he did some things which are open to censure and even to grave reproach—but as a man greatly suffering and sorely ill-used, but boldly daring, supremely competent, and greatly achieving. Not without reason is a special room set apart for him and his relics in the Victoria Memorial Hall at Calcutta, in the place where he strove and wrought. Not without good cause is his story taught to every student of history in English schools.

The two most conspicuous features in the character of Warren Hastings, as seen in his Indian career, were an overpowering sense of civic duty and his devotion to his wife ; and of these two, while the former carried him unscarred through the hurricanes of his public career, it was to the latter that he owed all the happiness of his life.

Mrs., or as she was called the Baroness, Imhoff was not the first wife of Hastings. Among the victims of the Black Hole tragedy whose names were inscribed on Holwell's pillar was one Captain John Buchanan, who comported himself well during that fateful time. He left a widow, Mary, whom Hastings married either late in the same year or early in 1757. There were two children of this union—a son, George, born 1st December, 1757, who died in England in his eighth year ; and a daughter, Elizabeth, born 5th October, 1758, who only lived for three weeks. The mother died before she had reached the age of thirty, on the 11th July, 1759, and was interred in the old burial ground at Kasimbazar (Cossimbazaar), where I saw her tomb and perused the inscription upon it when in India.

Hastings remained a widower for eighteen years, until at length, in August 1777, in his forty-fifth year, he married the woman who had won his heart eight years earlier and who retained undisputed dominion over it for the remainder of his long life. At that time she was thirty years of age and possessed of attractions of face and form which, although she lived until her ninety-first year—dying in the year when Queen Victoria ascended the throne—she never wholly lost.

In the lives of great men, many of whom have been passionate

---

[1] A summary of the main issues is given in a well-compiled little book by a member of the Hastings family, entitled "A Vindication of Warren Hastings," by G. W. Hastings (1909).

lovers, there does not exist a record of a fiercer or a more faithful devotion than that of Hastings to his second wife ; and in the published love letters of such persons—to which subject a book, from which Hastings is strangely omitted, has recently been dedicated—there cannot be found any tributes of a more romantic and consuming admiration than those which, whenever absent, he addressed to her. If such intimacies are to be made public to the world—as to which I express no opinion—it is perhaps a pity that none, or next to none, of the wife's letters have survived, having presumably been intentionally destroyed by her after her husband's death.

There may be something to our ears a little stilted and absurd in the use by the adoring husband of such epithets as " elegant " and " amiable " and " most deserving." But when a man of the intense reserve of Hastings can address his wife as " My heart's beloved," " My most beloved," " My sweet," and can pen to her such lines as these : " The sweet Music of her Voice which none but myself has ever heard, and the Looks of Heaven which I am sure have never been cast but on me alone "; " I would give half of my Life for the Certainty of beginning the other Half with you to-morrow "; " Remember with what Delight you have known me frequently quit the Scene of Business and run up to your Apartment for the Sake of deriving a few moments of Relief from the Looks, the Smiles, and the sweet Voice of my beloved "; " Yes, my beloved, we will have many Walks together and infinitely more delightful than those of Allipoor—And many an Excursion too from home. I have a Variety of Schemes of Pleasure playing in my Imagination which will all derive their Relish from your Society and your Participation of them. Let me but follow and be once more in Possession of my Heart's Treasure. I care not for what may happen without Doors, if I have but that which I wish within " —who can doubt that all the strength of this strong man's being was concentrated on the woman he had chosen ? That the replies to these rhapsodies were written in a similar, even if a less exalted, vein is clear from the quotations from them which appear in some of Hastings' letters.

The famous picture of Marian Hastings by Zoffany, which I succeeded in recovering for Calcutta, gives, as she herself thought, a very inadequate impression of her charms. Her striking figure, her abundant auburn ringlets which she declined to powder, her tasteful but rather showy mode of dressing, her fondness for jewels, received the admiring if sometimes acidulated testimony of her contemporaries.[1] In addition she was a capable financier and an excellent woman of business. She managed to accumulate a considerable fortune in India, where she was not above receiving handsome presents, particularly in the form of jewels ; and with the means thus acquired, though partially dissipated in unsound investments, she was able to provide handsomely for her family by her first husband. She was thought by her critics, at any rate in England, to be rather over-queenlike and assuming. But no such verdict was passed upon her by her intimates, still less by the husband who found perfection in all she said or did.

The shafts of malice have sometimes been sharpened at the expense of the earlier connection of this romantic couple, which indeed exposed itself to such attack ; and when Macaulay spoke of them as " lovers " and talked about " extenuating their fault," he appeared, whether deliberately or not, to favour the imputation. Other contemporary writers, such as Wraxall, and some subsequent historians have used similarly ambiguous terms. Sir Alfred Lyall more definitely accepted the charge as well founded, and said that " the facts, which are quite plain and speak for themselves, prove against Hastings a breach of the moral and social law upon which everyone must pass his own judgment according to his estimate of the gravity of such offences in the circumstances of this particular case ; nor will the verdict have been much affected by the attempts which the biographers of Hastings have made to address public opinion in mitigation of an austere sentence." [2] And yet from a careful study of the available evidence I am far from clear that this verdict is just. During the long years in which Mrs. Imhoff was awaiting her divorce in the Franconian Court and was residing in Calcutta, she had the protection at different times either of her first

---

[1] Of these perhaps the best known, though not the best natured, is that of Mrs. Eliza Fay, the young wife of a dissipated English barrister who went out to practise in Calcutta in 1780 :

" Mrs. H—— herself, it is easy to perceive at the first glance, is far superior to the generality of her sex, though her appearance is rather eccentric, owing to the circumstance of her beautiful auburn hair being disposed in ringlets, throwing an air of elegant, nay, almost infantine simplicity over the countenance, most admirably adapted to heighten the effect intended to be produced. Her whole dress, too, though studiously becoming, being at variance with our present modes which are certainly not so ; perhaps for that reason, she has chosen to depart from them. As a foreigner, you know, she may be excused for not strictly conforming to our fashions ; besides, her rank in the settlement sets her above the necessity of studying anything but the whim of the moment. It is easy to perceive how fully sensible she is of her own consequence. She is indeed raised to a giddy height and expects to be treated with the most profound respect and deference."

This was Mrs. Fay's not always grammatical record of the first meeting. Later she spoke of Mrs. Hastings with a less qualified admiration.

[2] " Warren Hastings," by Sir A. Lyall (Rulers of India Series), p. 25.

2—K

husband or of her mother ; and in all the correspondence and comments of that scandal-loving and backbiting age, when a woman in her peculiar position was exposed to unavoidable misrepresentation, I have only come across one passage in which the definite accusation was made ; and that, it is not surprising to learn, is to be found in a letter of the arch-adder Francis.   On the 19th July, 1777, he wrote to his friend Godfrey in England :

"To complete the character, as it will probably conclude the history of this extraordinary man (*i.e.* W. H.), I must inform you that he is to be married shortly to the supposed wife of a German painter, with whom he has lived for several years.   The lady is turned of forty, has children grown up by her pretended husband, from whom she has obtained a divorce under the hand of some German Prince.[1]   I have always been on very good terms with the lady and do not despair of being invited to the wedding.   She is an agreeable woman and has been very pretty."[2]

It is a sufficient comment on this characteristic outburst that within three weeks of the marriage the slanderer was "supping at the Governor's," where "Mrs. Hastings very handsomely acknowledges my constant attentions to her"; while a fortnight later he writes to his wife : "The lady herself is really an accomplished woman.   She behaves with perfect propriety in her new station and deserves every mark of respect."

Such a verdict could hardly have been penned by a personal enemy upon one who was the recent mistress of the Governor General.   Indeed the best answer to the charge is to be found in the history of the time. Is it likely that in Calcutta Society, where Hastings was at that time surrounded by implacable foes, and still more after his return to England, where every avenue of tittle-tattle and lying was explored to provide material for the attacks of his enemies, so promising a field for defamation or innuendo would have been ignored ?   And yet in the voluminous and festering literature of the period, while no effort was spared to prove Hastings a tyrant, a taker of bribes, a public criminal of the deepest dye, not a hint was given that to his other villainies this monster had added that of living for years with another man's wife.

We might find a similar and perhaps an even more cogent refutation in the characters of the couple themselves.   Hastings, though an

---

[1] She was not more than thirty, her children were not grown up, and there was no "pretence" about her marriage to Imhoff.

[2] "Memoirs of Sir Philip Francis" (ed. J. Parkes and H. Merivale), Vol. II, p. 92.

WARREN HASTINGS

From a medallion presented by him to the Raja of Benares.

ardent lover, was far too strict and punctilious in his observance of the accepted codes, and his wife was too superior to passion, being of a colder temperament than her husband, to indulge in relations which, if they had been true, must have been known to all, and would have covered both their position and their prospects with open shame.[1]

I hold, therefore, that the relations between Hastings and his second wife, during the five and a half years in which she resided in Calcutta before the divorce was procured and they were married, were probably innocent. Unhappily, in the long years of their wedded life, Mrs. Hastings bore him no children ; although his letters to her during her journey home in 1784, when there was for a time good reason to believe that their joint hopes might be gratified—the trials of the long sea voyage doomed them to disappointment—are among the most tender and pathetic of the entire series. How lavishly he provided for her comfort may be shown by the prodigious price that he paid for her passage to England with that of a female companion—no less a sum than £5,000[2]—and the sums that he expended upon the furniture and decoration of the round-house and the state cabin which he retained for her accommodation. The popular account of Mrs. Hastings' departure from Calcutta by river, so frequently quoted from " Hartly House," I believe to be mythical and to have been composed in England, since the writer represents Hastings as having left India at the same time as his wife, whereas he stayed on for more than a year. In the annals of lovers' meetings is there, however, a more affecting scene than that of 17th June, 1785, when the returned Governor General, who had landed at Plymouth four days before and had posted straight to London, after seeing Mr. Pitt in the afternoon, set off at 4 p.m. by road, having summoned his wife from Cheltenham, and met her towards sundown on the Bridge at Maidenhead ? In that town they spent the night, returning on the morrow to London, all unconscious of the stormy future that lay before them.

I should not have devoted so much space to the relations between Hastings and his wife, were it not clear that in his love for her, even more than in his own courage and sense of rectitude, lay the main source of

---

[1] In the latest edition of " Echoes from Old Calcutta " (1908) Dr. Busteed printed an Appendix on " Hastings and the Imhoffs," in which he retracted the less favourable opinion which he had previously formed.

[2] Sir Elijah and Lady Impey are said to have paid £6,250 for the entire passage accommodation on the ship by which they returned to England.

the strength that enabled him to sustain the burden of the last decade of his service in India.   I doubt if in the entire history of public affairs any man has been so cruelly persecuted or more persistently tried. Surrounded by vindictive enemies, daily outvoted and insulted in his own Council, accused by his colleagues of the meanest of crimes, confronted by a series of situations that might have daunted the most heroic spirit, with an empty Treasury and a discontented Service, and beset by frequent ill-health, Hastings showed a patience, a fortitude, a fertility of resource, and a self-control that could only have proceeded from a character profoundly conscious both of its own integrity and its power to prevail.   To no great statesman can the hackneyed quotations be more truthfully applied—*mens conscia recti* ;   and

> *Justum et tenacem propositi virum*
> *Non civium ardor prava jubentium,*
> *Non vultus instantis tyranni*
> *Mente quatit solida, neque auster,*
>
> *Dux inquieti turbidus Hadriae,*
> *Nec fulminantis magna manus Jovis ;*
> *Si fractus illabatur orbis,*
> *Impavidum ferient ruinae.*

The motto (inscribed over his portrait in the Council Room of the Government of India), of which he was proud, and which, had he been made a peer, he intended to retain—*Mens aequa in arduis*—describes with fortuitous but incomparable accuracy the main quality by which he met and triumphed over his adversaries.   He was indeed endowed with equanimity in a superlative degree.   Naturally mild of temper and not prone to wrath, he never lost his head, never wavered in his patience, and even associated without apparent resentment with those by whom he was daily thwarted and overruled.   But he never shirked a fight, he did not readily forgive an enemy, and with a tireless purpose he eventually wore him down.

Perhaps the most famous incident in the Calcutta career of Warren Hastings was the duel with Francis, his victory in which was the beginning of the end of that particular phase.   Among the papers which only during the past five years have come into the possession of the British Museum by the death of Miss Marian Winter, daughter of the old Rector of Daylesford and great-niece of Mrs. Hastings, is the actual

MRS. HASTINGS

From the painting by Zoffany.

account, written by Hastings himself, of this duel, in his private diary on the same day. It is contained in a little paper booklet of forty-five MS. pages, in a marbled cover, in which Hastings appears to have entered his daily record before he began to use the small calf-bound books with a metal clasp, a series of which has been for long in the British Museum and has been dipped into by at least one writer. But these little booklets, of which there are two, have so far escaped notice ; and I give the following entry, in Hastings' own spelling, both because of its intrinsic interest and also because of the light which it throws upon the unswerving and resolute character of the man.

Hitherto we have been dependent for our knowledge of this historic duel, which was fought near Belvedere at 5.30 a.m. on 17th August, 1780, upon a letter of Colonel Pearse (Hastings' second) to Lawrence Sulivan, written two months afterwards, upon Francis' own account in his Journal and Correspondence, upon a letter of Sir Elijah Impey, upon two brief but reassuring notes sent by Hastings to his wife in the morning and in the evening of the same day, and upon a passage in another letter written by him to Lawrence Sulivan a fortnight later, the full text of which is given by Glieg.[1] But none of these has the value of the actual record made by the principal actor on the same day and within a few hours of the event which it describes.

" Aug. 17th. The next morning Col[l] Pearse by Appt. called on me, but before ye Time, at about a Qr. after 4. I laid down again on ye Couch for half an Hour. Then dressed and went w[h] him in his Carriage. Met ye Troopers on ye Way and dismissed y[m.] Arrived at Belvidere exactly at ye time proposed—at 5.30, found Mr. F. and Col[l] Watson walking on ye road. Some time was consumed in looking for a private place—went along the road to Mr. Barwell's,[2] stopped between ye Village and the House. Our Seconds proposed y[t] we s[d] stand at a measured Distance w[h] both (taking a recent Example in Eng[d])[3] fixed at 14 paces, & Col[l] Watson paced & marked 7. I stood to ye Southward. There was (as I recollect) no wind. Our Seconds (Col[l] W. I think) proposed y[t] no advant[e] sh[d] be taken, but each chuse his own Time to fire— I s[d] have said y[t] Col[l] Pearse loaded my pistols on ye ground w[h] two Cartridges w[h] he had prepared. I had resolved to defer my Fire y[t] I might not be embarrassed w[h] his. He snapped but the pistol missed Fire. The Second put a fresh priming to it and chapped y[e] Flints. We returned to our Stations. I still purposed to receive

[1] " Memoirs of the Life of Warren Hastings," Vol. II, p. 307.
[2] This was the house afterwards known as Kidderpore House.
[3] The allusion was to the duel between Charles James Fox and Adams in 1779.

ye first Fire, but Mr. F. twice aiming and withdrawing his pistol, I judge y[t] I might seriously take my Aim at him. I did so and when I thought I had fixed ye true Direction I fired. His pistol went off at ye same Time, & so near ye same Instant that I am not certain w[h] was first, but believe mine was first, and that his followed in ye Instant. He staggered imm[y,] his Face expressed a sensation of b[g] struck, and his limbs shortly but gradually went under him, & he fell saying but not loudly, 'I am dead.' I ran to him, Shocked I own at ye Information, & I can safely say without any immediate sensation of Joy for my own success. The Seconds also ran to his Assistance. I saw his Coat pierced in ye right side, & feared ye Ball had passed through him; but he sat up without much Difficulty several Times and once attempted w[h] our help to stand, but his Limbs failed him, & he sank to ye ground. Col[l] W. y[n] proposed y[t] as we had met from a point of Honor & not for personal rancour, we s[d] join Hands (or that Mr. F. s[d] give me his). We did so ; Mr. F. chearfully, & I expressed my regret at ye cond[n] to w[h] I saw him reduced. He found most ease lying on his Back. A cot was bro[t] from Major Tolley's, he hav[g] no palikeen, & he was conveyed upon it to Belvidere, where he remains. Col[l] P. & I returned to my House in Town. We went to seek Dr. Campbell & I desired Dr. Francis to follow. Both immed[y] went. They found ye Wound not dangerous, hav[g] ent[d] the side before ye seam of ye waistcoat a little below ye Shoulder, and passing through both Muscles & within ye skin w[h] covers ye backbone, was lodged within a visible distance of ye skin in ye opposite side.

"As soon as I returned home I sent Mr. Markham to S[r] E.[1] to inform him of what had passed, & that I sh[d] wait ye Event, w[h] if fatal I s[d] instantly surrender myself to him, that ye Law m[t] take its Course ag[t] me."

This account is in close accord with, but adds a few not uninteresting details to, Colonel Pearse's narrative ; and it demonstrates with unerring clearness the firm deliberation with which Hastings acted and fired.

From this slight but, I hope, excusable digression, I return to the character and personality of Hastings. Side by side with this deep tenacity of purpose, there was to be found in his nature a tender-heartedness and generosity which, while it was constantly imposed upon by the crowd of blood-suckers, mendicant friends, and impoverished relatives who infested him on every side, and while it tempted him sometimes in its public aspect to repose undue confidence in quite unsuitable and unworthy persons (witness his unfortunate selection of Major Scott as his Parliamentary Agent in England), rendered him incapable of parsimony in his own interest, and left him, almost alone

---

[1] *I.e.* Sir Elijah Impey, Chief Justice.

among the higher Civil Servants of that time, in constant need of money and, when he retired, in possession of a fortune which in those days might fairly be regarded as modest and which had been acquired by honourable means. Even Macaulay pauses in his full-throated declamation to offer a halting tribute to Hastings' " general uprightness with respect to money."

There were many other attractive features in the character of the Governor General. He was almost the only one in the long list of the British rulers of India who took a real interest in literature, scholarship and the arts. His correspondence with the " Great Cham," which is referred to and in part quoted in Boswell's Life, is well known. So is Boswell's appreciation of him as " a man the extent of whose abilities was equal to that of his power, and who, by those who are fortunate enough to know him in private life, is admired for his literature and taste, and beloved for the candour, moderation and mildness of his character." Hastings was well versed in Persian and Arabic literature, and tried to establish a Persian Professorship at Oxford University. He founded with Sir William Jones the Asiatic Society of Bengal, instituted the Mohammedan *Madrassa* or College at Calcutta, and patronised, even if he did not understand, Sanskrit. His library, both in India, where it was constantly replenished from England, and after his return, at Daylesford, testified to the wide range of his reading. Like most cultured men of that day he dabbled in versification, of a somewhat academic and pedestrian character, whether it took the form of translations from the Classics[1] or of poems to his wife. On the other hand, he was the master of a nervous and polished literary style, and even the author of " Junius," no mean authority, admitted that " there was no contending against the pen of Hastings." Macaulay acclaimed him as the real founder of the school of official writing in India. He was the friend and patron of painters, as was testified by the many portraits of him by the foremost artists of the day ; and he encouraged the visits to India and the artistic work of Hodges, Zoffany and Devis. Nor is it the least among his claims to the admiration of the present writer that he sought to open up those political and trading

---

[1] In a sale in London I found and purchased the original holograph MS. of the rhyming paraphrase of Horace, Odes II, 16, which was composed by Hastings on board the " Berrington " during his return journey to England in 1785, and dedicated by him to his fellow passenger, John Shore, afterwards Governor General and Lord Teignmouth. It is mentioned by Macaulay in his Essay. The Manuscript is now in the Victoria Hall at Calcutta.

relations with Tibet and Lhasa, which it was reserved for one of his successors 120 years later to carry into practical effect.

I have spoken of Hastings' ill-health, and his letters are full of complaints about his dyspepsia and other ailments inseparable from overwhelming toil in the trying climate of Bengal, from which not even in the hot season did he obtain any relief. His constant boat journeys up and down the river, and his recourse to the various riverside residences which have been noticed in the first Volume of this work, were his chief prophylactic against the lassitude induced by these attacks. But he owed much more to his own abstemious habits and to the regular hours which he kept. As he wrote in one of his letters, he was always in bed by 10 p.m. and he dressed before sunrise, while his fondness for riding and his interest in agriculture and in horticultural experiments, which he practised with equal assiduity at Alipore and later at Daylesford, tended to keep him in a sound condition of body. With a more prophetic acumen than characterised the bulk of his actions towards Hastings, Francis wrote in a letter to an English correspondent in 1775 : " As for Hastings, I promise you he is much more tough than any of us, and will never die a natural death." His life was indeed prolonged to his eighty-sixth year.

I have before said that in this chapter I am more concerned with the private character than with the public performances of the men who have ruled India. But it is impossible to speak of Warren Hastings in the terms which I have employed without at least briefly indicating the nature of the achievement which rendered him so pre-eminent among the great Indian servants of the Crown.

Hastings' policy in India may be regarded in its relation to the character and fortunes of the Company which he served, to the progressive development of Indian administration, to the fortunes of the Indian people over whom he ruled, and to the destinies of the British Empire. In all these respects he left a deep and enduring impression upon the interests entrusted to his care. Under his wise guidance the Company passed from being a narrow and selfish commercial oligarchy, concerned only with profits and culpably indifferent as to means, into a governing organisation in which the tradesman was replaced by the statesman. He laid the foundations of the revenue and financial system, of the civil and also of the judicial administration, that were henceforth the basic principles of British rule. His interest in the welfare of the *ryot* or peasant, founded on intimate personal knowledge and wide personal sympathy, was profound and genuine ; and for a generation the Bengali population remembered and revered his name. By his bold and masterful foreign policy at a moment when British dominion was threatened throughout the world and had already crumbled in America, he saved the British Empire in India. No more courageous spirit was ever shown by a ruler than by Hastings in his Mahratta campaigns. Though no friend of fighting, he conducted the wars that were forced upon him with indomitable energy. He did not shrink, where the necessity arose, from dismissing a Governor of Madras. Annexation was no part of his policy, and yet he left a British Dominion larger and more secure than he found it. Above all, with the vision that bears the hall mark of genius, he foresaw, as early as 1779, the rôle that his country was destined to fill in the political evolution of the Indian Continent.

" I am morally certain," he wrote, " that the resources of this country, in the hands of a military people and in the disposition of a consistent and un-divided form of Government, are both capable of rare internal improvement and of raising that power which possesses them to the dominion of all India; and I believe myself capable of improving them and of applying them to the real and substantial benefit of my own country."

In the pursuit of these policies Hastings met with an antagonism and with obstacles from home such as no other Governor General has ever encountered, and which might well have prepared him for the yet baser ingratitude that he was to experience after his return. At the end of the 18th century India was, to an extent that now seems in-credible, the sport of political parties in England : Ministries rose and fell upon Indian issues ; the representatives of Britain in India were the skittles to be set up or knocked down in this indecent Parliamentary brawl ; and English Prime Ministers would openly denounce and scheme for the dismissal of the man or men whom it was their duty, if not to support, at least to defend. In this sordid conflict—notwith-standing that in its decision great principles of administration were involved—Hastings became at different moments the symbol, the scapegoat, and the victim. The amazing system of Government or non-Government that has been described in the preceding chapter found its most lurid illustration in his case. I have spoken of the open disloyalty of his colleagues in India. But this was nothing to the envenomed distrust and obstruction of Governments at home. At one time he had to face a King, a Prime Minister, and a Cabinet all scheming for his overthrow. Five times he was only saved from disgrace by some unexpected revolution in the political wheel of fortune in London. As early as March 1775 he had written as follows to the Prime Minister, Lord North, who was an ill-concealed antagonist, and who a little later put all the pressure in his power on the Directors to get Hastings recalled :

" I now most earnestly entreat that your Lordship—for on you, I presume, it finally rests—will free me from the state I am in, either by my immediate recall or by the confirmation of the trust and authority of which you have hitherto thought me deserving, on such a footing as shall enable me to fulfil your expectations and to discharge the debt which I owe to your Lordship, to my country, and my Sovereign.

" The meanest drudge who owes his daily subsistence to daily labour enjoys a condition of happiness compared to mine, while I am doomed to share the responsibility of measures which I disapprove, and to be an idle spectator of the ruin which I cannot avert."

At the same date he incautiously put in the hands of his Agent then in England, Colonel Maclean, a conditional resignation of his office, the unauthorised production of which a year and a half later was the cause of one of the most dramatic incidents in his career and of the unparalleled incident of the "Governor General of a day."[1]

In May 1776 a motion (arising out of the conduct of the Rohilla War) was carried by a majority of one in the Court of Directors, for an Address to the King praying for the removal of Warren Hastings. This, however, was defeated on a vote by ballot of the Court of Proprietors, who always stood by the Governor General, by a majority of 106 (? 108). A few weeks later the Directors cancelled their former decision by a majority of two.

In 1780, when he was in sore trouble in the South of India, he again had cause to complain to the Directors of having been treated by them " with every mark of indignity and reproach."

In 1782 he was confronted both by the angry Directors and by a

---

[1] An interesting testimony to Hastings' conduct on this occasion is to be found in a letter from his colleague, Richard Barwell, to his sister, Mary Barwell, of 28th June, 1777 : " Few men could have stood so severe a trial or could have been so collected under a provocation of such magnitude. Firm, decided, and just in every measure, he may challenge the severest test to which his enemies shall subject his conduct throughout the whole of this extraordinary attempt to turn him out of his office and debase him in the eyes of the people of the country."—" Bengal Past and Present," Serial Nos. 33-34, p. 241.

hostile House of Commons ; for on this occasion, after a Parliamentary Enquiry into the affairs of India, a motion was moved by Dundas and carried, calling upon the Directors to recall him.   The Directors, nothing loth, acquiesced in the suggestion.   But once more the Court of Proprietors, encouraged by a change of Ministry, came to his rescue, and reversed the decision of the Directors, on the ground that they had by law the right of nomination and removal, and that they were not bound by the decision of a single branch of the Legislature.

In 1783 a further set of Resolutions came out from the Court, disapproving of the Governor General's conduct in the Benares affair as improper, unwarrantable, and highly impolitic, to which the injured man replied by threatening instant resignation if Cheyt Singh were restored, and asking to be relieved as soon as possible from a thankless task.   This threat brought the Court to their senses ; and for the moment there was a suspension of active hostilities.

But Hastings himself was now becoming anxious to go, and after the departure of his wife in January 1784, which left him desolate and miserable, he continued to press his resignation upon his official superiors, declining to remain beyond the beginning of 1785, although at one moment he seems to have contemplated staying on, provided that he could obtain from the Home Government an extension of the powers of the Governor General in overruling his colleagues, such as was afterwards conceded to Cornwallis.

Pitt, however, whose entire conduct to Hastings was open to much reproach, was indifferent or hostile.   And so at length in February 1785 the great Proconsul laid down his post after a service of thirty-five years in India, thirteen of which had been spent in the discharge of the highest office.

One of the little calf-bound diaries in the British Museum contains Hastings' brief and modest summary of his departure, of which Macaulay has given the following picturesque account :

" On the day on which he delivered up the keys of office, a crowd of friends and admirers formed a lane to the place where he embarked.   Several barges escorted him far down the river; and some attached friends refused to quit him till the low coast of Bengal was fading from the view, and till the pilot was leaving the ship."

Macaulay must, I think, have borrowed this description from the purely imaginary picture given in " Hartly House " :

"He would have taken leave of his friends at Diamond Point, but they would not hear of such a thing—their bugeros were well stored with provisions and every requisite, &c.; so with pendants flying and bands of music, to the last man and instrument to be found in Calcutta, they attended him to Sawger, the extremity of the river."

Now for the facts in Hastings' own words :

"Feb. 1   Council before 11.
           Delivered keys and minute of Farewell.
           returned home and received farewell of the English inhabitants.
           wind high from the South.   Therefore did not go by water.
           At 1 went with McPherson[1] and others by coach to Powder Mills.[2]
           dined with Mr. Hay.[3]
           Went on board his budgerow 4 p.m. (raining).
           came to off Budgebudge.
 Feb. 2   Fulta.
   „ 3   Culpee.
   „ 4   Kedgree.
           6—shifted to Charlotte Yacht.
   „ 5   Berrington in sight.   went on board at 12.15.
   „ 6   Most of day at anchor because of wind.
   „ 7   1.30 p.m. lost sight of land.
           Mrs. Hastings' Birthday.   Departure reckoned from this time."

Such were the real conditions of the departure of a Governor General in days when row-boats and sailing yachts were the only means of exit from the treacherous reaches of the Hugli ; and in such manner did the greatest of the rulers of India slip away from the scene of his sufferings and his triumphs.

I do not know a fairer account of the circumstances in which, four and a half months later, Hastings arrived in London, or of the appearance which he then presented, than that which is contained in the not always veracious pages of Wraxall, who appears to have entertained for the returning Governor General a sincere and unbiased admiration :

"In his person he was thin, but not tall; of a spare habit, very bald, with a countenance placid and thoughtful, but, when animated, full of intelligence.

---

[1] His successor.
[2] Eight miles down the river.
[3] Under-Secretary of the Governor General in Council.   The party, as we know from other sources, consisted of some fifty of Hastings' warmest friends.

Never perhaps did any man who passed the Cape of Good Hope display a mind more elevated above mercenary considerations. Placed in a situation where he might have amassed immense wealth without exciting censure, he revisited England with only a modest competence. Animated by the ambition of maintaining, perhaps of extending, the dominions of the East India Company, he looked down on pecuniary concerns. Mrs. Hastings, who was more attentive to that essential article, brought home about £40,000, acquired without her husband's privity or approval: but she had the imprudence to place it in the hands of a London merchant, who shortly afterwards proved bankrupt. The *fact* not the *loss* chagrined Hastings, when the circumstance became known to him.

"In private life he was playful and gay to a degree hardly conceivable, never carrying his political vexations into the bosom of his family. Of a temper so buoyant and elastic that the instant he quitted the Council board, where he had been assailed by every species of opposition, often heightened by personal acrimony, oblivious of these painful occurrences, he mixed in society like a youth on whom care had never intruded." [1]

For a time on his return to England Hastings was the hero of the hour, and contemporary writers are full of the favourable impression that he made upon the Society of the metropolis, and notably upon the feminine element. Fanny Burney was " extremely pleased with the extraordinary plainness and simplicity of his manners and the obliging openness and intelligence of his communication." [2] Hannah More found him " a man of remarkable simplicity of manners, dress and deportment, full of admirable good sense ; nothing of the Nabob about him." Elizabeth Montagu, Queen of the Blues, wrote to her sister (1785) : " The great Hastings is to drink tea with me this evening. I am charmed with the humility and simplicity of his behaviour and manners. He has none of the airs of a Nabob, nor the pride of a Hero." It will be observed that in all these comments the simplicity of the returned Governor General is the feature that attracts attention. While the impeachment was dragging its weary course, the poet William Cowper, who had been a schoolfellow of Hastings at Westminster and who held to the view that *Nemo repente fuit turpissimus*, sent from his retreat at Weston (5th May, 1792) to his cousin Lady Hesketh the

---

[1] " Posthumous Memoirs," Vol. I, pp. 329, 331.

[2] This was in a letter to her father of 26th September, 1785, soon after Hastings' return to England (" Diary and Letters of Madame D'Arblay," Vol. II, p. 353). In the following year her Diary of 24th May, 1786 (*ibid.*, p. 414), shows that her admiration had even grown in the interim. " He appears to me to be one of the greatest men now living as a public character ; while as a private one his gentleness, candour, soft manners and openness of disposition make him one of the most pleasing."

following lines, which, though without merit as poetry, are memorable as a tribute :

> Hastings ! I knew thee young and of a mind
> While young, humane, conversable, and kind;
> Nor can I well believe thee, gentle THEN,
> Now grown a villain, and the WORST of men;
> But rather some suspect, who have oppress'd
> And worried thee, as not themselves the BEST.

Nor is my own interest in the persecuted man diminished by the knowledge that some years later (on 5th August, 1806), when spending a night in Derby on his way by road to pay visits in Scotland, the Diary of Hastings in the British Museum records that he " deviated to Keddleston Hall and saw Keddleston House "—then in the occupation of my great-grandfather, and famous as the architectural masterpiece of Robert Adam, who had died not many years before.

Into his retirement, broken by the seven years' nightmare of the Impeachment, it falls outside the scope of this work to follow Hastings. But in view of the account that has been given in a previous chapter of the rewards or otherwise that have been conferred upon the retiring Governors General of India, it may be worth while to record the measure that was meted out to this great man. Though Hastings was personally indifferent to honours, it was notorious that he would have accepted a peerage, both as some public recognition of services that had been grossly traduced, and still more for the sake of his wife. But Pitt hesitated and evaded until the Impeachment itself provided a more plausible excuse. There is rather a pathetic passage in a letter from Hastings to G. Nesbitt Thompson of 19th December, 1785, before the blow had fallen :

" My reputation stands as high as I can wish it, and I see or think I see the beloved Partner of my life stand as high in the public estimation; which I prize far beyond my own credit. . . . As to rewards and honours I have almost given up the expectation of either, though the wishes of many, and of many to whom I am personally unknown, are sanguine yet in the belief that they are yet in store and ready for me. With respect to the former I have been informed that they were withheld by Mr. P[itt] when proposed a little before my arrival, on the plea that, Mr. Burke having threatened to bring some criminal charges against me in the approaching meeting of Parliament, it would have been indecent to forestall them. Whether this man really means what he has threatened, I know not." [1]

[1] " Bengal Past and Present," Vol. XVI, Serial No. 32, p. 209.

Ten years later, after the death of Pitt, Hastings thought, not without reason, that a reversal of this unfeeling sentence might be expected from the Regent and his new Ministers, and in an interview with the Prince at Carlton House on 14th March, 1806, he mentioned his desire for a title in which his wife might participate. But he wanted this favour to be accompanied by a formal reversal of the Impeachment. The Prince was ready to bestow the peerage, but did not relish the idea of a quarrel with the Cabinet, some members of which had been implicated in that ill-starred measure, or with the House of Commons, who might not like to acknowledge their error. Lord Moira, the subsequent Governor General, who was always friendly to Hastings, represented to the latter the difficulties of the case, upon which Hastings made the following dignified reply :

" I beg, my Lord, that the affair may go no further. I am content to go down to the grave with the plain name of Warren Hastings, and should be made miserable by a title obtained by such means as should sink me in my own estimation."

Six years later Hastings was made a Privy Councillor, the sole official distinction that was ever conferred upon this great public servant — now in his eighty-second year and within a measurable distance of the grave. As plain Warren Hastings he had lived, and as plain Warren Hastings it was, perhaps, not unfitting that he should die.

This book is not the place in which to attempt a final judgment upon the career of this remarkable man. That his name, however, stands supreme in the list of those who have served India and have suffered for that service will not be disputed. In the attributes which Carlyle deemed essential to his conception of the hero-man—namely sincerity, valour and intellect—Hastings excelled ; nor can we dissent from the Chelsea sage when he added : " We cannot look, however imperfectly, upon a great man without gaining something by him." Hastings was undoubtedly cast in the heroic mould. He did many wise, courageous and far-sighted things ; he also, in the face of almost unexampled temptation, did some irregular and unwise things from which a more fastidious sense might have shrunk.[1] But he never lost sight of the double aim of his entire career, the good of the Indian

[1] Perhaps the most impartial summary is to be found in the pages of Sir Alfred Lyall.

people and the glory of England ; and it was with some approximation to the truth, though with an excess of self-depreciation, that in later years he described himself, in an inscription in a book which he sent to his former Secretary, G. N. Thompson, as " a man more sinned against than sinning."

I have narrated elsewhere the peculiar circumstances in which John (afterwards Sir John) Macpherson came to act as Governor General for a year and a half before the arrival of Lord Cornwallis. This person had an extraordinary career, being a combination of the political adventurer, the adept intriguer, and the society darling. Originally going out to India in 1767 as the nominal purser of his uncle's ship, and embarking at once on a career of local intrigue, he succeeded in 1770, by influence in England, in obtaining a writership in the Madras Service, from which, however, he was dismissed in 1776 by the Governor, Lord Pigot, for intriguing with the Nawab of the Carnatic. Returning to England, his social connections procured him a seat in Parliament which he held from 1779-1781, when he was reinstated by the Directors of the East India Company and was appointed by Lord North to Barwell's vacancy in the Council in India. Arriving in Calcutta in October 1781, he almost invariably sided against Hastings, whose political star he believed to be on the wane, but who never quarrelled with him ; and there he managed with singular success to excite the dislike and contempt of all his associates. When Hastings retired, as senior Member of Council he became Governor General pending the appointment of a successor from home, and in this capacity endeavoured to curry favour with the Directors, with a view to securing the definite reversion of the office, by a policy of ruthless but hypocritical economy. Meanwhile he utilised his Indian opportunities to become rich himself. Hastings, who frequently mentions Macpherson in his letters, saw through him completely, and was not deceived by " the most imposing talents and an elegant and unceasing flow of words." When Cornwallis arrived, greatly to Macpherson's disappointment, the latter lingered on in the hope of ingratiating himself with the new ruler. But Cornwallis also soon found him out, describing his administration in a letter of 1st November, 1788, to Dundas as one " of the dirtiest jobbery." He spoke in another letter of his " flimsy, cunning and shameless falsehoods," and of his " duplicity and low intrigues," while in a letter of 1st November, 1789, he added : " I think him weak and false to a degree and he certainly was the most contemptible and the most contemned Governor that ever pretended to govern."[1]

A similar opinion appears to have been entertained of Macpherson by Hastings' correspondents from India. Thompson spoke of his duplicity and passion for intrigue, and described him as a snake in the grass. Colonel Pearse, who commanded the Artillery in Fort William, wrote to Hastings gleefully about the final departure of Macpherson in February 1787 :

"He stole away and thus preserved his real character to the last. . . He set off to go to Madras for his health, now he is going to the Cape for the same purpose, where I suppose with the rest of the people he will find a French frigate to carry him to the South of France for his health or safety. What a misery it must be to be conscious of deserving contempt."[2]

When he arrived in England, Macpherson, who had already received a Baronetcy, continued to badger the Government for some recognition or compensation for his disappointment, and was eventually consoled with a grant of £15,000 and a pension. He found a greater solace in the attentions of society, where his handsome presence, agreeable manners, and numerous accomplishments, combined with the warm friendship of the Prince of Wales, secured for him an excellent position. But even there he seems to have been unable to conceal the flaws in his real character ; for I find in Lord Glenbervie's Journal this caustic entry (dated 10th November, 1793) :

"Sir John Macpherson is a very good-natured man and not without abilities (as his success in life proves), and I believe him sincerely attached to the family of his patron, the late Lord Guilford ;[3] but he is, alas, such a flatterer, such a placebo, such an universal and habitual sycophant, that it is difficult to get at his real object or his real sentiments from what he says. His slow, soft, drawling manner is very tiresome, and even Lady Anne North never said a better thing than when she observed that Sir John Macpherson's words ' come from his lips like drops of laudanum from a vial and that they produce the same effect.' "[4]

On the other hand, the social attractions and the unquestionable gifts of this very composite personality won the enthusiastic encomiums of his friends, among whom Sir N. Wraxall delivered this panegyric :

[1] "Correspondence of Marquis Cornwallis" (ed. C. Ross), Vol. I, pp. 415, 441.
[2] "Bengal Past and Present," Vol. VII (1911), p. 108.
[3] Better known as Lord North, the Prime Minister, who had died in 1792.
[4] "Glenbervie Journals," p. 51.

2—L

" Convivial, formed for society, master of French and Italian, singing with ease and grace the airs of almost every nation, he chained his guests to the table. . . Nor was his talent limited to one language. Venetian, Hindoo, French, but above all Highland ballads he gave with the same facility. Never did any man display more unaffected hospitality. It was only eclipsed by his liberality. . . His manners were the more ingratiating because they formed a contrast with his person. If his figure reminded of Hercules, it was Hercules in the Court of Omphale, gentle, subdued and disarmed. Who can wonder that such talents should raise their possessor to eminence ? " [1]

These talents retained for Macpherson the close friendship of the Prince of Wales (George IV) from 1788 to 1802, after which the intimacy came to an end. But this professional charmer, proceeding abroad, at once replenished the void by courting with equal success the favours of the Emperor Leopold and Frederick William II, King of Prussia.

There we may leave Macpherson, the least esteemed, and the most volatile, of all the men who have occupied the Governor General's seat. In India he did not fill it long enough to produce any permanent effect on the administration, though his adversaries declared that he did what little harm he could.

A very different type of man now appears upon the scene in the person of Lord Cornwallis—a man with quite ordinary abilities but with a sterling character, a great fund of common sense and a superb and untiring devotion to duty—who left a considerable mark upon Indian administration. Cornwallis was one of those men upon whom Governments rely to do their business straightforwardly, efficiently and well. For twenty years he was the *deus ex machina* to whom successive Ministries turned to extricate them from muddles or to place disordered affairs upon a stable basis. Even his failures never counted against him. The surrender of York Town brought with it no censure, but was followed by other and higher employment. Twenty years later the Treaty of Amiens, which Cornwallis was sent out to negotiate, proved to be obsolete almost as soon as it had been signed. But no one blamed its author. It was always felt that Cornwallis had done his best in an honest, capable, commonsense way, and that no lower consideration than the honour of his country had guided his action. Thus, although destitute of any pretension to genius and with quite mediocre intellectual gifts, he filled post after post in the

[1] " Posthumous Memoirs," Vol. II, pp. 5, 6.

STATUE OF LORD CORNWALLIS

Sculpt.: John Bacon.

internal and external service of Britain, and was regarded as having comported himself in each with credit and success.

I have already described the repeated efforts made by the Home Government to enlist the services of this honourable and worthy soldier for India, and I have further given an account of his simple habits at Calcutta, his unpretentious but not undignified social régime, and his general popularity. He enjoyed advantages which had been denied to Warren Hastings, and which relieved him of many of the troubles by which the latter had been encompassed. For Cornwallis always had the Home Government and the Directors behind him ; he had insisted as a condition of going out upon powers which his predecessors had never enjoyed ; his rank and station gave him an immense local prestige ; and, moreover, he was both Governor General and Commander-in-Chief.

On 12th September, 1786, Lord Cornwallis landed at Chandpal Ghat, and walked on foot, escorted by the Body Guard, to the Fort, where he took the oath and assumed the reins of government. He was the first Governor General to come to India from the outside, the advance guard of the long procession of statesmen from England to take up what was rapidly becoming one of the foremost posts under the British Crown. Nothing indeed more directly demonstrates the changes which Hastings' régime had brought about in the scale and importance of the Indian Dependency than the fact that a member of the Indian Service, however eminent, was no longer thought adequate for the office, and that Ministers, Cabinet Ministers, and men of public fame were henceforth regarded as almost indispensable.

From this time forward the ceremony of the arrival and, a few years later, the departure of the man from home was invested with special dignity and display ; and the contrast—always dramatic and sometimes pathetic—between the high hopes of the one occasion and the sadness or, it may be, the disappointment of the other, has made a vivid appeal to the historian or the biographer who has subsequently chronicled the scene.

Here, therefore, it may be permissible to diverge for a moment in order to acquaint my readers with the various phases through which these ceremonies have passed, leaving individual instances to take their place in the ensuing narrative.

For a century from the arrival of Cornwallis to the time of Lord

Northbrook, who was the first Viceroy to enter Calcutta by rail, the approach was invariably made by river from the sea. But the maritime journey was itself divided into two epochs, the first—which lasted from Cornwallis till the first Lord Hardinge—in which the Governor General came out from England in one of the King's or the Company's ships, spending a period of from four to six months on the journey,[1] halting maybe at Madeira, St. Helena, the Cape and Madras (possibly even having to cross the Atlantic as did Lord Auckland to Rio), and upon arrival at the mouth of the Hugli trans-shipping into the State flotilla of the Governor General, which brought him with great pomp and pageantry up the stream ; the second, in which, after the opening of the Overland Route through Egypt towards the middle of the last century, the journey was made by sea from England to Alexandria, by land to Cairo and Suez, and then by sea from Suez to Calcutta, where the earlier ceremonial was still observed. In these cases the journey was reduced in length by more than one half.

The third and latest phase was that in which the incoming Viceroy came out, no longer in a frigate, but in a passenger steamer to Bombay, whence he crossed the Indian peninsula by rail to the Howrah Station at Calcutta.

Until the railway was opened, and as long as the arrival was by sea and river, the landing place was invariably at the well known Chandpal Ghat on the left bank of the Hugli, in close proximity to the official quarter of the town. At this famous spot, which took its name, as so many Calcutta sites and streets have done, from an obscure and forgotten native shopkeeper, Governors General, Commanders-in-Chief, Judges, and Bishops set their foot for the first time on Bengal soil, for a space of nearly a hundred years ; the actual spot at which they disembarked being a little to the North of the present landing stage and steps. From here the incoming Governor General walked in full uniform on foot through the streets lined by troops to the North entrance of Government House,[2] where he was received by the outgoing head of the Government and the leading officials on the great outdoor

---

[1] When Clive went out to India in 1742 he took over a year on the way. Warren Hastings' first outward journey occupied from 8 to 9 months. After the middle of the century the voyage consumed as a rule from 4½ to 6 months. Hastings' return journey in 1785 occupied a little over 4 months. But in 1789 a Dutch East Indiaman took 14 months to sail from Amsterdam to Bengal with many long halts on the way. As late as 1815 the news of Waterloo did not reach Calcutta for nearly 5 months. Lord Auckland's outward journey in 1834-6 also occupied 5 months.

[2] Before the building of Government House by Wellesley he walked to the Fort.

staircase ; at a later date the distance was traversed in the Viceroy's carriage attended by the Body Guard.

Upon his arrival the newcomer was escorted by his host to the Council Chamber where he at once took the oath and assumed the reins of office ; the retiring Governor General remaining sometimes for days with his successor in Government House in the ambiguous position, half of host and half of guest. As I shall explain subsequently a more sensible practice was adopted in later years.

When the railway was opened and the change was made to the Howrah Station, a longer and more brilliant pageant was the natural sequel ; and the procession of the incoming Viceroy and his staff, with the full Body Guard and an additional escort of the Calcutta Mounted Volunteers, through streets crowded with thousands of natives, to the Government House compound was a spectacle not to be forgotten.

Corresponding changes marked the official exit of the ruler who had laid his office down. Up till nearly the middle of the 19th century Chandpal Ghat was the scene of departure as of arrival. But about that time there was built in memory of James Prinsep, celebrated as scholar, architect and engineer, the Ionic archway on the bank of the river some way lower down, which was intended henceforward to be the point of departure—and also, if they came by river, of arrival—for the rulers of India. Lord Ellenborough was the first Governor General to embark from this spot, and thither the newly arrived Viceroy was in the habit of escorting his predecessor and taking formal leave, if the latter were making his exit by sea. The river has receded so rapidly in the last half-century that the archway, from which a flight of stone steps originally led straight down to the water, now stands inland, and there is a broad space, as well as the main roadway, between it and the river-bank. But the surroundings of the Howrah Station are so ill-adapted for ceremonial display that Royal personages arriving at Calcutta are almost invariably taken down the river by boat and invited to land at Prinsep's Ghat, which serves its purpose sufficiently well.

Readers of this narrative will now be able to realise the *mise en scène* in which for a century the British rulers of the Indian Empire took up or laid down their onerous task, and they will understand the poignant emotions which the scene and the situation have more than once provoked.

From this digression I will return to Cornwallis, whom we left, so to speak, on the landing-stage, about to assume his great office for the first time. Like more than one of his successors he came out with the avowed intention of pursuing a policy of peace, but presently found himself at war. Like others of them, he came out with the idea that his predecessor (in this case, Warren Hastings) had been wrong in many things, only to discover before long that he had been right in most. Indeed one of the most conspicuous incidents in Hastings' trial in Westminster Hall, eight years later, was the appearance of Cornwallis, to testify to the universal esteem in which his predecessor was held by the natives of India and his immense services to his country.

The administration of Cornwallis, which was prolonged for seven years in spite of his frequently expressed desire to return, was remarkable for his internal reforms, in which, with a courage that cannot be over-praised, he set his face against the jobbery and corruption that still permeated the Civil Service, carrying the now forgotten crusade of Clive to its logical conclusion by the grant of decent salaries to the Writers in return for the prohibition of private trade. The Civil and Criminal Courts were reformed, and the inefficiency in the military services, which had reached the dimensions of a scandal, was severely taken in hand. The Permanent Settlement in Bengal, which is invariably associated with the name of Cornwallis, but which was really the work of his civilian advisers (albeit the best of them, Sir John Shore, who advocated a decennial term, was unfortunately overruled), is now generally regarded as having been a mistake, and has happily not been followed in any other province. Perhaps however the most characteristic, as also the most creditable, of Cornwallis' achievements was the fearless courage with which he fought against jobbery in any form, refusing to yield a jot to the shameless pressure that was brought to bear upon him from the highest quarters in London, including the Prince of Wales. Sir John Shore wrote of him : " The honesty of his principles is inflexible ; he is manly, affable, and good-natured, of an excellent judgment, and he has a degree of application to business beyond what you would suppose " ; and again : " His situation was uncomfortable on arrival ; he now receives the respect due to his zeal, integrity and indefatigable application."

A study of Cornwallis' character and a survey of his administration leave us with a very pleasant impression of the service that can be rendered in an Oriental dependency—or, indeed, anywhere—by transparent honesty of purpose, a total absence of self-seeking, and an unswerving devotion to duty.   Cornwallis neither did nor attempted anything brilliant, but he never spared himself in making things better than he found them and in diffusing a general sense of contentment and stability.   It was not surprising that, when at length he persuaded Pitt to let him return to England, his services in India should have been commemorated not only by the fine statue that stood for a century hidden in the dingy basement of the Calcutta Town Hall—from which I obtained a promise of its release for the Victoria Memorial Hall where, in one of the Courts, it now stands—and by the full-length painting by Devis that hung in my day in the Council Chamber at Government House, but also by effigies at Madras and Bombay.   It is true that the ample figure of the old soldier when garbed as a Roman Consul, holding a laurel wreath in his hand, is calculated to evoke a transient smile ; but the statue, executed by John Bacon the younger, is a fine work of art, and there is something not inappropriate in the classical representation of a personality that reproduced many of the Roman virtues.

It was a tribute to the character of Cornwallis that his successor, Sir John Shore, was willing to spend seven months quietly in Calcutta after his arrival in March 1793, without employment or responsibility of any sort—for he did not even sit in Council[1]—until Cornwallis was ready to start for England.   In October the retiring Governor General left for Madras in the " Swallow " ; the King's ship, which was to have taken him home, being compelled to go into dock at Bombay.   He left, and—entirely to his satisfaction, for the two men esteemed each other highly—Shore reigned in his stead.

It cannot be said that in his five years' rule Shore left any mark. He was a typical Bengal Civilian of the best type, a great revenue expert, an upright, dull, respectable, friendly kind of man, hating pomp of any sort, loving peace and economy, very pious, declining to work on Sundays though not attending the services of the Church, and ultimately joining the Clapham Sect after his return to England.   As Major Toone, who had been one of Hastings' A.D.C.s, remarked : " A good man, but as cold as a greyhound's nose."   Shore had some of the tastes of a scholar, being a student of Urdu, Persian and Arabic ; he wrote a journal in Latin, kept up his knowledge of Greek and

---

[1] He lived during this period at a Garden House next door to Sir William Jones, in Garden Reach.

composed mediocre verses and translations in the decorous 18th-century fashion. While in India he did not enjoy good health, and was always chafing at the absence of his wife and family.

Shore's strong views about economy had made him a strenuous critic of Hastings' régime, and he was popularly regarded as a member of the Opposition or Francis' camp, until he was won over by personal contact with Hastings, notably on the return journey of the latter to England. This conversion excited the not too kindly comment of William Hickey, who wrote in his Memoirs :

" Mr. John Shore suddenly and most unaccountably from an inveterate and bitter enemy became that gentleman's [*i.e.* Hastings'] sworn bosom friend."

This, he goes on to say, was the foundation of Shore's fortunes, since it was through Hastings' influence alone that he first procured a seat in the Supreme Council, then became Governor General and a Baronet, and ultimately an Irish Peer with the title of Lord Teignmouth.[1]

As a ruler Shore was not a success, being nervous and irresolute. He nearly came to grief over the Mutiny of the Officers of the Bengal Army, to placate whom he offered unheard-of concessions. But he showed greater strength in handling the question of the Oudh Succession. In the annals of India his name has long been forgotten ; nor is history ever likely to question the decent obscurity into which it has been allowed to subside. He sailed for England on 7th March, 1798, without waiting for his successor.

And now we come to a very different era and a very opposite type of man. On 17th May there stepped ashore at Chandpal Ghat a little man, thirty-eight years of age, short of stature, slight of build, with clear-cut aristocratic features and a haughty mien, who was destined to leave an indelible mark both upon the Capital City and upon the Empire of which it was the head. This was the Earl of Mornington, elder brother of the Duke of Wellington, sometimes designated by his admirers " The Great Marquis " and " The Great Proconsul."

In the earlier parts of this work we have come across this little man in many of his acts and accomplishments. We have seen him building one palace at Calcutta and another at Barrackpore. We have observed his spectacular parties and balls and parades. We have noticed his

---

[1] " Memoirs," Vol. III (1782–1790), p. 262.

self-centred labours in almost every sphere of activity ; and we have watched the long-drawn struggle between him and the Directors of the Company who had sent him out—a struggle inflamed by an angry cross-fire of verbal invective from which neither party emerged wholly victorious ; in which, on the merits of the case, the Governor General was usually in the wrong, but where he generally prevailed because he did what he wanted to do, and could afford, with his censors separated from him by 14,000 miles of ocean and twelve months of time, to snap his august fingers in their faces.

There hardly exists in the gallery of British celebrities a man upon whose character and achievements more opposite verdicts have been passed, or whose career more fairly justifies such a clash of opinion. One class of writers has seen in Wellesley the courageous and far-sighted architect of Empire, who carried out and expanded the great work of Warren Hastings and reared the central edifice, lofty and strong, of British dominion in the East. The opposite school regards him, if not as the " brilliant incapacity " of Croker, at any rate as the embodiment of vanity in high places, the " Sultanised Englishman " of Mackintosh, who, by an excess of arrogance and self-esteem, failed in India, as later in England, to attain the goal which his self-confident ambition had marked out for him. The truth does not lie midway between these extremes. It is to be found in both of them. Wellesley was at the same time both great and small, a man of noble conceptions and petty conceits, a prescient builder of Empire and a rather laughable person. On the Indian side of his career the balance is, however, decidedly in his favour ; and if his Letters had not been published, which reveal him in his most petulant as well as in his most majestic moods, the credit balance would probably have been even larger.

The Indian Despatches and Correspondence of Wellesley were published in five big volumes in his own lifetime (1836–1837) by the Court of Directors, as a sort of *amende honorable* to the vainglorious old man whom they had once disparaged and condemned. Memoirs or Biographies of him have been written by R. R. Pearse in 1846, by W. M. Torrens in 1880, by W. H. Hutton in 1893 ; two volumes entitled " The Wellesley Papers " appeared in 1914 ; there are said to be 400 volumes of MSS. still lying unexplored in the British Museum. " The Wellesley Papers," from which so much was expected, turned out to be a very disappointing publication, for the greater part of the correspondence in the two volumes consists of letters written not by him but to him, and, so far at least as his Indian career is concerned, they add little to our knowledge, and that of a rather damaging nature.

I think there can be no doubt that, while Anglo-Indian society stood aghast at Wellesley's pretensions and was considerably awed by his magnificence, it regarded the presence and the patronage of the little autocrat as a compliment to itself, and saw a reflection of the nimbus which he habitually wore floating about its own head. Whether it would have been equally pleased had it read his opinion of " his sub-jects," as he characteristically designated them in his letter to Lord Grenville of 18th November, 1798, from which I quoted in Chapter IX, is more doubtful. No society likes to be called " vulgar, ignorant, rude, familiar and stupid "; no ladies like to be described as " not even decently good-looking "; no community welcomes an intima-tion, such as the following, that their official head means to put them without compunction and with some contempt in their proper places :

" I am resolved to encounter the task of effecting a thorough reform in private manners here, without which the time is not distant when the Europeans settled at Calcutta will control the Government, if they do not overturn it. My temper and character are now perfectly understood, and while I remain no man will venture *miscere vocem* who has not made up his mind to grapple instantly with the whole force of Government. But it required some unpleasant efforts to place matters on this footing, and you must perceive that I am forced to fly to solitude for a large portion of the twenty-four hours, lest I should weaken my means of performing my public duty."

Matters might have been different had there been a lady to preside over Government House, and perhaps to modify some of the idio-syncrasies of its official head. But one of the main sources of weakness in Wellesley's career, upon which his biographers appear uniformly to have turned a blind eye, was his relations with women. For many years before his appointment to India he had lived with a young French woman, Mlle. Hyacinthe Gabrielle Roland, irreverently described by a critic as " a nymph of the Palais Royal," who had borne him five children, and whom he had only married as recently as 1794. She was a clever and attractive woman, and at that time he was much devoted to her. Considerations of social expediency rendered it undesirable that she should accompany him when he started for India, but at one moment he thought seriously of bringing her out, and only desisted because her care was wanted for the children at home. He consoled himself for her absence by taking out a full-length portrait by Hoppner of her and the two eldest boys, which he hung on the walls of the new Government House.

Soon after the return of Wellesley to England, this rather ill-assorted pair separated,[1] and the lady died in 1816. In 1824, at the age of sixty-four, he married the American widow of an American merchant named Patterson,[2] who accompanied him, when he was Lord Lieutenant of Ireland, to Dublin, and who survived him for some years. His relations with her did not prevent him from renewing the gaieties of his youth ; and the irregularity of his private life affords, I think, a partial explanation of some of the disappointments of his career.

Many of Wellesley's enterprises in India, apart from the Mysore and other campaigns, which added so much both to the glory and the territory of the Empire, and which incidentally laid the foundations of his younger brother's fame, were characterised both by wisdom and imagination. But there was always a flavour of self-advertisement about them, and they were as a rule too expensive, particularly in a country like India which is liable to such sharp oscillations of policy, to be sure of a prolonged existence. These remarks apply to his project for a College of Fort William for the education of the young European Cadets, which was first vetoed by the Directors and then only sanctioned in a very modified form, and to his schemes for the encouragement of agriculture and horticulture and the study of the flora and fauna of India (which led to the institution of the Gardens and Menagerie at Barrackpore).

But, unquestionably, in all that he did or planned in India Wellesley was actuated by the highest sense of public and personal duty, always operating, however, as a gracious dispensation from a benign Providence. His administration was conscientious, laborious and upright, and was untouched by any of those public scandals that had disfigured the reign of some of his predecessors. Even his pomp and show were dictated by the desire to do full justice to a great station and a supreme responsibility.

---

[1] We find Mrs. Creevey writing to her husband in 1805 : "We [i.e. Mrs. Fitzgerald and herself] had a long discourse about Lady Wellesley. The folly of men marrying such women led us to Mrs. Fox."—" Creevey Papers," Vol. I, p. 70.

[2] The second Lady Wellesley was a lady of much charm. William IV paid her many compliments, and Creevey said that in his life he never found a more agreeable companion.—" Creevey Papers," Vol. II, p. 248.

The most absurd form which was taken by his sensitive egotism was his quite unconcealed disappointment that more honours were not heaped upon him, and his almost shameless pleading for titles and orders. After the fall of Seringapatam in 1799, when he had only been in India for a year, he asked Lord Grenville for a Marquisate or the Garter, and intimated that he thought a Dukedom an even more appropriate reward. He even hinted not obscurely at resignation if his hopes were disappointed, nor was he consoled by a money grant of £5,000 per year for twenty years from the Company. When he found that he had only been made an Irish Marquis his indignation boiled over at the gift of what he described as " This double gilt potato." Throughout his public life he did not cease to plead with a deplorable importunity for honours and positions in excess of those—and they were not inconsiderable—that he received ; and in 1840, when already eighty years of age and nearing the end, he renewed his almost piteous supplication for the Strawberry-leaves.

Such a man, with such a passion for aggrandisement and with such a conception of his own services and deserts, was bound to come into speedy collision with his employers at home, all the more that they had sent him out with the strictest injunctions to keep the peace, not to meddle with the Native States, and to husband the depleted resources of the Company. His seven years of Indian service were therefore a constant series of explosions, with censures and rebukes on the one side, and protests and resignations on the other. In none of the Lives of Wellesley have I found any clear or consecutive account of this prolonged and mortal encounter. But, as far as I can ascertain, the following were its phases. My information is derived from the published Despatches and Correspondence of Wellesley, and the Life of Lord Sidmouth (Addington), to whom as Prime Minister a large number of his letters were addressed.

His case against the Court of Directors was that they had censured his appointment, disapproved of his policy, interfered with his prerogative, and shown a want of confidence in himself. His first letter of resignation to them was written as early as 28th September, 1801, and this was followed by two others of 1st January and 13th March, 1802. Simultaneously he wrote an explanatory letter to Addington of 10th January, 1802. In the letter of 13th March he showed that his proffered resignation must not be taken too seriously, since he added that " so convinced was he of the public importance of his continuance in India that he was ready to remain on certain conditions until the close of January 1804."   Before the replies to these letters had reached him, Wellesley, who was clearly apprehensive that they might contain an acceptance of his offer, wrote again on 24th December, 1802, to say that in consequence of the Mahratta troubles he had determined to remain on till affairs assumed a more settled aspect.

The Government and the Directors were happily of the same opinion, and letters poured in upon the gratified Proconsul, which flattered his conviction that he was indispensable.   Castlereagh, who was then President of the Board of Control, wrote a private letter of 10th September imploring Wellesley to stay, and an official letter of 27th September to say that he had made representations to the Court, who had concurred in the Governor General's request to continue. Addington wrote a private letter on 26th September in the same sense, and the official letter of the Court, dated 29th September, begged Wellesley to postpone his departure for another year, *i.e.* till January 1804.   Wellesley's reply to the Court, dated 11th February, 1803, announced his willingness to act upon this request ; and on the following day he wrote private letters thanking both Castlereagh and Addington, to the latter of whom he said with a fine disregard of truth :

" I desire neither power, emoluments nor honours on my return to England ; my wish is to preserve the regard of my friends for myself and to restore their union for the preservation of the country.   In such a course office or honours will not engage my attention."

In September 1803 Addington, mindful of the engagement, spoke in a letter to Wellesley of " the individual who is likely to succeed you." In a private letter of the same date Castlereagh revealed the identity of this individual as Sir George Barlow, explained that the Court, regarding the stipulated year as a fixed term, had appointed the latter, and added that though Wellesley had the unabated support of His Majesty's Government, he could not perceive a corresponding disposition in the Court.   He therefore put the whole case before Wellesley and left him to decide as to his return.   Before these letters could reach him the Governor General had already made up his mind that duty compelled him to make a further stay ; and on 3rd December, 1803, he wrote to the Court that in consequence of the military operations and political negotiations still pending in India, he deemed it a public duty to relinquish the idea of embarking for Europe in January 1804. In March 1804 (Castlereagh's letter having in the meantime arrived) he wrote a polite letter to the Court saying that he intended to embark for England at the end of the year.

These civilities however were only intended for public consumption ; and the real sentiments of Wellesley towards the body who were alternately recalling him and asking him to remain in their service, were revealed in a letter to Castlereagh of 19th June, 1804, in which he " let himself go " in denunciation of the " vindictive profligacy of the Court " and the " ignominious tyranny of Leadenhall Street," and ended with the following highly characteristic explosion :

" Your Lordship may be assured that as no symptoms of tardy remorse displayed by the Honourable Court in consequence of my recent success in India will vary my present estimation of the faith and honour of my very worthy and approved good masters, or protract my continuance in India for one hour beyond the limits prescribed by the public interests, so no additional outrage, injury or insult which can issue from the most loathsome den of the India House will accelerate my departure while the public safety shall appear to require my aid in this arduous station."

When such were the real relations between the two parties, it was not likely that a further and final rupture would be long postponed. Wellesley was still reluctant to hand over, and in March 1805 he wrote to the Court that the continuance of hostilities and disturbances had delayed him and he could not abandon his station without a dereliction of duty. He proposed, however, to embark at the earliest opportunity in the present year, as soon as affairs had assumed a more settled aspect. Meanwhile, early in 1805 the Court, disgusted at Monson's retreat from the Mahratta forces (for which Wellesley was not responsible) and annoyed at his unabated escapades, had decided finally to recall the Governor General, and on receipt of their despatch he finally resigned and announced his intention of embarking in August. So ended this protracted and rather indecent conflict, and so concluded a Proconsular reign that was to form the theme of political controversy for at least another century. In what form the actual conflict was revived in England has already been narrated.

When, after a five months' journey, Wellesley landed at Portsmouth, to be met only by his wife and children and a few friends from town, he could not conceal his mortification at the complete absence of any demonstration in honour of the returned potentate who had ruled the East with such unparalleled splendour for so many years.   Nor did he ever lose his sense of the gross and inexplicable ingratitude of his countrymen.

I have said on an earlier page that in estimating the conduct or careers of persons in this narrative I would largely rely upon the opinions of their contemporaries.   In the case of Wellesley we may find, without going to his enemies or detractors, a significant consensus. Already, while he was still in India, Warren Hastings, writing from the seclusion of Daylesford to his friends in Bengal, had remarked with much sagacity :

" Lord Wellesley has constructed a political system of vast strength and extent, but of a weight which will require that it should be continually upheld by an arm as strong as his ; but that if they nominate a successor to him, of abilities much inferior to his, and of an activity of mind not equal to his, the whole structure will fall to pieces and all that we formerly possessed be lost in the same ruin."

And again :

" The Governor General has committed the heinous crime of using expressions of Ridicule and Contempt about the Company at his table and the words have been carried home.   If I was in his confidence, I would tell him that civility costs little."

Long before he returned to England the reports of Wellesley's airs and graces in India, and his incessant quarrels with the Court, had created an atmosphere of prejudice against him which permeated all grades of society.   In 1804 we find the King (George III) unbosoming himself to George Rose in the following terms :

" Lord Wellesley was spoken of by His Majesty as having considerable merit in the conduct of affairs in India, but as inflated with pride and with his own consequence, assuming to himself the exclusive merit of all that had been done in the East, and demanding ceremonious respect beyond what was due to his station ; that when he had more than once been reminded that he was exacting from those about him more than the King did, his Lordship replied : ' Then the King is wrong, but that is no reason why I should improperly relax also.'   His Majesty added, ' When he returns his head will be quite turned, and there will be no enduring him.' " [1]

---

[1] " Diaries and Correspondence of Rt. Hon. G. Rose," Vol. II, p. 165.

A more discriminating judgment was that of Lord Holland at a rather later date :

" He had more genius than prudence, more spirit than principle, and manifestly despised his colleagues as much as they dreaded him. Unlike most English politicians, he was rather a statesman than a man of business, and more capable of doing extraordinary things well than conducting ordinary transactions with safety or propriety."

And again :

" Yet there was a smack, a fancy of greatness in all he did; and though in his speeches, his manners and his actions he was very open to ridicule, those who smiled and even laughed could not despise him." [1]

The recently published Diary of the gossiping Academician, Joseph Farington, contains two references to Lord Wellesley that confirm a good deal that has appeared in these pages :

" April 8, 1811. Sir T. Lawrence spoke of Lord Wellesley. With all his abilities he has so great a share of vanity that, at the age of about 53, Lawrence has noticed that when His Lordship sat to him for His Portrait His Lips were painted." [2]

" June 15, 1811. The Marchioness of Thomond spoke of the Marquess Wellesley, who by His Excessive extravagance has Expended His Fortunes. Yet under these circumstances he had a George made for him as a Knight of the Garter which is wholly composed of diamonds and the price of it £2,000. It is now at Picket & Rundall's, the jewellers, who however will not deliver it until the money is paid. Though He is an Ugly little man his personal vanity is excessive."

I cannot help regarding the criticism upon the looks of Lord Wellesley as unkind, for he possessed singular beauty of feature and was, indeed, a better-looking man than the Duke of Wellington, who shared his partiality for the fair sex and was known in London society as the Beau. So also must have thought Macaulay when in 1833, before proceeding to India, he went to call upon the retired Governor General.

---

[1] " Further Memories of the Whig Party" (1807-1821), by Lord Holland (ed. Lord Stavordale), 1905, pp. 113, 116.

[2] This is the beautiful picture that hangs in the Corridor at Windsor Castle. It is to be regretted that the remark about the facial decoration was well founded. When the second Lady Wellesley had returned on one occasion from Dublin to Leamington, the unkind Jekyll wrote : " The Lord Lieutenant, though by no means in despair at this Catholic emancipation from wedlock, shuts himself up in total seclusion. Whenever he does deign to appear in public he presents a singular spectacle —a hoary head with eyebrows artificially blackened, cheeks highly rouged, and a forehead painted white. Grimaldi in a pantomime is a less picturesque Viceroy. It is said Lady Glengall some time ago forced her way to his toilette and caught him in the very act of repairing himself."

" I am particularly curious, and always was, to know him.   He has made a great and splendid figure in history, and his weaknesses, though they make his character less worthy of respect, make it more interesting as a study.   Such a blooming old swain I never saw : hair combed with exquisite nicety, a waistcoat of driven snow, and a Star and Garter put on with rare skill." [1]

Vulnerable as Wellesley was to attack, and even to ridicule, no words can be found too strong to condemn the monstrous persecution that was directed against him in the House of Commons after his return. The example of Warren Hastings, so far from deterring the experiment of impeachment, had set in motion a ghastly epidemic.   Lord Melville was attacked, but escaped.   A miserable creature named Paull, who was the son of a Scotch tailor and, having traded in India, bore a grudge against Wellesley for something that had happened there, purchased a seat in Parliament in 1805 and launched an attack upon the retired Proconsul, backed by a considerable number of the Directors, for his alleged treatment of the Nawab of Oudh.   These charges were first brought before the House of Commons in a number of motions for papers in the Session of 1806, and finally in a series of Resolutions in March 1808, which were rejected by a majority of 182 to 31.   A Resolution approving the conduct of the Governor General was then passed by 180 to 29. [2]   In May 1808 another M.P., Sir T. Turton, moved for the actual impeachment of Wellesley on the same grounds. This was negatived without a division, and a motion approving his conduct was then carried, with a minority of 15.   That a man who, whatever his faults or foibles, had nobly sustained the honour of England, and in the case in question had been guilty of no offence, should have been thus assailed in the Parliament of Great Britain, is an additional illustration of the manner in which some of the greatest of England's servants abroad have been recompensed on their return to this country.

The picture which I have drawn will perhaps have assisted my readers to form some idea of a man who was nearly, though not quite, in the first rank of those who have governed the Indian Empire.   The fact is that Wellesley's estimate of himself was always a little in excess of that which other people, whose views were important, held of him ; and he could not conceal his surprise at the stupidity or malevolence of those who were capable of such misjudgment.   In India, however,

---

[1] " Life and Letters of Lord Macaulay," by Sir G. Trevelyan, Vol. I, p. 312.
[2] Paull having taken to gambling and lost heavily, and being in constant pain from the wounds which he had received in a duel with Sir Francis Burdett, cut his throat in the following month.

2—M

he will always be regarded as one of those who strove mightily and builded well ; and the generous tributes which were paid to him in his declining years by the East India Company were acclaimed by the general sense of his countrymen.

It was not after all to Sir George Barlow, but to the veteran Cornwallis, that Wellesley was to hand over the sceptre. When the old soldier was once more pressed to go out, he said in a letter of 24th October, 1804, with a devotion to duty that set a magnificent example :

" It is a desperate act to embark for India at the age of sixty-six ; prepared however as I am to forego all further comforts and gratifications in this world for the sake of my family, I cannot sacrifice my character and my honour." [1]

Cornwallis arrived on 30th July, 1805, in the Company's yacht " Charlotte"; he landed at 6 p.m., and took the oaths and his seat as Governor General at 8.30 p.m. Wellesley stayed on at Government House for three weeks after the arrival of his successor, received an Address on 5th August, left Government House at 8 a.m. on 20th August after a public breakfast given by the Commander-in-Chief, Sir Alured Clarke (at which Cornwallis was not present), and, attended by the Body Guard, drove to the Calcutta Gate of Fort William. From this point he passed through the troops and the Water Gate, where he was met by the European inhabitants of Calcutta, who escorted him to the " Charlotte," on which he embarked and went down the river to join H.M.S. " Howe."

It is unnecessary to add anything here about Cornwallis' second and abruptly suspended reign. I have spoken elsewhere of his too eager and exaggerated retrenchments. Of more serious import was his public repudiation of Wellesley's policy, which he openly announced that he had come out to reverse, and the consequent rupture of negotiations by Scindia. Before he had time to measure the consequences of these retrograde steps, Cornwallis was stricken down by a mortal illness and, though he had saved his honour, his family knew him no more.

Sir George Barlow, a member of the Service and senior Member of Council, who was compensated for his earlier disappointment by receiving the succession to Cornwallis, continued the policy which the latter had been sent out to adopt. He was an upright and worthy man, with a high sense of duty, but no width of outlook and not much warmth

[1] " Correspondence " (ed. C. Ross), Vol. III, p. 520.

LORD MINTO (1813)

From the painting by G. Chinnery.

of heart.   Lord Minto, under whom he continued to serve for months, wrote of him :

'A constitutional coldness and apathy of temper which has exposed him to the reproach of indifference to the interests of other men, and has enabled him to discharge many harsh duties pretty inflexibly, seems at the same time to have kept his personal feelings in a temperate state and to render a second place less irksome and irritating than it would be to ninety-nine men in a hundred who had filled the first."

Barlow, however, had not the strength of character to enable him to ride the Indian or any storm, and contemporary writers or correspondents almost uniformly deplored his political feebleness and incompetence.   I have described elsewhere the political intrigues and shuffles in England that were responsible for leaving him in possession for as long a period as nearly two years.   At the end of that time he was withdrawn and sent to Madras—the first Lord Minto, who came out in the frigate "Modeste," commanded by his second son, George Elliot, having, after a voyage of nearly six months, arrived at Calcutta and taken over the Government on 31st July, 1807.

Lord Minto had had considerable experience, if not of India, at any rate of Indian affairs, in more than one capacity.   In 1783, as Sir Gilbert Elliot, he had been designated one of the seven Parliamentary Directors to be appointed under the abortive East India Bill of Fox. In 1787 he had been appointed one of the Managers for the House of Commons of the impeachment of Warren Hastings, who never forgave the part that he had played, and always spoke of him with dislike and contempt.   In 1788 he had moved the impeachment of Sir Elijah Impey for perversion of justice in the case of Nuncomar.[1]   In 1806 he had served for five months as President of the Board of Control, before being translated to the most important office in India.   He was a warm personal friend of and disciple of Burke, and had had, as mentioned in the preceding chapter, a somewhat varied external experience of public affairs.

While Lord Minto was on his way out to India in 1807, the Government which had appointed him fell over the Catholic Bill, and was succeeded by the administration of the Duke of Portland.   Lord Grenville, the head of the retiring Government, wrote to Minto and expressed an earnest hope that he would not think it necessary to resign

The motion for impeachment was defeated, in May 1788, by 73 votes to 55.

his office, to which the other replied that he had already placed his conditional resignation in the hands of his son at home, but was prepared to continue if invited to do so, because " on public grounds I am sure that this distant Government ought not to change with every turn in domestic politics "—a doctrine of unimpeachable soundness which in more modern times has become an accepted canon of Indian administration.   The new Ministry very properly confirmed the nomination of their predecessors.

Lord Minto was one of the class of Governors General who leave no particular mark on history and cease to be remembered either for good or ill.   Coming out to pursue the policy of peaceful isolation which had been unsuccessfully practised by his immediate predecessors, he soon found himself driven into courses which even Wellesley would have approved.

I have before disclaimed the intention of writing the political history of any Governor General, and therefore I shall say nothing here of Lord Minto's expeditions that resulted in the capture of the Ile de Bourbon and Mauritius, which were a reflex of the European Wars, or of Java, which had also passed temporarily into French hands from the Dutch.   The Governor General accompanied the second of these expeditions himself—a most undesirable proceeding, undertaken on his own responsibility and without orders, but from a desire to regulate personally the administration of the conquered territories.   Nor need I comment upon the Missions which he despatched to the Courts of Lahore, Kabul, and Teheran, all with the most excellent intentions, but with meagre, if not barren, results.[1]

His internal administration was marked by more than one serious anxiety : a trouble with the Missionaries in Bengal, arising out of the circulation of the Scriptures and rather indiscreet religious propaganda ; and a military mutiny in Madras, which kept him for fourteen months absent from headquarters in that Presidency.

Lord Minto's time in India was further saddened by the absence of his wife, to whom he was devotedly attached, but who had been unable to accompany him, and by the death of their youngest son, William, at Madras.   I have spoken elsewhere of his social régime at Calcutta, and of his love for Barrackpore.   He was extremely popular in Bengal.

---

[1] The Mission to Persia was sadly bungled, for Lord Minto's Envoy, Colonel Malcolm, and an Envoy from the British Government, Sir Harford Jones, appeared simultaneously on the scene, with the result of a good deal of bad feeling.

and was a man of kindly disposition and considerable culture, with a sense of humour which is apparent from some of his published letters.[1] But his main interests were domestic, and while conscientiously and uncomplainingly performing his public duties, he was all the while longing to return home.

This desire was aggravated by the deep disappointment felt by the Governor General at what he regarded as the inadequate recognition, both by the Court of Directors and by the Home Government, of his administration in general, and more especially of his services in adding so materially to the territories of the Crown. After his return from Java his spirits flagged somewhat, while the burden of his work seemed steadily to increase. There is a passage in one of his letters to his wife which reflects this increasing lassitude, while at the same time it throws a light upon the conditions in which a Governor General did his work in the early years of the 19th century. It may deserve therefore to take its place in the panorama which this book has endeavoured to present.

" I feel anxious to tell you why, with the same good intentions, I have fallen lately so far short of my former voluminous virtues in correspondence. One grand reason is that I have too much to do by several hours' work every day. Our conquests, among other causes, have increased our labours greatly. But since you will know my infirmities, the honest truth is that I am older every birthday,[2] which is very common in the East, and I find, first and foremost, that writing in windy weather by candlelight is a thought more *kittle* than it was last century ; secondly and lastly, I used to write to Minto between the evening's drive and supper which is now called tea ; but now-a-days, getting up to open my shop at five or half-past, and slaving like a maid-of-all-work the whole day, I am ashamed to own that between 7 and 8 p.m. I am so thoroughly done up that I *coup o'er* like a leaden statue, on a sofa ready set in the breezy verandah, and doze and dream of Minto ; but am fairly *unable* to sit up and write, fighting with the flare and with the darkness and the mosquitoes, as I was wont in my youth a year or two ago. This is the melancholy truth."[3]

These were the sentiments of the tired and ageing man, who had

[1] On his way out to Calcutta he stopped for a fortnight in Madras, where in the month of June everyone was suffering from the prickly heat. " To give you some notion of its intensity," he wrote to his wife, " the placid Lord William (Bentinck) has been found sprawling on a table on his back ; and Sir Henry Gwillin, one of the Madras Judges, who is a Welshman and a fiery Briton in all senses, was discovered by a visitor rolling on his own floor like a baited bull."

[2] He was now in his sixty-second year.

[3] " Lord Minto in India," p. 332.

already asked to be relieved not later than January 1814 (by which time he would have had six and a half years of office), when, in the summer of 1813, he suddenly learned that six months earlier it had been decided to supersede him and to confer the appointment on Lord Moira, who, he was told, would reach Calcutta in October 1813. This very invidious form of recall had been forced upon the Court of Directors by the Board of Control, acting under strong pressure from the Prince Regent, who was a bosom friend of Lord Moira. The Court endeavoured to atone for their discourtesy by sending out a simultaneous Resolution warmly acknowledging Lord Minto's eminent services, and the Government made him an Earl. Thus, however, once more was a Governor General sacrificed to the exigencies of Party politics or Governmental indifference at home.

Lord Minto bore the rebuff with much dignity, and finally started homewards in December 1813, his successor, Lord Moira, having arrived at the stipulated date in October. England was reached in May 1814; but the circumstances of the home-coming were sadder even than the incidents which had provoked it. Lady Minto was awaiting the return of her husband in Scotland, and the meeting was ardently looked forward to by each. Sundry duties retained the Governor General a fortnight in town. He then caught a chill while attending the funeral at night of his brother-in-law, Lord Auckland, who, though previously in perfect health, had been found dead in his bed. Nevertheless Lord Minto insisted on starting upon his Northward journey by carriage to the wife and the home that he loved so dearly; but he had not proceeded beyond Stevenage when on 2nd June, 1814, he sank and died. The Abbey was deemed the sole compensation for such a tragedy.

The arrival of Lord Moira[1] and Lady Loudoun at Calcutta was a typical illustration of the solemnities, but also of the long-drawn-out stages, of the arrival of a Governor General in the olden times. Sailing from England on 14th April, 1813, in H.M.S. "Stirling Castle," they reached Saugor on 29th September and embarked in the "Hastings" pilot vessel. On 1st October they exchanged into the "Phœnix" yacht, and reached Diamond Harbour on the 2nd, where the State flotilla met them. On the 3rd they moved into the *Sonamukhi*, and were towed

---

[1] At that time he was Earl of Moira, and she was Countess of Loudoun in her own right. In 1818 he was made Marquis of Hastings.

up the river to Kyd's Dockyard.   On the 4th at 6 a.m. they landed at Chandpal Ghat.   Lady Loudoun and the children were put into a carriage and despatched to the private door of Government House. Lord Hastings, accompanied by the General Officers and Staffs, walked on foot through a lane made by the troops along Council House Street to the North front of Government House, where he was met by Lord Minto (as in the common fashion) at the top of the steps, introduced to the Members of Council and others in the ante-hall, conducted to the Council Chamber and sworn in, and then entertained at an official Breakfast in the Marble Hall.

Lord Minto then retired to a house in Chowringhi which had been rented for the purpose,[1] and there he stayed till 11th December, taking part in a public banquet on 9th November to celebrate the launching of the " General Kyd."

As time has passed these formalities have been greatly reduced in number and duration, and the anomaly of the two potentates residing for a considerable period in the same place has fortunately disappeared.

This may be a suitable moment at which to mention a point by which I was for long considerably puzzled.   In the chronicles of my predecessors I found it placed on frequent record that the incoming Governor General, immediately upon arrival, was conducted to the Council Chamber, where he took his seat at the table and was sworn in.   Apparently this was a *pro forma* meeting of the Council held for the purpose.   On one occasion the retiring Governor General accompanied him.   On the other hand, when I arrived in January 1899, not only did I not assume the office, as will be explained later on, until my predecessor had left Calcutta, but I took no oath at all.   I merely walked to the Council Room, where I stood at the upper end, under the portrait of Warren Hastings, while the Warrant of my appointment was read out by the Secretary in the Home Department.   I bowed, everybody bowed, not a word was exchanged, and I then retired while the guns boomed the salute from Fort William.   The entire ceremony had not occupied so much as five minutes.   The explanation of the difference is as follows.

Up till the arrival of Lord Northbrook in 1872, every Governor General and Viceroy took the prescribed oaths on being admitted to

[1] *Vide* Chapter II.

office. In 1873 was passed the Indian Oaths Act which, except in certain cases mentioned in the Act, dispensed persons in India from taking an oath or affirmation on the assumption of any office. Accordingly there was a period of nearly half a century in which no oath was taken, until in November 1918 a Royal Warrant was issued requiring the Governor General and other high officials to take an oath of allegiance and an oath for the due execution of justice ; and the Indian Oaths Act of 1873 was amended accordingly.

But to revert to Lord Moira. In England he was best known as a personal friend of the Prince Regent, at whose invitation he had in the previous year all but succeeded in forming an Administration with himself as First Lord of the Treasury. When this fell through, the Prince insisted on his crony being appointed to India, and Lord Minto was recalled for the purpose. In earlier times Lord Moira had attacked Warren Hastings and criticised his policy. But more recently he had become a convert and an admirer, and the old man at Daylesford could write thus to Charles D'Oyly on his appointment : " He possesses none of the faults attached to a good character. His predominant quality is a high sense of honour, and his understanding both solid and brilliant. His lady, not beautiful, is most amiable."

It may be added that the absence of beauty was a characteristic that was shared by her spouse, for, although a man of fine appearance, tall of stature, and athletic in build, he was, as his portraits show, not an Adonis.

In an earlier chapter I have described the extraordinary state and style which were observed by the new Governor General and which came as a shock to Calcutta Society after the modesty of recent régimes. I have there cited the evidence of General Palmer, who had been both Military and Private Secretary to Warren Hastings, and was now Resident at a native Court, and who found " the Transition too abrupt to please."

These formalities, as I have before observed, did not really indicate any excess of pride or vanity on the part of the Governor General, and were compatible with much affability and kindness of heart. On the other hand, his love of display tempted him into an extravagance which had a ruinous effect upon his own fortunes, and left him in an impoverished condition in the later part of his life. It was said of Hastings that " fidelity was both the strength and the weakness of his character.

He was very faithful to his friends and sometimes allowed the man to prevail over the ruler, lacking the sterner stuff required to restrain the promptings of good nature and warmth of heart."

The sharp reaction in ceremonial observances initiated by Lord Hastings was reproduced in his public policy. The wheel had now performed a complete revolution ; and the interrupted policy of the earlier Hastings and of Wellesley was pushed to its logical conclusion by the later wearer of the name. The successive campaigns in which he overcame Nepal, crushed the robber league of the Pindaris, and finally broke the Mahratta power, himself, as Commander-in-Chief, leading an army against them in 1817 of 120,000 men with 300 guns, carried the spread of British dominion over Northern and Central India to a stage which it was only left for Lord Dalhousie, a quarter of a century later, to complete. Simultaneously he resumed Wellesley's policy by extending British supremacy and protection over every available Native State. By these achievements Hastings unquestionably stands forth as one of the foremost architects of the India we know.

This policy, it may well be believed, did not at all meet with the approval of the Court of Directors, with whom Hastings found himself in the customary trouble. In 1819, in gratitude for his victories, they had voted him a gratuity of £60,000 for the purchase of an estate ; but two years later his conduct in relation to the case of the banking firm of Palmer & Co., at Hyderabad, provoked both their suspicion and their censure, delivered in no adulterated terms. Hastings resigned in disgust and left India, to find himself greeted with coolness by the India Board and with open hostility by the Court of Proprietors, although they acquitted him personally of any corrupt intent in the Hyderabad transaction.

Returning to Europe a poor man, he was compelled to accept the Governorship of Malta in 1824, and it was while serving there that the news reached him of the qualified censure passed on him by the Court of Proprietors after the publication of the papers relating to the Palmer case. The veteran was greatly distressed, and contemplated returning home to clear his character. Shortly afterwards, however, he had a fall from his horse from which he never recovered ; and, being taken to sea, died on board his vessel off the Bay of Naples in November 1826. His extravagance had left him so impoverished that upon his death the furniture in the palace was seized and his entire property had to be sold to pay his debts.[1]

This excellent and hard-working ruler deserves recollection for two other achievements. It was he who made up for the loss of Java, foolishly given back to the Dutch, by the purchase of Singapore, which has since become the most important naval base and coasting station in the East. He earned the undying gratitude of Calcutta by his efforts to cleanse and beautify the city, which commemorated the service by attaching his name or titles to more streets or quarters than preserve the fame of any other Governor General. Loudoun Street, Rawdon Street, Hungerford Street, Moira Street (Hastings Street had already received the title in honour of an earlier and more famous Hastings), the colony of Hastings in the South-west corner of the Maidan, Hastings Bridge, erected by public subscription over Tolly's Nullah in honour of his Administration—all keep alive his name. With the proceeds of a great lottery he built the Strand Road along the river bank, and added greatly to the amenities of both the City and the Maidan. Perhaps he rendered a more doubtful service in removing the historic *pipal* tree, under which Job Charnock was said to have sat and smoked his *hookah*, as well as the battered pillar which Governor Holwell had set up over the remains of the victims of the Black Hole and which it was left to me, 80 years later, as narrated in a previous chapter, to replace.

Lord Hastings was a man of strong domestic affections ; and he felt very deeply the prolonged separation from his wife and family. Lady Loudoun and their children had to go home in January 1816. She returned alone in 1819 to be with him in the remainder of his stay. When dying, he directed that his right hand should be cut off and clasped in that of his wife when she should follow him. This strange but pathetic request was faithfully carried out. The hand, enclosed in a small box, was deposited in the family vault at Loudoun in Ayrshire, and when Lady Hastings died, fourteen years later, it was placed in her coffin.

The biographers of Hastings seem as a rule to have forgotten or to have been ignorant of the fact that he was the father of the ill-fated Lady Flora Hastings, Lady of the Bedchamber to the Duchess of Kent, against whom a foul and baseless charge was made in 1839, that precipitated her early death at the age of thirty-three. He was also the

---

[1] " Journal of H. E. Fox " (Lord Holland) (edited by the Earl of Ilchester), pp. 206–7.

grandfather of the spendthrift Lord Hastings, whose disasters on the Turf and early death are among the most vivid recollections of my own childhood—brought up as I was in the same English county.

When Lord Hastings retired, the Court of Directors wished to appoint Lord William Bentinck, who had been Governor of Madras, in his place, and Bentinck ardently desired the office. But in view of the political attitude which he had taken up, Lord Liverpool's Government would not hear of the selection, and the Prime Minister himself wrote to the Court that he " thought it would be humiliating to the Government and productive of the very worst effects, to appoint to such a station a man who had taken so strong a part in Parliamentary opposition." George IV replied that he thought it " highly inadvisable that Lord W. Bentinck should be the successor of Lord Hastings." [1] Bentinck's ambitions accordingly had to be postponed, and Lord Amherst's name was put forward by the Court and accepted by the Government. His nomination to India was understood to be a sort of consolation for the failure of his Mission to Peking.

Pending the arrival of the new Governor General there was a short interregnum of about three months, in which John Adam, a narrow-minded official, acted as senior Member of Council. In August 1823 Lord Amherst assumed charge.

After the strenuous and victorious reign of Hastings, neither the new-comer nor his employers at home anticipated any prospect but that of continuous peace. It is true as regards internal affairs that Amherst's term of office was both uneventful and sterile. But in external matters he found himself involved in a series of military expeditions which ended in the conquest of Assam, Arakan, and Tenasserim, and the storming of the renowned fortress of Bhurtpore. Arising out of the Burmese campaign occurred the melancholy and badly handled incident of the mutiny of the Sepoys at Barrackpore in 1824, to which I have referred in my first Volume. The Burmese War, which in its early stages was attended by great calamities and was much mismanaged, had been severely criticised in England ; nor did the tale of the mutiny and its fierce punishment produce a better impression. From the end of 1825 the ship of Amherst was labouring in very heavy waters, and he was only saved for a time by the robust common sense

---

[1] C. D. Yonge, " Life and Administrations of the 2nd Earl of Liverpool," 1868, Vol. III, p. 204.

of the Duke of Wellington, who thus addressed the Prime Minister, Lord Liverpool, on 10th October, 1825 :

" I am aware of the power of the Court of Directors to remove the Governor General. But in my opinion it would be better, both for the public interest and for the honour of the individuals concerned, that they should remove him against the will of the Government than that we should be guilty of injustice."

In March 1826 the news reached the Governor General that he was about to be recalled. Calcutta took his side, and so in a halting manner did the Home Cabinet, who, having read Amherst's defence, declared that they would be no party to his dismissal, which they thus rather pusillanimously left to the Court.

For months the unhappy Governor General, separated by nearly six months from English news, was left in almost daily expectation of being recalled—not the least among the cruel experiences to which the British people have been apt to expose their Indian servants. In August 1826 he had made up his mind to resign. But in May 1827 there arrived a Resolution of thanks and compliments from the Court, as a belated solatium for his previous sufferings. Nevertheless his resignation, proffered on the score of ill-health, was accepted, and in March 1828 Lord and Lady Amherst left Calcutta after a chequered reign. In spite of the ill-health he lived for nearly thirty years, but held no further post of distinction, though nominated in 1835 to the Governor Generalship of Canada. Among the British rulers of India Amherst leaves one of the most inconspicuous and impalpable of impressions. In a previous chapter I have noticed his extravagant attention to ceremonial, and have cited the opinion of a high official who knew him well.

It was a curious coincidence that while one of the contributory causes of Amherst's recall was the Sepoy mutiny at Barrackpore, his successor had already been recalled from Madras over twenty years before for his failure to deal with a similar rising at Vellore. This was Lord William Bentinck, who under the Charter Act of 1833 became the first Governor General of India as distinct from Fort William in Bengal, and during the last years of his Administration was also Commander-in-Chief—the last British ruler of India to combine the two offices. Bentinck had been brought up as a soldier ; because of his military experience he had been sent as Governor to Madras in 1803, at the early age of twenty-nine ; after his recall from that Presidency he had commanded the British Army in Sicily.   And yet it was reserved for this soldier to enjoy and to take advantage of the most peaceful and tranquil period of office that had yet befallen any Governor General of India.

Bentinck, who thought, with justice, that he had been very badly treated over Vellore, was always longing, as we have seen, to get back to India—but only in the highest place.   He refused Madras when it was offered to him a second time in 1819.   When Lord Hastings left Calcutta, he had asked for but had been refused the succession to Bengal.   When Amherst left, he was at last successful.   Nominated in July 1827, he assumed office in July 1828, the interval of four months after the departure of Amherst having been filled by the acting appointment of W. B. Bayley.

The new Governor General, being free from external troubles, had time to devote himself to the problems of internal administration, and his term of office was distinguished by many moral and educational reforms.   At one time he incurred a storm of obloquy from the European community because of the reduction of *batta*, and the curtailment of the posts in the higher ranks of the Civil Service which were open to Englishmen.   But a certain quiet tenacity, and the knowledge that he was acting under orders from home, enabled him to recover from this unpopularity with his countrymen.   On the other hand his encouragement of native aspirations and his opening to them of many avenues of employment previously closed rendered his name very popular with the Indians, who have ever since cited him as one of the most sympathetic of Governors.   That he was a man of sterling sincerity and deeply devoted to the interests of the country cannot be doubted ;   and the abolition of *sati* (suttee), the suppression of *thagi* (thuggee), and the adoption, under Macaulay's inspiration, of English Education in the State-aided Schools, have invested his name with a sort of halo that has never lost its lustre.

Macaulay, however, who as Law Member was his colleague (but only for nine months in 1834-35), as usual exceeded in eulogy as he was apt to do in invective, when he wrote on the base of Bentinck's statue at Calcutta the following inscription :

" To William Cavendish Bentinck, who during seven years ruled India with eminent prudence, integrity and benevolence ;   who, placed at the head of a great empire, never laid down the simplicity and moderation of a private citizen ;[1] who infused into Oriental Despotism the Spirit of British Freedom ; who never forgot that the end of Government is the happiness of the governed ; who abolished cruel rites; who effaced humiliating distinctions; who gave liberty to the expression of public opinion ; whose constant study it was to elevate the intellectual and moral character of the nation committed to his charge."

And still greater was the exaggeration when he concluded his Essay on Clive by referring to " the veneration with which the latest generation of Hindus will contemplate the statue of Lord William Bentinck."

Greville, himself an admirer of Bentinck, and still more of his wife, who was a great help to him in India, and whose full-length portrait was the only picture of a Governor General's wife that hung on the walls of Government House, was a more discriminating critic when he wrote :

" He is a man whose success in life has been greater than his talents warrant, for he is not right-headed and has committed some great blunder or other in every public situation in which he has been placed ; but he is simple in his habits, popular in his manners, liberal in his opinions, and magnificently hospitable in his mode of life."[2]

I have previously quoted H. T. Prinsep on Bentinck's methods of work. But I may here cite from his (unpublished) Memoirs two other passages about the same Governor General, whom he knew intimately and with whom he had not always agreed. Prinsep shared Greville's admiration for Lady William.

" It was not in Lord W. Bentinck's nature to give his implicit confidence to anybody except his wife, and he never took any important step without consulting her. She had been trained to diplomacy at Naples and in Sicily, and I cannot say that her advice and influence was other than beneficial."

Prinsep spoke of Bentinck as being " of a suspicious and ungenerous character," and added :

" He had a great love of change and desire to meddle with every institution or practice that he found in work or prevailing. It is impossible to deny that some of his changes were beneficial, but he as often muddled what he meddled

---

[1] For the manner in which the simplicity of the Bentinck régime at Government House impressed the European community in Calcutta, where, if Lord Hastings went to one extreme, Lord William was regarded as having gone to the other, *vide* Chapter IX of this work.
[2] " Memoirs of the Reigns of George IV and William IV," Vol. II, p. 339. " Memoirs of the Reign of Queen Victoria " (1837–1852), Vol. III, pp. 157–158.

with as improved it, and he left a great deal to be done by those who succeeded him in order to bring the machine of Government back into good working order."

These criticisms are not dissimilar from those which dog the path of any innovator on unconventional lines. But that Prinsep also sought to be just is apparent from the following :

" Lord W. Bentinck wrote more Minutes than all the other Governors General of India put together, but they were mostly on subjects of little moment. If he had to discuss a great question, he did not bring to it any originality of view or commanding intelligence and power of reasoning that carried with it the conviction of those who read and had to carry out the ideas and propositions he desired to see adopted. But there never was a more honest man in his intentions, and in the distribution of his patronage."

After nearly seven years of unremitting labour, in the course of which he set the example of extensive tours in many parts of India, Bentinck resigned in 1835 on the score of failing health, having, indeed, spent the concluding months of his tenure of office in the Nilgherries on that account. He was then sixty-one years of age and, though he was elected to the House of Commons on his return to England—after issuing an extremely Radical Address to the electors of Glasgow (the sole ex-Governor General to become an M.P.)—he only lived for another four years. Having no children, he had declined the peerage which was offered to him.

For a year the Government of India was administered by Sir Charles (afterwards Lord) Metcalfe, one of the ablest and most liberal-minded of Indian Civilians, who experienced to the full at the hands of the Court of Directors that refined caprice of which they were the accomplished and inveterate masters. At one moment they were struggling to confirm his officiating appointment. A few months later, after Metcalfe's action in liberating the Indian Press, they would not even send him to Madras.

CHAPTER XII (*Continued*)

PART II

AUCKLAND TO MINTO, 1836–1910

LORD AUCKLAND, the new Governor General, arrived in March 1836, and for the next six years we have the advantage of the lively Memoirs and Letters of his two accomplished sisters, who came out to preside over his bachelor establishment. The arrival by river was attended by a combination of misfortunes. The "Jupiter," on which the party came out, was towed up the Hugli from Diamond Harbour, the *Sonamukhi* being towed astern. The "Jupiter" then ran aground, and the *Sonamukhi* collided with the "Jupiter," and recourse had to be had to the steamer to continue the journey. Finally, the landing at Chandpal Ghat was not effected till 10 p.m., when the party drove to Government House to find Sir Charles Metcalfe and a party of eighty already at dinner. The new Governor General was promptly sworn in and the banquet was resumed.

These contretemps might, in a more credulous age, have been regarded as prophetic of an Indian career that, beginning with fair promise and continuing for a while in a rich glow of sunshine, was destined to end in disaster and gloom. Auckland is thus depicted by his biographer :

"Cold-mannered, reticent, shy, good-natured, robust of figure, disliking all pomp or parade, and delighting in regular official work, Lord Auckland was eminently fitted by temperament and long experience to discharge the most exacting duties of *quiet times*." [1]

Greville also spoke highly of him :

"He was a man without shining qualities or showy accomplishments, austere and almost forbidding in his manner. Silent and reserved in society,

[1] " The Earl of Auckland " (Rulers of India Series), by Capt. L. J. Trotter, p. 16.

196

unpretending both in public and in private life, and in the House of Lords taking a rare and modest part in debate. . . . Nevertheless he was universally popular . . . His understanding was excellent, his temper placid, his taste and tact exquisite ; his disposition, notwithstanding his apparent gravity, cheerful ; and under his cold exterior there was a heart overflowing with human kindness."[1]

Next let us take the contemporary opinion of the Service.   These are the views of H. T. Prinsep :

" He was a good man of business, an assiduous reader of all papers, and very correct and careful in any of the drafts he approved and passed ; but he was much wanting in promptness of decision, and had an overweening dread of responsibility which caused the instructions he gave, which were often penned by himself, to be so unsatisfactory that his agents had generally to decide for themselves what to do in any difficulty."

And again :

" Lord Auckland was much esteemed by the society of Calcutta, native as well as European.   He had many amiable qualities, and his two sisters, especially the elder, contributed much to establish his popularity.   But he was the author of no great measure to improve the internal administration, and in his general policy he showed a hesitation and want of decision that prevented his being looked upon as a Governor General of whom India might be proud.

" He was considered to have yielded too much to his Private Secretary (John Colvin), who, on occasions when the Governor General called his Members of Council and others into private consultation with himself, would take the whole initiative of the discussion while his Lordship sat listening with his hands at the back of his head; and from having thus so much thrown upon him he got the nickname of Lord Colvin among the younger Civil Servants."

A man who is both weak and diffident may emerge without discredit from normal situations.   But in times of stress, where ordinary rules and ordinary men are equally misplaced, those qualities become the parents of inevitable disaster.   It would be quite foreign to the scope of this work to discuss the Afghan policy of Lord Auckland, conceived in haste, disapproved by the best authorities—on this occasion the Court of Directors happened to be in the right, and the Ministry and the President of the Board of Control, Sir John Cam Hobhouse, in the wrong—and culminating in appalling tragedy.   To us at this distance of time it seems inconceivable that any man or body of men should have committed themselves to such an initial sequence of

---

[1] " Memoirs of the Reign of Queen Victoria " (1837–1852), Vol. III, pp. 254–5.

blunders as the deposition of Dost Mohammed, the setting up of Shah Shuja, and the posting of a British Resident in Kabul : inconceivable that such a display of incompetence and vacillation should have been given on the spot in Afghanistan as followed the murder of Sir A. Burnes and accompanied the retreat of the British forces ; inconceivable also that at Calcutta a Governor General and a Commander-in-Chief should have shown such consistent incapacity to grapple with a situation the most critical that had ever confronted British arms and British prestige in Asia. But so it was, and the ruler, however amiable or well-meaning, who was responsible for such a series of catastrophes, stands self-condemned. Greville however thought that Auckland was most unfairly blamed, and eulogised his " laborious and con-scientious administration." He further quoted the opinion of Lord Fitzgerald, who was President of the Board of Control from 1841 to 1843, and who testified to the ability of Auckland's State papers and Despatches and to the justice of his government.

Auckland, whose health had suffered from the strain, was abruptly recalled, Sir Robert Peel, who had re-entered office in September 1841, never having forgotten the slight inflicted by Lord Melbourne upon his own nominee, Lord Heytesbury, in 1835. Seven years later he died from an apoplectic seizure while shooting in Hampshire ; and except for the Eden Gardens, which Calcutta owed to the liberality of his sisters, and for his own statue, inscribed with an almost fantastic panegyric, his name in that city is forgotten.

The Court of Directors, with almost complete unanimity, sent out Lord Ellenborough in his place, and the knowledge of Indian affairs possessed by that statesman, who had already three times been President of the Board of Control, combined with his brilliant abilities and powers of speech, must have been regarded by them as guarantees of a certain success. Perhaps the worst omen that was forthcoming was provided by his own parting speech at the India House, where he defined his mission as being " to restore peace to Asia "—neither the first nor the last time in Indian history when such a boast by an outgoing ruler has been the presage of immediate and sanguinary wars.

Arriving at Calcutta on 28th February, 1842—the last Governor General to come out from England in a frigate by the Cape route—he was met by his predecessor at the *bottom* of the steps (a solitary departure, if the report be not mistaken, from the established precedent), and the

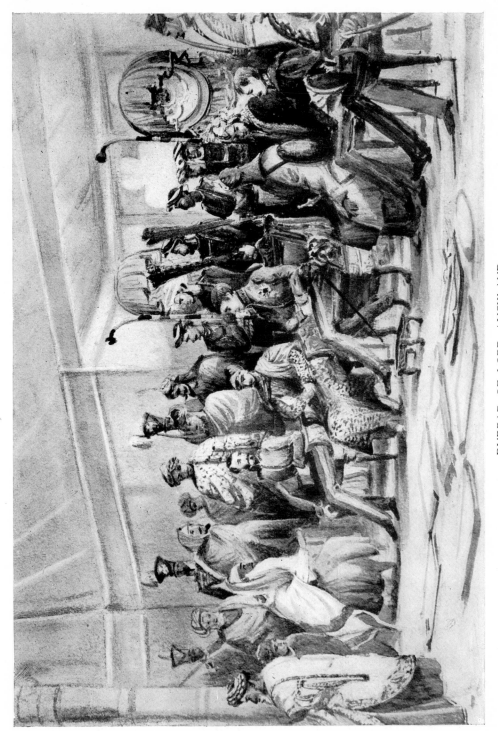

DURBAR OF LORD AUCKLAND

From the drawing by Miss Emily Eden.

two satraps with the ladies lived together in Government House for a fortnight, during which there can have been no phase of the Afghan situation, where the tide of disaster had already turned, that was not discussed between them.   In view of this friendly interchange, Auckland was indignant at the manner in which Ellenborough subsequently attacked and flouted his administration.

Ellenborough soon got to work in his own peculiar way, for which India and a series of campaigns provided an excellent opening ; and the military parade at Ferozepore, in honour of the returning troops, when the arches collapsed and the elephants bolted, was not more ridiculous than the bombastic proclamation about the Somnath Gates, which the Governor General wrote himself and published at Simla, without consultation with his Council and against the advice of some of his colleagues, followed by the triumphant procession of the fraudulent trophies to India.   I have myself been both to Somnath, from the Hindu shrine at which place the gates of sandalwood were declared to have been originally torn ; to Ghazni, where they were said to have adorned the tomb of Sultan Mahmud ; and to the place in the Fort at Agra, where in dishonoured obscurity they now repose.   They never were at Somnath, they are not Hindu in character or workmanship, they are not made of sandalwood but of pine and deodar, and they are a patchwork of late Mohammedan fabrication.   Such was the character of the trophies that were intended to be the lasting memorial of the Ellenborough reign.   Well might Macaulay say in the House of Commons on 9th March, 1843 : " We have sometimes sent them Governors whom they loved, and sometimes Governors whom they feared, but they never before had a Governor at whom they laughed." Even the Duke of Wellington, who was a firm friend of Ellenborough and sided openly with him in his final downfall, found the Somnath Proclamation and the Ferozepore parade too much for him ; and when Greville told him of Ellenborough's dispositions for the latter, at which the Indian Army was to be arranged in the form of a star, with the guns at the point of each ray, and a throne for himself in the centre, the old warrior broke out—" And he ought to sit upon it in a strait-waistcoat." [1]

In the pages of Greville we may read a good deal about the chorus

[1] Greville," Memoirs of the Reign of Queen Victoria " (1837–1852), Vol. II, p. 139.

of condemnation that burst forth in England when the escapades of the Governor General became known :

"Ellenborough is certainly not happy in his measures, his manners or his phrases. He began by his much abused orders for retreat, he lost no time in quarrelling with his Council, and making himself personally obnoxious, and his present Proclamation is very objectionable in many respects."[1]

Auckland, with a vivid recollection of these conversations in Government House, thought that Ellenborough was mad from the moment of landing in India. He had told Auckland that he meant to "come Aurungzeb over them," and that he intended to "turn the old Royal Family out of the palace at Delhi and convert it into a residence for himself."

These impressions were somewhat mitigated by the appearance of the Parliamentary Blue Book in February 1843, in which Ellenborough argued his case with great ability, but they were further confirmed by his subsequent conduct.

The annexation of Sind, which few have been found to condone, followed the victories in Afghanistan ; and all the time the temper of the Directors at home was steadily rising, aggravated by the insubordinate and hectoring tone in which they were addressed by their Governor General. The Duke of Wellington, who on more than one occasion seems to have exercised an arbitral and sagacious influence in such matters, warned the Governor General of the gathering storm, and blamed him for his long absence from the seat of Government— among other follies he accompanied Sir Hugh Gough's army in the field against the Mahrattas, and narrowly escaped being shot on the battlefield of Maharajpore (28th December, 1843)—and Ellenborough himself was conscious that recall was in the air. There was an exchange of heated amenities between the Governor General and the Court, in which the former declined to resign, and challenged the Directors to remove him.

Finally, in June 1844, they took him at his word, and the Governor General, though supported by the Board of Control, was ordered by the unanimous vote of the Court to return. Apart from the histrionic escapades to which I have referred, Ellenborough, by identifying himself at every stage with the Army and with military policy, had not

---

[1] Greville, "Memoirs of the Reign of Queen Victoria" (1837–1852), Vol. II, p. 125.

LORD ELLENBOROUGH

From the painting by F. R. Say.

merely alienated but exasperated the European Civil Service,[1] and although he was much esteemed by the Army, whose side he had so openly espoused,[2] his departure was witnessed without regret. That his errors sprang, not from accident or ill-fortune, but from a congenital lack of self-restraint and an overweening temper, was shown not merely by the incidents which I have recorded, but by the events of fourteen years later, when, again without consulting his Cabinet colleagues, he sent his notorious Despatch of 8th May, 1858, to Lord Canning upon the confiscation of the soil of Oudh, and was obliged in consequence to resign his place in the Government.

With better judgment and less vanity Ellenborough might have been a considerable ruler : for he had conspicuous talents, and I remember Mr. Gladstone telling me that he thought him the best speaker of his day in the House of Lords. As it is, he was the shortest-lived and the least successful of all the Governors General. Nor was it out of keeping with his own erratic character and career, that his second wife, after being divorced from him, should have married a Bedouin sheikh, and taken up her abode in an Arab camp near Damascus.

Ellenborough was succeeded by his brother-in-law, Sir Henry Hardinge. The Government and the Court were agreed in thinking that the situation in India required military experience ; and they accordingly sent out to India the most capable soldier-politician at their disposal. Hardinge was indeed a doughty warrior, for he had already been present at sixteen battles (he was now fifty-nine years of age) and had lost a hand at Ligny. Moreover, on the civil side he had sat for many years in the House of Commons, and had there been Secretary of State for War. He was the first Governor General to go out by the Overland Route, halting in Egypt on the way, where he was received with honour by Mehemet Ali at Alexandria and by Ibrahim Pasha at Cairo. He arrived in the Hugli on 22nd July, 1844, but the customary misadventures prevented him from stepping ashore at Chandpal Ghat, where a great crowd was awaiting him, and he had to be driven from Garden Reach, the guns at Fort William not announcing that a new Governor General had taken office until 8.30 p.m.

---

[1] In the Nerbudda territories he had dismissed the entire body of Civil Servants and replaced them by military officers.

[2] For this reason the Duke of Wellington steadily supported him, and, when he was recalled by the Court, described their act as " a gross political outrage."

Three out of the four years of Hardinge's tenure of office (he was made a peer after Sobraon in 1846) were spent away from Calcutta, and accordingly the seat of Government saw less of him than of almost any Governor General. But what they saw they liked, and he left the impression of being a hard-working, common-sense, and unassuming man, who did what was expected of him with integrity and credit.

That he should have been permitted to accompany Sir Hugh Gough in the First Sikh War and even to exercise a secondary command on the battlefield, was, in my judgment, wholly improper; and the feeble defence of the step that was offered by Lord Ripon, who was then President of the Board of Control, affords no justification. The latter thus wrote on 24th February, 1846:

" It has a very strange and somewhat unseemly appearance that the Governor General should be acting as Second-in-Command to the Commander-in-Chief in the field; and as these Punjab affiars are, and must necessarily be, so much mixed up with political matters, it is quite reasonable that the same head should direct both."

The Government therefore proposed to send to Hardinge the same Commission of Captain General and Commander-in-Chief that had been given to Lord Wellesley in 1800. Later on, so much technical difficulty was experienced in drawing up the Letters Patent that it was decided, on the suggestion of the Duke of Wellington, to send out a Letter of Service from the Queen enabling the Governor General as Lieutenant General on the Staff to command personally the troops in India. Before, however, this letter had been despatched, Sobraon (10th February, 1846), at which Hardinge was present, although he did not as at Firozeshah command a wing of the army, had been fought, Lahore had been entered, and the campaign was over. In 1846, when Sir Robert Peel, whose friend and follower he was, went out of office, Hardinge was tempted to resign. But the Government asked him to stay on. In 1848, however, having completed his task, he sought leave to retire. It would have been better for his reputation as a prophet, though it would not have been in accord with tradition, if he had not upon leaving declared in a public speech that " it would not be necessary to fire a gun again in India for seven years." He did not realise the quality of the ruler by whom he was to be succeeded.

On 11th November, 1847, there had left England in H.M.S. " Sidon " the youngest man since Wellesley to take up the rôle which the elderly soldier was laying down.[1]   At Cairo he was received with almost regal honours and lodged in a palace of the old Pasha Ibrahim. The Company's ship " Moozuffer " took him on from Suez.   The old *Sonamukhi*, as it was towed up the Hugli behind the " Moozuffer," performed its usual trick of nearly swamping ; and the new Governor General had to land in a common *baulia* or country boat.   After he had taken the oath, as he gaily remarked in a letter home :

" For the first three days the outgoing Governor General feasts the incoming man ; for the next three days, or as long as he stays, the Governor General in the present tense is host to him who has reached the praeter-pluperfect. So on the next day I gave the same great dinner to Lord Hardinge that he had given to me : all the same people, whisker for whisker among the gentlemen, pin for pin among the ladies.   Then came Sunday and we sat together in the Cathedral under the same canopy."

The young man, not then thirty-six years of age, who had thus taken over, was James Andrew Broun Ramsay, Earl of Dalhousie, who in the course of the next eight years was destined to leave a mark upon India inferior to none of his predecessors, and to acquire a reputation second only to that of Warren Hastings.   The career of Dalhousie did, indeed, provoke at the time and has ever since aroused, though in a diminishing degree as time has proceeded, a controversy that recalls the fate of his famous predecessor.   The formidable figures of Gough and Napier, whom he encountered and overthrew, the forceful personality of the two Lawrences, whom he alternately conciliated and coerced, the tremendous sweep of his territorial acquisitions, and the range of his administrative reforms, the masterful character of the man himself, and the appalling nature of the convulsion with which India was shaken to its foundations almost immediately after his retirement, and which might, not without plausibility, be in some measure regarded as the consequence of his rule—all of these combined to make the reign of Dalhousie a theme of legitimate and even embittered disputation which did not die down till long after the subject of the controversy, at once too ill and too proud to defend himself, was in the grave.   The protagonists in this furious polemic, Sir John Kaye and Edwin Arnold on the one side, the Duke of Argyll and Sir Charles Louis Jackson on

[1] An old aunt, when Dalhousie announced his appointment, replied with curt brevity : " My dear James, I received your letter on your appointment. Although I cannot think you fit for it, I nevertheless send you my congratulations."

the other, filled the arena with their vehement denunciation or defence. Later, the ranks of the defenders were strengthened by the powerful aid of Captain L. J. Trotter, Sir William Hunter, and Sir Richard Temple, while the biographer of Sir John Lawrence held a midway position between. Dalhousie himself looked for his vindication to the subsequent publication of his own papers and correspondence, although, with a self-restraint that perhaps had in it more of dignity than of wisdom, he left in his will a direction that " no portion of his private papers should be made public until at least fifty years after his death."

In the year 1904, six years before the stipulated half-century had expired, these secret sources of information having been entrusted by the Dalhousie family to the late Sir W. Lee Warner, the latter brought out the " Life of the Marquis of Dalhousie " in two volumes. Even so, but little use was made of the private correspondence in which Dalhousie while in India abundantly indulged, particularly with his great friend Sir George Couper, with whom he exchanged letters by nearly every mail for eight years ; and it was reserved for the husband of one of the grand-daughters of the Governor General to give a selection from these to the world in a further volume in 1910.[1] For the first time, therefore, assuming that these two publications have made a fair and representative use of the immense mass of material upon which they were founded, we are able to apply to Dalhousie's character and administration the test which he himself desired. The question that the modern writer will put to himself and to his readers is accordingly this—how does the Governor General emerge from the ordeal ?

Sir W. Lee Warner's volumes are more in the nature of a speech of Counsel for the defence than they are of a judicial summing up, although they have done much to vindicate the high place in the estimation of his countrymen which has been assigned to Dalhousie by an ever-increasing consensus of expert authority. As for the Letters, it is only fair to remember that they represent the eager and often contradictory outpourings of an impatient spirit, finding in the confidential intercourse with a lifelong friend the outlet for sentiments and emotions—even for prejudices and passions—which he dared confess to no one else, and which he never intended for publication, either early or late.

---

[1] " Private Letters of the Marquis of Dalhousie " (ed. J.G. Baird), 1910.

Indeed, I cannot help doubting if Dalhousie would himself have authorised the appearance of some of the series, although we are informed by
the Editor that many of the most outspoken communications have been
purposely withheld.   The letters are in reality more in the nature of a
personal document than a political *dossier* ; and they reveal to us, with
a candour that is at times almost terrifying, the struggles and ambitions,
the tempers and the trials, of one of the most ardent but sensitive spirits
that ever wielded supreme authority.   If I here anticipate my final
opinion that in revealing his foibles they also establish his essential
greatness, I shall not be suspected, when I quote from them, of being
desirous to wrest a verdict either in one direction or the other.

Let us first follow the Governor General in the main controversies
by which his reign was disturbed.   We have in previous chapters seen
the uncompromising directness with which he expressed himself on
every subject that came under his penetrating and remorseless eye, and
shall not therefore be surprised at the occasional acerbity of tone.
Moreover, let it always be remembered that Dalhousie came out to
India with an overwhelming but in no sense an egotistical sense of
the dignity of his position, of the political mission which it was his duty
to discharge, and of the obligation incumbent upon him to "stand
no nonsense" from any community, class, council or individual that
was disposed to thwart his deliberately conceived and righteous plans.
Hence a disposition on his part to scent opposition even where not
intended, and to put a possible antagonist in his proper place with the
least possible delay.   His conflicts with his two Commanders-in-Chief
are typical of these predilections.   But they also reveal a claim to dictate
and even control the military dispositions and operations of the Indian
Army and its chief, which I do not hesitate to say that no modern Viceroy
would dream of attempting, and which must have rendered hearty
co-operation very difficult, particularly with so fiery a Paladin as Sir
Charles Napier.

When in the course of the Second Sikh War Lord Gough was
desirous to advance, the Governor General thus addressed him (17th
December, 1848) :

"Your Excellency is responsible for the Army ; I am responsible for the
Empire ; and it is on my head if everything is not done or forbidden which
the general interest of that vast charge requires.   I need not repeat the grounds
on which I rested my injunction to your Lordship not to advance.   They are

very fully set forth in my letter of the 27th ultimo.   The injunction was based upon certain circumstances, and in its terms required that you should not advance *without previous communication with me.*" [1]

In a letter, five days later, to Sir George Couper, Dalhousie defends the above injunction, and adds—

" I hope this will satisfy H.E.   If not he shall obey my orders, when I know I am right, whether he likes it or not.   We have been very good friends hitherto, and, as far as I am concerned, it shall continue so ; but, as I have said before, there can't be two masters here and shan't be." [2]

On 13th January, 1849, Lord Gough fought the doubtful and costly action of Chilianwalla, about which the Governor General wrote on the 22nd to the Duke of Wellington as follows :

" The conduct of this action is beneath the criticism even of a militiaman like myself.   I need therefore say nothing about it to you.   In public I make, of course, the best of things ; I treat it as a great victory.   But writing confidentially to you I do not hesitate to say that I consider my position grave. I have put into the field in the Punjab a force fit to match all India.   In the hands of the Commander-in-Chief I do not now *consider that force safe* or free from the risk of disaster." [3]

To me, I confess, it does not appear at all surprising that the Home Government, on receipt of this letter, should at once have recalled Lord Gough.   But what is surprising is that, when the news reached India, the Governor General should have expressed both astonishment and indignation, should have declared that the recall was a surrender to panic, and have protested that he had never recommended it.   What he really resented in the matter was the interference of the Home authorities with a prerogative which he thought belonged to, and ought only to have been exercised by, himself.

Nevertheless Dalhousie, whose explosions were essentially evanescent, and who had a genuine regard for his Commander-in-Chief, was soon found declaring, particularly after the victory at Guzerat :

" The old Chief and I are all right again.   We have agreed to kiss and be friends ; and we are both glad of it, I believe."

A little later Gough is "a fine old fellow" and a "genuine old fellow"; and the two parted on the best of terms—which is perhaps

---

[1] " Life," Vol. I, pp. 200-1.   [2] " Private Letters," p. 40.   [3] " Life," Vol. I, p. 209.

not strange, seeing that after Guzerat, which terminated the campaign, the Commander-in-Chief was made a Viscount and the Governor General a Marquis, and that both were covered with well-earned glory.

Gough was grateful for the magnanimity with which he had been treated by Dalhousie in the concluding stages ; and his biographer and apologist pays this handsome tribute to the latter's generosity :

" In his sorrow (*i.e.* at being superseded by Sir C. Napier) Gough derived no small comfort from the gentle and considerate kindness which he received from his successor and from the Governor General.   With Lord Dalhousie anger never degenerated into malice, and the past had left on his mind no trace of bitterness and no consciousness of injury received or done.   He ordered that during Lord Gough's stay in India he should receive all the honour that had been his due as Commander-in-Chief, and he was unremitting in his efforts to show him all possible deference." [1]

Sir Charles Napier was a much tougher nut to crack ; and anyone who knew the character of the two men might have foreseen trouble and even disaster.   This is not the place in which to re-open that historic engagement in which Napier put himself in the wrong from the start, and in which Dalhousie, in his vindication of the civil as against the military authority, received the unflinching support of the Duke of Wellington, the Court of Directors, and the Home Government—a support which at a later date was denied to at least one of his successors. But the personal incidents of the encounter, which are for the first time revealed in the published Letters, are of value in the light that they throw upon the character and methods of the Governor General.

Already, when Napier's appointment was announced, Dalhousie had written to his friend in terms that recall his admonitions to Lord Gough :

" He shall have full military authority and shall have every confidence and support from me in those military duties which belong to him ; but, by George, he shall not interfere with me in Civil matters, or touch them with the point of his beard." [2]

At the same time Dalhousie had promised the Duke of Wellington, and he honestly intended, to get on with the fiery veteran who now arrived in India, and their honeymoon relations were for a brief period

[1] " Life and Campaigns of Viscount Gough," by R. S. Rait, Vol. II, p. 299.
[2] " Private Letters," p. 70.

all that could be desired. But already the clouds were rolling up on the horizon, and presently they burst in a prodigious storm. Napier, hot-headed, alarmist, and extravagant, could not stand the restraint that was placed by the Indian Government, and the Governor General in particular, on his military movements ; he profoundly mistrusted the administration of the politicals, especially in the Punjab, and he disagreed altogether with Dalhousie in his estimate of the Indian political situation. But he was in the grip of an antagonist just as intrepid, far abler, and much more tenacious than himself ; and the end was certain. When the Commander-in-Chief issued his celebrated Order with regard to compensation to the native troops for the dearness of provisions, suspending, without the sanction or knowledge of the Governor General, the Regulations which had been promulgated by Lords Hardinge and Gough, and declared he would do it again, the rupture was complete. Dalhousie thus wrote on 16th April, 1850 :

" I have told him that consideration of these papers makes it necessary for me to say for H.E.'s future guidance that I will not permit the C.-in-C. under any circumstances to issue orders affecting the pay of the Army in India, and so to exercise an authority which does not belong to him, and which has been reserved, and most properly reserved, for the Supreme Government alone. He will be furious, I daresay, but I have him on the hip." [1]

Napier resigned ; and his resignation was at once accepted by the Government at home, who, together with the Court of Directors, unswervingly supported the Governor General. But the final exchange of compliments between the two protagonists was of the most vitriolic description ; and when Napier, in a State paper, quoted from Dalhousie's private letters, the latter thus exploded to Couper :

" It is the act of a blackguard to begin with ; and the act of a fool in this case, for they ludicrously contradict all that he calls them to prove." [2]

The disappearance of Napier did not bring unruffled peace to the military arena, for a little later we find the Governor General having a tiff with Sir Colin Campbell, then in command at Peshawar, giving him a piece of his mind, and telling Couper that " I have with difficulty abstained from forthwith removing him from his command, and unless he eats his words I will do so now." And even the new Commander-in-Chief, Sir William Gomm, whom Dalhousie calls Gummidge, and

---

[1] " Private Letters," p. 121.   [2] *Ibid.*, p. 152.

describes as " quiescent and acquiescent," is soon depicted as " growing very unsatisfactory," although " he submits the moment I show a tooth or growl never so gently, but he tries it on when he ought not to do so."

These pleasantries must not be too gravely regarded, for they represent the vicissitudes of a situation and the ebullitions of a temper that varied from week to week and almost from day to day.   But it may be interesting to follow them into the Civil domain, and to see how the despotic little Governor General fared with his colleagues in India and his official superiors at home.   Here we shall note the same mingling of a rather fretful impatience with bursts of sincere and generous emotion.

It may seem strange that of the two Lawrence brothers Dalhousie should have got on with the masterful and practical John, who shared many of his own characteristics and with whom he ended by being on terms of the most intimate familiarity, while he failed either to attract or to be attracted by the finer and more idealistic spirit of Henry. The first collision between the two men arose out of the milk-and-water Proclamation with which Henry Lawrence proposed to open his career as Resident at Lahore in the early part of 1849.   Lee Warner gives the text of Dalhousie's letter to Lawrence,[1] Baird gives the simultaneous explanation to Couper.[2]

" I told him this sort of thing would not do at all ; that I had great confidence in him, but that I could not permit him to substitute himself for the Government whose servant he was, or permit a word to be said or an act done which would raise the notion that the policy of the Government depended in any degree on the agent who represented it. . . . I ended by forbidding this Proclamation at all, and desiring that nothing should be said or done without my approval. . . . Lawrence has been greatly praised and rewarded and petted, and no doubt naturally supposes himself a King of the Punjab ; but as I don't take the Brentford dynasty as a pattern, I object to sharing the chairs, and think it best to come to an understanding as to relative positions at once.   It will soon be settled."

When, after annexation, Lawrence did not much like the creation of the Board of Advice which the Governor General had set up, in order to avoid what he considered " the greater evil of a sole authority vested in Sir H. L.," Dalhousie explained to Couper :

" He has tried restiveness once or twice.   Upon this I tipped him a little of the 'Grand Seigneur,' which I had not given him before, and the storm sank into a whisper in a second."[1]

The fact is that Dalhousie never understood or really liked Henry Lawrence, whose qualities were in such sharp contrast to his own, and of whose paper on Sir Charles Napier in the "Calcutta Review" of 1854 he wrote:

"It is a transcript of the character of the man—with undoubted ability, plenty of energy, and a good deal of power, but scrambling, unconnected, and losing half its force from total want of method and arrangement."[2]

It was certain that so forceful a personality as the Governor General would not have relations of unbroken tranquillity with the President of the Board of Control, or with the Company at home; and though Dalhousie was far too wise to quarrel openly with either, and generally retained their support by adopting in his semi-official correspondence a tone of reasonable conciliation, the ears of both would have tingled had they been acquainted with some of his more confidential impressions. Sir John Cam Hobhouse, the President, afterwards Lord Broughton, had great experience and was not quarrelsome, and Dalhousie ended by feeling for him a warm esteem. But there were anxious moments in the interval. When they disagreed over Gough and Chilianwalla, in which affair I have already said that in my judgment Dalhousie was in the wrong, Hobhouse's letter was described to Couper as "insolent and ungentlemanlike in the worst degree." A few weeks later Hobhouse is "very civil and obliging." Two months pass, and "I despise him and consequently nobody can expect me to forget what has passed and be a familiar friend. If I correspond with him freely, treat him with irreproachable civility and perform all the demi-official duties of my office as before, nobody has a right to demand for him from me inward respect or regard." In another four months: "Sir John Hobhouse is very civil now and is supporting my views against those of the Court"—no doubt the correct explanation of the latest veering of the Indian vane. This genial phase continues, and so amiable are the relations that when, two years later, Hobhouse, now Lord Broughton, seems likely to go, Dalhousie with happy forgetfulness can write (21st February, 1852): "I greatly fear I shall lose Lord Broughton. I know he is not held highly; but, with the exception of one tiff in 1849

---

[1] "Private Letters," p. 78.   [2] *Ibid.*, p. 295.

about Lord Gough, we have got on admirably. He has been a fast friend to me and, so far as I know, has always supported my views and fought my battles. I shall therefore regret him."

These fluctuations of attitude and utterance are probably to be found in the relations of every Viceroy and Secretary of State, though rarely given to the world. They illustrate, not so much the temperament of the individuals concerned, as the inherent difficulties of the two-headed system, which not even the electric telegraph has since availed to overcome. There were the same ups and downs in the intercourse of Lord Dalhousie with Hobhouse's successor, Sir C. Wood. In June 1854, " he has written me in a very disagreeable style, quite unlike his usual courteous tone. . . . It galls one to be rated by a man whom you feel to be so much inferior to you." In September, "I can't say I like Sir C. Wood as well as they did at the India House, or as I did at first. He is fidgety and meddlesome. Under him it is not the Board of Control it was meant to be, but a Board of Interference, which it was not meant to be." In October the speeches and despatches of Wood are "nothing but personal claptrap." But in April of the following year, when Wood too has gone, the Governor General writes to his relative, Lord Panmure : "It has vexed me very much to lose Sir C. Wood from the India Board. A change at all, just at this time in my last months, would have been unpalatable ; but Sir C. Wood has treated me with confidence and frankness—he was a very honest worker, sincerely interested in his duties ; and thus his transfer is a personal loss to me, as well as a detriment to the public service in India." [1]

Upon this harmonious chord it is well that the matter should have ended. The references by the rather irritable little man in India to the Court of Directors in England, in spite of his ostensibly correct relations with them, are however more acrid and at times diverting. In May 1850, when Dalhousie is evidently in a bad humour, he spits the following fire :

" I despise both the understanding of the Court and its political conduct as a body, whatever the members may be individually ; for I need not tell you, who have lived sixty years in the world, that the conduct of a gentleman in his own room and the same gentleman as member of a body are widely divergent." [2]

---

[1] " Life," Vol. II, p. 56.   [2] " Private Letters," p. 124.

In December 1851, after receiving a Despatch from the Court which he did not relish, he bursts out :

" The fact is these Despatches are penned for the most part by head clerks and signed by many without being read and by all *as members of a body.* The penmen—d . . . . d fellows who do the mechanical work which others sign— fancy themselves the hidden springs by which this Empire is in reality moved, and they write in a tone which no Secretary of State would address to the Lt. Governor of the bulls and bisons in the Falkland Islands." [1]

Here it may be remarked that the tone of the India Office to its chief representative in India has not always, even in modern times, been beyond reproach.

In 1853, when the Court had asked Dalhousie to stay on in India— in granting which request he thought that he was doing them a much greater favour than they were offering to him—there is an outpouring of exceptional bitterness :

" Honoured I have been in India and rewarded—highly, richly ; but by my Sovereign, not by the East India Company. To them I owe nothing— not even civility. There is more warm and cordial praise in any one single despatch to my predecessor during '45-'46, when the public voice here will tell you he jeopardised their Empire, than in all their despatches to me put together ; though I have already added four ancient sovereignties and about two millions of fresh annual revenue to their territorial rent-roll. I ask nothing from them and expect nothing, but I am not disposed to bear myself as though I was favoured in continuing to be their Governor General." [2]

It is only fair to add that the writer of these words went on to say that they had " never been penned or uttered before to mortal — except to my wife," and that they were " made to the confidence of an old friend alone." Finally, when in 1856 Dalhousie is on his ship steaming down the Bay of Bengal, the spleen of the departing satrap finds vent in the following outburst :

" I have left India without receiving one word of thanks or civility from the Court of Directors or from H.M. Government. For two mails before I ceased to be G.G. the Chairman did not write to me at all. For one mail I received no letter from the President of the Board of Control. After I ceased to be G.G. I had letters from each, but not a civil word from either." [3]

Dalhousie was not the only Governor General who might have made or did make a similar complaint ; we have already heard the same

---

[1] " Private Letters," p. 184.   [2] *Ibid.*, p. 241.   [3] *Ibid.*, pp. 371-2.

accents from other lips ; and if the foregoing excerpts reveal a nature hypersensitive and at times querulous, they nevertheless have their value, not only in the light that they throw upon the personality of the man, but also in their revelation to the British people, who are apt to picture a Viceroy's career as one of effortless and equable splendour, of the real conditions under which he labours and the mortal anxieties by which he is sometimes oppressed.

Sir George Couper more than once rebuked his excitable correspondent for a warmth of expression which he felt might, in letters to others who knew or loved him less, make them think that he was of an over-anxious and unstable temperament. Dalhousie's reply, in so far as his letters to Couper were concerned, was that he treated his two greatest friends at home, Couper and Fox Maule (afterwards Lord Panmure), as a safety valve through which he could blow off the feelings that could be expressed to no others. When Couper said that the Directors endorsed the criticism, Dalhousie retorted in one of his most characteristic passages :

" It is quite true that I have refused to allow the Court to insult me as they were used to insult my predecessors. It is quite true that I have not allowed them to blame me when I was right, and to tell me that ' they desire the G.-G. will forthwith ' undo something which he had done, which he was perfectly right in doing, and which they were forced ultimately to confirm, simply because it *was* right. It is quite true that I have not allowed the *clerks* of the house, who word the despatches which the Directors sign (with that carelessness which makes the collective members of a Joint Stock Company do what no individual gentleman among them would do), to address me as no well-bred gentleman would address his gamekeeper. All this is true. It is true also that when such things have been attempted, I have resented, resisted and overcome them. It is true that thus I have refused to allow them at home to treat me as my predecessors often were treated—that is as though I were no more than a head clerk. *They* call this ' over-sensitiveness.' I call it a proper and politic maintenance of the authority of a mighty office, whose responsibilities are in danger of being increased, its character lowered, and its usefulness marred, by the undue assumption and vulgar expression of a disproportionate authority at home." [1]

At this stage it is pertinent to mention that Dalhousie suffered throughout his Indian career from an ill-health that may have partially explained his fretfulness, but that rendered his ubiquitous and manifold

[1] " Private Letters," p. 326.

2—O

exertions truly heroic. In one letter, as early as July 1849, he declared that he was broken in health when he started from England, and that he had landed in Calcutta an invalid, almost a cripple, and had seldom been free from pain. There was some slight exaggeration in this; but as time passed and he refused to spare himself, he became a prey to a lamentable combination of maladies : ulceration of the mouth, ending some years later in almost complete loss of voice; lameness in the right leg, which, accelerated by more than one accident, developed into an open and incurable sore or canker of the shin-bone; frequent attacks in the head and other members of what was then called ' tic '—and many subsidiary ailments. An interesting and pathetic account of these sufferings and of the splendid fortitude with which they were borne is contained in a book by Dalhousie's surgeon in India, Dr. Alexander Grant, known to his friends as Sandy Grant, for whom he cherished a warm regard.[1] And it is not too much to say that on every day of the eight years which he devoted to India, the life-blood of this indomitable man was drop by drop being drawn away. There were times, during the middle part of his service, when he represented himself as free from trouble and stronger than ever. But these phases only tempted him to exertions which were beyond his strength; and the hardships of his prolonged tours, pursued under conditions of fatigue and exposure from which the perfectly organised processions of the modern Viceroy are completely immune, were largely responsible for the final collapse both of his own health and that of his wife. Unable to leave the country himself, owing to the unfeeling law that denied to the rulers of India any return to England during their tenure of office, Dalhousie sought in prolonged journeys, at one time to Chini in the Himalayas on the border of Tibet, at another to the Nilgherries, at another to Ceylon and the Straits Settlements, or again to Arakan and Burma, the relief which could never be found in India itself. These excursions may have retarded, they could not avert, the inevitable doom.

But for his partner no such respite was to be allowed. The sufferings of Lady Dalhousie in India and her uncomplaining endurance were scarcely inferior to his own. Leaving their young family at home in order to share with him the toilsome burden of the Indian throne, she was the consort of all his troubles as well as his triumphs, or, as he himself expressed it, " my only friend, and my only companion in this

[1] " Physician and Friend " (ed. Dr. G. Smith), 1902.

country." In 1852 she had been ordered to return to England, but not being strong enough to stand the journey, was sent to Ceylon instead, whence she returned to Calcutta but little improved in health. Finally, in January 1853, she sailed for England ; and the feelings and the letters of the lonely husband recall, alike in their desolation and in their devotion, the already quoted experiences of Warren and Marian Hastings seventy years before. But for Dalhousie was reserved no happy meeting at home, no resumption of a serene married existence, no tranquil march hand in hand down the lengthening vale of years. As her vessel entered the Bristol Channel the gentle spirit fled from the frail body, wasted by sea-sickness and already enfeebled by five years of India ; and the desolate husband poured forth the anguish of his soul to his old friend in England in accents that even now bring tears :

" I do not know whether I submit in deed and in truth. I try to do so, and try to pray to be able to do so. But I feel all the severity of the scourge, and feel, too, that the circumstances which attend the chastisement have added scorpions to the lash. The severance of two souls bound together ' till death shall them part ' is the bitterest drop in the cup of mortality. But to be called upon to drink it suddenly when comforting my loneliness by anticipations of the joy of mother and children reunited, to see her who had battled with and conquered so many perils sink under no distemper, but from the very sea that all thought was to be her restoration—to hear of her children looking upon her face again, but dead—to hear of her return to her home, but only to the grave—surely, surely God will pardon me if, for a time, I feel it almost too hard to bear.

" It is done. I pray God I may say in truth ' Let it be so '—if one may dare to adopt the words, ' Not as I will, but as Thou wilt.' I shall not again revert to this miserable topic, but my whole future is shivered by it." [1]

This passage, which if it has not been too sacred to publish, it is not too sacred to quote, brings me to an aspect of Dalhousie's character which might not be readily inferred from the very human character of its ordinary demonstrations, but which is of profound value in the testimony offered to its combined purity and strength. Who could doubt that the writer of the following lines was not merely a great patriot and a great statesman, but also a true Christian ?

" You say that I have cause for thankfulness that the blessing has rested on my administration. Most true ; and I am deeply—devoutly—thankful.

[1] " Private Letters," p. 257.

It is my belief that the blessing has so rested for four reasons : 1st, Because I have never undertaken anything which in my soul I did not believe to be honestly right ; 2nd, Because when I had once resolved upon it, I fought with all my human might and main to accomplish it; 3rd, Because I always wished, and I believe I seldom failed, to ask God's blessing on the fight ; and, 4th, Because I have *never* failed, publicly and privately, to give Him the glory when all was done. I know very well that I am no better than my neighbours—worse than many of them and good for nothing at all in His pure sight ; but He has said, ' Ask and ye shall receive,' and having done so through my public life, in which, with no extraordinary abilities, I have gained as much reputation and honour as most men at 42, I feel implicit faith in that Refuge, and feel no wish to escape from India ' lest something should go very wrong ' and mar the fairness of the past."[1]

And now that I have said so much about the personal and human attributes of this very exceptional man, as shown in his own correspondence, let me pass to the impression that he left upon his contemporaries and to his place among the British rulers of the Indian Empire.

Expende Hannibalem ! Quot libras in duce summo
Invenies ?

The very weaknesses and foibles of which we have witnessed his unpremeditated betrayal, are also a key to the qualities that make him superlatively great as an administrator and ruler of men. His impetuosity was the reflex aspect of a spirit that was never satisfied until it had attained its goal ; his assertiveness and self-confidence were the endowments that enabled him to drive the chariot with such unrelenting force ; his somewhat dictatorial nature secured for him the unquestioning allegiance of those who comprehended his purpose and were proud to subserve his lofty ambitions.

But first let us see what manner of appearance was presented—to use his oft-repeated designation—by the Laird of Cockpen. For the obligations of his family, his race, his birth and birthplace were the goads that were always spurring him on. Small of stature but erect of mien, with a fine head, a lofty forehead, and clear unquestioning eyes, he wore an air of unchallengeable command, and was recognised even by those who trembled at his nod as a king of men. He always knew more about a subject than the acknowledged experts, he had a carefully thought out plan for every emergency—the result not of a hasty inspiration, but of a profound study and a balanced foresight.

---

[1] "Private Letters," p. 309.

Even his faults, it has been remarked, were those not of a small man but of a great man.

Where he erred, it was from a certain hardness of texture that prevented him, though far from lacking in sympathy, from realising the human side of the problems of Government, and making sufficient allowance for the susceptibilities and weaknesses of others.   His quickness of temper sometimes led him into passing injustice—" the Lord Sahib is a pepper-pot," remarked Sir John Peter Grant—but it was injustice of utterance rather than of thought or deed ; and his capacity for wrath, which was great, was compatible with real magnanimity. The parallel or rival gift of equanimity, which was the glory of Warren Hastings as it was of Dalhousie's successor Canning, he certainly did not possess.   His dignity enjoined him to keep silence under calumny and abuse ; but he chafed visibly under the restraint.

Accordingly, while Dalhousie won the love of the few, he appealed with overpowering force to the admiration of the many ; but it was an admiration tempered by awe.   Sir James Outram told Dr. Grant that he had had interviews with the Duke of Wellington, Sir Robert Peel, and other leading statesmen in England, but that he never felt such awe or such a sense of inferiority as in his conversations with Lord Dalhousie.   When, at the moment of departure, the latter stepped on to the quay with death written in his eyes, all felt that there was disappearing a king in Israel.

To his subordinates Dalhousie was apt to be exacting and even severe ; and, as we have seen, he never shrank from a reprimand where he thought it called for.   He could expostulate but not plead ; he knew how to order but not how to cajole.   In all he said or did there was the ring of the military commander's voice, rapping out in tones of unassailable authority the generalissimo's orders to the officers or the battalions in the field.   But he had an infallible eye in the choice of these officers ; he collected around him and was faithfully served by an exceptional body of men ; and to these he gave not merely his support but his trust.

Among the many contemporary appreciations from which it might be possible for me to quote, I select the testimony of his physician, who, in a chapter of well-balanced eulogy, thus diagnosed the attributes and character of his Chief :

" His intellectual power was not unbalanced by any activity of heart, and many no doubt looked upon him with more of fear than of love ; but all coveted his praise, as it stamped deserving merit with the seal of valued recognition. . . . His high notions of duty and work, his inexhaustible and indomitable energy, were constantly the subject of remark in Indian society. . . . His ambition as a statesman burned with a pure flame.   He and Lord Wellesley will perhaps ever remain the most striking personages in the history of British India, for there lay something very spirited and fascinating in the policy and bearing of both—the same forethought governed by precaution, the same prompt decision, the same vivacity of style and precision of thought.   There was an instinct of sovereignty about them both, and they never discarded the state and personal consideration due to their position. . . . Lord Dalhousie's speeches were concise and clear, for he never cloaked his thoughts and opinions in ambiguous language. . . . Of all the members of the Supreme Council not one could approach him in skill and force of argument ; in writing his mind seemed to be overpowered by ideas and words. . . . He did not crave for popularity but sought to command it, for he was not so much indifferent to fame as assured of it. . . . He had a fiery, impulsive spirit which, controlled and disciplined, was productive of a harvest of good. . . . Although perhaps wanting in the genial nature which gives sway over equals among statesmen in England, he easily obtained authority, and at once took and kept the lead . . . for besides conciliation of manner and skilful amenity of language he had all the other qualities which attract and command attention.   Yet he was ready for any strife and never indulged in repose. . . . In business he was the most orderly of men ; no loose papers were ever seen on his desk ; he was so methodical that he never appeared hurried. . . . His habit of concentrated thought on any subject was indeed remarkable. He revolved it in his mind and, having thoroughly examined and thought it out—built it up, in fact—committed his views to paper clearly, rapidly, and without an erasure. . . . He had in some respects an intuitive knowledge of character; a rare faculty of penetrating and judging what was in men.   Having an instinctive sympathy for lofty aims, he sought out officers of this stamp and gave them his confidence. . . . He had . . . an unhesitating faith in his own judgment in whatever measure he undertook.   Thwarted, controlled, and restrained as he often was by the Home Authorities—especially the Board of Control—he never lost heart or yielded. . . . He had a powerful fancy and play of whimsical allusion ; he had also a keen sense of the ludicrous in persons and things, with a great deal of Scottish humour, making things doubly amusing by his way of saying them through a vein of mockery and grotesque exaggeration. . . He never, however, while in India admitted to anything approaching to great intimacy or companionship so as to encourage undue familiarity.   He was one with whom it was impossible to take a liberty. . . . He was the little man whom everyone feared, as was said of Nelson ; one felt in his presence a sort of awe, such a feeling as might be excited by the presence of a being of another nature.   Yet his manner was in general cordial, rarely official. . . . Like Pitt, he was perhaps too prone to feel and to show disdain ; yet his demeanour was generally gracious, and he had, more than any public man I ever saw, the kingly art of inspiring the greatest confidence, of instantly winning people of all classes ; it was the dominion which a strong will exerts at pleasure over feebler ones.   He seemed at times to be pleased and gratified by the admiration and the fear he alternately excited ; thus his praise was anxiously looked for, his censure deeply felt."[1]

I have quoted at unusual length this description, both because it is that of a witness who was brought into the closest daily contact with Dalhousie for many years, and also because it gives the fairest account that I know of the composite personality of this extraordinary man.

As an Imperial administrator Dalhousie was not inferior to the greatest of the great men whose genius for organisation has built the British Empire in the East.   He was splendid in his organisation of war, an Abraham Lincoln in the Orient.   But he was even more splendid in his organisation of peace ; and no sooner had he annexed a Province or confiscated a State than his plans for the new régime, elaborated in the most minute detail, were ready, and he began to erect the new structure almost before the débris of the old had been removed. Whether such a man, after his eight years of Indian autocracy, would ever have bent his neck to the yoke of official life in England, even though he had excelled in it in his pre-Indian career, is more than doubtful.   He himself again and again repudiated both the capacity and the desire.   Public life on a lower plane than that on which he had moved, and on what he considered the sordid stage of British politics, possessed for him no attraction.[2]   Whether the retention or the recovery of health would have altered his attitude it is impossible to say ; that he would have been willing to rust from idleness is unbelievable ; that some form of public service would have claimed his incomparable talents is more than likely.   While on his return journey he even discussed the possibility of accepting the War Office if offered to him, but this would only be on terms which he could hardly expect to be conceded : since he was, he confessed, " a curious compound of the radical and the despot."   That he would have re-entered a Cabinet or, had he done so, that he would have succeeded in showing that a

[1] " Physician and Friend," by Dr. A. Grant, Chap. IX *passim*.
[2] In May 1852 he wrote : " I am sick of public affairs, and especially of public men on all sides, and really am inclined to regard the career of a modern English statesman as an ungentlemanlike occupation, and therefore I have no temptation to engage in it again."   He said the same thing in August 1852, and again in July 1853.

Governor General of India can also be a Prime Minister of Great Britain seems to me improbable.

When he came out to India in 1848, Dalhousie did not contemplate more than the normal five years' reign. But the ever-expanding range both of his ambitions and his achievements, the combined pressure of the Government and the Directors in England—although, as we have seen, he despised the compliments of the latter—and above all his own exalted conception of public duty, compelled him twice to accept an extension, the first time for two years, and then again for a third, the Crimean War being the dominating reason on the last occasion. And even though he knew that he was signing his own death warrant by remaining on, his hand never faltered on the page, and he uttered neither remonstrance nor regret.

Here, as in the case of his predecessors, I have purposely abstained from attempting to pass judgment upon Dalhousie's administration. Such a task would demand, if not a volume, at least a chapter to itself. The storm of obloquy with which he was assailed when the Mutiny broke out has long ago died down, and I have no desire to rake up the embers of a forgotten controversy. The causes of the rising, both immediate and remote, were many and complex, and I see no shame for any defender of Dalhousie in admitting that the annexation of Oudh, which after all was not, in the form in which it was carried out, the act or the policy of the Governor General so much as of the Government at home, may have been and probably was a contributory cause of the movement in that part of India, or that the policy of annexation by lapse produced a considerable and a natural ferment in the Native States. Personally I hold that the annexation of Oudh, as of the Punjab and Pegu, was right and inevitable, and that the Native State policy of Lord Dalhousie, which was wisely reversed by Lord Canning, was wrong. But his own motives in both cases were impeccable, and were dictated by considerations, not of personal egotism or aggrandisement, but of broad Imperial policy. He was profoundly convinced that it was for the good of the peoples of India that they should pass from the then too frequently corrupt and cruel administration of Oriental potentates, themselves in many cases upstarts, to the secure and equitable protection of the British Raj ; and while to the Company he proudly pointed to the lacs and crores of rupees that he thus poured into their exchequer, he was prouder by far of the addition that he was thereby making to the range of British authority and what he believed to be the happiness of the governed.

Quite apart from his conquests and acquisitions, which placed Dalhousie in the direct line of lineal descent from Wellesley and Lord Hastings, and which rounded off the British dominions in India to the approximate shape which they have since borne (Upper Burma has been the main subsequent acquisition), his administrative reforms were greater and more ambitious and have been more durable than any which had been before congregated in a similar space of time. *Nihil Indici a me alienum puto* might have been his motto ; and whether we regard his policy in respect of public works or railways (which began in his time) or telegraphs or roads or irrigation or posts or education or industries or jails, or the institution of the first Indian Legislative Council or the creation of a separate government for Bengal, or the reduction of interest on the public debt, or the reform of the medical and commissariat services of the army, we are equally astounded at the range of his activities and the extent of his accomplishment. In all these respects modern India has been built upon the foundations which Dalhousie laid, and the famous Minute on his administration, written on his back by the sick man as he sailed homeward to die, is a monument of achieved endeavour such as few rulers can boast. That he should have remarked on leaving India that he was guilty of no presumption in saying that he should leave the Indian Empire at peace without and within, was his single act of conformity to a popular Viceregal aberration. That he did not foresee the Mutiny is true, but how many did ?

Those who have attacked Dalhousie complain that by the extent and vehemence of his reforms he galvanised India into the discontent that blazed out in May 1857. Those who have defended him aver that it was only owing to his policy that British rule was enabled to withstand the shock. Neither contention contains more than a half truth. That a rule so strenuous should have been followed by a sharp revulsion, and that as soon as the stern hand was removed every element of disaffection or disorder should have reared its head, is a natural law of which the history of India has provided and will continue to provide many illustrations. It is the fate of the strong ruler to provoke this form of reprisal. But the measure of his responsibility is far from being the measure of his reproach.

And now the time drew nigh when this indomitable fighter must put off his harness, and retire from the scene of so much endurance and so much glory. The parting scenes have been described by the pens of many witnesses, who were conscious that they were gazing upon a spectacle that would live in Indian history. On 29th February Lord and Lady Canning made the usual procession up the river in the *Sonamukhi* to Chandpal Ghat. Lord Dalhousie met them at the top of the steps of Government House and conducted the new ruler to the Council Chamber, where he was at once sworn in. The Cannings were startled to see the havoc that eight years had wrought in the appearance of their host. " Oh, how sad," she wrote, " to see the change in him, and he but forty-three ! " John Lawrence, who had been standing at the open window, awaiting the arrival of the new-comers, asked him what were his feelings. " He drew himself up and with great fire replied : ' I wish that I were Canning and Canning I, and then wouldn't I govern India ! ' Then of a sudden the fire died away ; and with a sorrowful look he said : ' No, I don't. I would not wish my greatest enemy, much less my friend Canning, to be the poor miserable broken-down dying man that I am.' "

Dalhousie remained for a week in Government House until the Company's S.S. " Firoze," which had brought out the Cannings, was ready to take him back. He spent the interval for the most part in his rooms, and in receiving Addresses. On 6th March in the late afternoon he and his daughter, Lady Susan, drove down to Prinsep's Ghat. The retiring ruler " barely tottered on board with the aid of crutches, and his countenance bore traces of his physical pain and his mental emotions." There was a death-like silence and many shed tears as the doomed man waved a last adieu to the country for which he had sacrificed his health and, as it was presently to appear, his life.

This was his own description of the scene :

" The ' Friend of India ' said some months ago that I was not personally popular. I don't know ; but if I am not, never were so many tears shed over the departure of an unpopular man as have been wiped away by bearded men within this week. We had a sad leave-taking in the Council on Thursday, and it was not much better in the Legislative Council on Friday. The deputation which brought me up the address from the community were unmistakably sorry. And I myself was miserable. To-day at the Government House, and on the Ghat where I embarked, there was silence like a funeral chamber. Half could not speak . . . I am quite done ; my leg is now giving me great pain and has a frightful wound in it." [1]

Dalhousie spent the greater part of his time on board the " Firoze," which took him as far as Suez, in writing the record of his administration, afterwards published as a Parliamentary Paper.   At Cairo, where he spent a week, his troubles recommenced, for whereas he had been led by Sir Charles Wood to think that a British man-of-war would be sent to convey him from Alexandria to Portsmouth, he now learnt, to his indignant disgust, that no better accommodation was provided for him than a 600-ton Holyhead packet boat, the " Caradoc," in which he was conveyed, through shocking weather and mountainous seas, to Malta.   There the Admiral, Sir Houston Stewart, acquainted with his sufferings and his wrath, gave him the " Tribune," an auxiliary screw frigate, to take him to England, and in this vessel, towed by the " Furious," he made the last stage of his journey home.   On the way he heard that the Company had settled £5,000 per annum upon him, and his long resentment against his employers for the first time melted into a genial recognition of their favour.   On 13th May, 1856, he landed at Spithead.

Here we must take our leave of Dalhousie.   During the less than four years of life that remained to the stricken man, he flitted uneasily, in pursuit of a relief that never came, to London, Scotland, Malvern, Malta for eight months 1857-58, Malvern again, Edinburgh, Bournemouth.   He spent the greater part of the last two years of his life a hopeless invalid at his Scottish castle, where his Indian ailments, aggravated beyond endurance, culminated in Bright's disease ; and then on 19th December, 1860, he died, not yet forty-nine years of age. No man ever gave his life to his country more completely or with a more consuming devotion.

The new Governor General started at Calcutta with every advantage —the possession of a great name, a wide official experience in England, the good wishes of his predecessor.   Dalhousie, when he first heard of the intended appointment, had written to Couper in August 1855 :

" You can never tell what a man will be in such a post as Governor General until you see him tried.   But Canning has plenty of ability, he has been long in office, he will work when it is requisite, his manners will please here and he will do the externals of his office exceedingly well.   He does not speak

[1] " Private Letters," p. 371.

well, but that is not required here. . . If times are quiet I believe he will do very well indeed. If he falls on troubled times it remains to be seen of what metal he is made."[1]

The test was soon to be applied. But it was early evident that a very different type of man now sat in the Governor General's chair. For the powerful concentration, the incisive vigour, and the all-embracing initiative of Dalhousie, were substituted a temperament abnormally cautious, a demeanour shy and reserved, a mind much prone to the weighing of evidence, the balancing of considerations, and the postponement of vital decisions. That the strong hand should be withdrawn, and that such a personality should be suddenly confronted with one of the greatest crises in history, might seem at first sight to be not merely a paradox but a misfortune.

And undoubtedly there were many moments before and during the Mutiny when the new Governor General displayed a lamentable inability either to forecast the situation or to realise the magnitude of the peril. No one at Calcutta or, indeed, elsewhere, saw the storm clouds rushing up the sky. In April 1857, after the military rising at Barrackpore, Lady Canning wrote: "All our troubles are over."

Even when things were at their worst and the long-drawn agony was dragging its bloody trail across the face of the Upper Provinces, Calcutta was always confident that Delhi had fallen, that Lucknow had been captured, that Lucknow was relieved, that the end was near. Canning declined the offer of the British community in the capital to raise a Volunteer Regiment; he delayed in ordering the disarmament of the Sepoys; he refused to disband the Body Guard; he seemed incapable of swift or resolute decision.

He worked with an uncomplaining and tireless devotion, but without method or precision. When first he started at Calcutta he took exercise by riding and driving; but gradually he became a slave to his desk and to the tasks with which he was powerless to cope, until he ended by exhausting his strength and ruining his health. His successor, Lord Elgin, wrote of him at a later date:

"Poor Canning certainly never gave himself a good chance; at least not during the last year or two of his reign here. He took no exercise and not even such relaxation of the mind as was procurable, though that is not much

---

[1] " Private Letters," pp. 350, 353. Canning in the course of his Indian experience developed the capacity of speaking very well on public occasions.

in the situation of Governor General.   When I told him that I should ask two or three people to dine with me daily, in order to get acquainted with all the persons I ought to know, and to talk matters over with them by candle-light, so as to save daylight for other work, he said : ' I was always so tired by dinner-time that I could not speak.' " [1]

The impression, accentuated by a shy and almost ungracious manner, got abroad that the Governor General was not adequate to the occasion, and that indecision at headquarters was fatal to prompt issues.   The former physician of Dalhousie, Dr. Alexander Grant, who was back in India, while extolling the magnanimity of Canning in " never throwing out a hint that the policy of his predecessor was the cause of the Mutiny and all the difficulties of the Empire," went on to say :

" A cultivated man of patient thought and perseverance, of most impartial yet inflexible mind, his great defect was want of decision in time of emergency ; but this irresolution and vacillation were undoubtedly the result of high con-scientiousness, of almost morbid scruples, which on some occasions during the Mutiny were extremely perilous.   The strength of his character and of his true devotion to his work was best seen on the establishment of order and in his dealing generously with the Native Chiefs." [2]

And yet all the while the defects of the Governor General's character were the reflex aspect or at least the concomitant of qualities that fitted him supremely not for the handling of the crisis itself but for the post-crisis settlement, not for the stamping out of revolt but for the assuagement of passions, not for the task of punishment but for the exercise of mercy.   What was caution viewed from one angle became patience from another.   Hesitation was combined with an unruffled calmness : slowness was compatible with a dauntless resolution.

The situation was one that might have frayed the temper and even shaken the mental balance of any ordinary man.   Disputes among the higher officers who were conducting the military operations, the con-stant break-down of arrnagements, arising from individual or depart-mental incompetence, the weight of personal anxiety and responsibility, the ferocious and unbalanced hostility of the European community and Press in Calcutta clamouring for vengeance, hurling at the Governor General the epithet which afterwards became his chief glory, and even

[1] " Letters and Journals of James, 8th Earl of Elgin " (ed. Th. Walrond), p. 402.
[2] " Physician and Friend," p. 172.

in the height of the crisis petitioning for his recall—failed to disturb an equanimity that was truly sublime. The position of the Governor General was not rendered easier by the abuse which was lavished upon him in the English Press, and by the very inadequate support which he received from the Ministry at Home. At length, in November 1857, Lord Granville, who was his personal friend, was spurred on to make a defence of Canning in a speech at the Mansion House, and there were evidences of some revulsion of feeling. The " Times," which had hitherto been foremost in attack, swung round in his favour.

The defence offered by Canning of his own conduct at this time, contained in a letter to Lord Granville, is one of the noblest apologies in English history :

" As long as I have any breath in my body, I will pursue no other policy than that which I have been following ; not only for the reason of expediency and policy above stated, but because it is just. I will not govern in anger. Justice, and that as stern and inflexible as law and might can make it, I will deal out. But I will never allow an angry or indiscriminating act or word to proceed from the Government of India as long as I am responsible for it. . . .

" I don't care two straws for the abuse of the papers, British or Indian. I am for ever wondering at myself for not doing so, but it really is the fact. Partly from want of time to care, partly because with an enormous task before me, all other cares look small. . . .

" I don't want you to . . . do more than defend me against unfair or mistaken attack. But do take up and assert boldly that, whilst we are prepared, as the first duty of all, to strike down resistance without mercy, wherever it shows itself, we acknowledge that, resistance over, deliberate justice and calm patient reason are to resume their way; that we are not going, either in anger or from indolence, to punish wholesale, whether by wholesale hangings or burnings, or by the less violent but not one jot less offensive course of refusing trust and countenance and favour and honour to any man because he is of a class or creed. Do this, and get others to do it, and you will serve India more than you would believe."

When the Town Hall of Calcutta was ringing with denunciations of the Governor General and demands for his recall, when at a later date the insolent Despatch of Ellenborough, condemning his Oudh policy, came out, and he learned that the Home Government, while dismissing their colleague for his procedure, had concurred in his censure, he remained quite unmoved, willing to be recalled but firmly resolved not to resign. As he wrote to the Home Government :

" No taunts or sarcasm, come from what quarter they may, will turn me from the path which I believe to be that of my public duty.   I believe that a change in the head of the Government of India at this time (1858), if it took place under circumstances which indicated a repudiation on the part of the Government of England of the policy which has hitherto been pursued towards the rebels of Oudh, would seriously retard the pacification of the country. I believe that that policy has been from the beginning merciful without weakness, and indulgent without compromise of the dignity of the Government. . . . Firm in these convictions I will not, in a time of unexampled difficulty, danger, and toil, lay down of my own act the high trust which I have the honour to hold."

These qualities at such a time endowed a man, who in ordinary circumstances would not himself have appeared as more than ordinary, with the vesture of real greatness—and have conferred a measure of immortality upon his name.

In "The Story of Two Noble Lives," *i.e.* of Lady Canning and her sister Lady Waterford, we obtain a vivid picture of Calcutta during the terrible days of the Mutiny—great ships laden with troops beating up the river and lying at anchor off the wharf, a perpetual stream of officers and regiments passing to and fro, telegrams pouring in at all hours of the day and night, agitated meetings in the Council Chamber ; but the normal life of the capital and Government House flowing on all the while undisturbed, with a succession of dinners, parties and entertainments, in order to keep up the spirit of the British community —it is a picture dramatic in its features and in its contrasts.

By the side of Canning we see the gentle and tragic figure of his accomplished wife, her youth and beauty ebbing away under the appalling strain, her happiness, though not her devotion, shadowed by a cloud,[1] the blame for which had been exclusively his, and for which after her premature death he felt an endless remorse.   After four years of the life which I have described, both were longing already to lay down the burden.   But the four years lengthened into five and the five into six ; and then, in November 1861, this sweet woman sickened of a fever in the circumstances which I have related in a previous chapter, and died in her husband's arms.

From that moment the light went out of his life.   Death was stamped upon his brow when he stepped on the home-going vessel, as surely as it had been on that of Dalhousie six years before.   On 5th May, 1862, he landed in England.   On 17th June the famous figures

[1] " The Story of Two Noble Lives," Vol. III, pp. 120-1.

of Clyde and Outram, rivals and all but antagonists in the storms of a few years before, followed the body of their recent Chief up the nave of Westminster Abbey.

Canning had not suffered at the hands of his official employers in England to the same extent as his predecessor claimed to have done. But he too had not been exempt from the ordinary lot. The attacks of Calcutta had found their echo in London ; and an attempt was even made to exclude the name of the Governor General from the Parliamentary Vote of thanks to the Indian Services in 1858. Ellenborough's Despatch, though it recoiled upon his own head, was an insult to the ruler of India such as no other British Minister would have perpetrated, and which few, if any, of those rulers would have treated with such calm and lofty disdain.

Canning was a man of fine presence, with a broad brow and well-cut features. His bust by Noble, one of the originals of which is in the possession of Lord Lascelles, who presented a replica to the Victoria Memorial Hall at Calcutta, shows him at his best. After the Mutiny he grew a short beard which transformed his face and converted him into an elderly and melancholy man. As such he was depicted in the portrait—a very bad one—that hung in Government House in my day. The pictures of him taken at the end of his time in India reveal an expression of settled sadness and seem to foreshadow the end. He stands in Indian history as one of the most pathetic but also one of the most heroic figures that have represented the name and upheld the honour of England.

Canning's successor was Lord Elgin, a man of wide diplomatic experience who had served his country in Jamaica, in Canada (as Governor General for eight years) and twice as envoy to China, and whose name had for long been frequently mentioned in connection with that which had now become the Viceroyalty of India. He himself ardently desired the post, and had already had an introduction to the official and social life of Calcutta when in 1857 he had diverted to Bengal the troops which he was taking to China, and had spent some time in the capital as the guest of Lord and Lady Canning. On 12th March, 1862, he took over from the departing Viceroy, and the scene was thus described by Sir Richard Temple, who witnessed it :

" Canning looked pale, wan, toil-worn and grief-stricken ; the brow and forehead had indeed their inseparable dignity ; but the complexion had become

LORD CANNING

From the chalk drawing by G. Richmond, R.A.

sallow, losing those hues which had so often lighted up his aspect on occasions of State ceremony. . . . Elgin on the other hand came up gaily, ruddy in face, massive and square in forehead, buoyant in manner and stalwart in frame, though of short stature." [1]

Who could have foreseen that little more than a year and a half later he would have joined his two immediate predecessors, Dalhousie and Canning, in the land from which there is no return ?

Lord Elgin was too short a time in India either to leave any mark on the administration or to demand more than a passing notice in these pages.   He spent the greater part of his first year at Calcutta or Barrackpore, where his genial manners and social tastes endeared him to the British community, who had never become entirely reconciled to his predecessor.   He was a sagacious, industrious, cheerful man who did all that he had to do conscientiously and without ever giving offence, but withal he possessed courage and no small common-sense.   Canning had advised him not to tie himself too closely to the Lower Provinces, but to get away as soon as possible to the North and North-west. Accordingly he spent the autumn of his first year in making preparations for his contemplated journey, and having been joined by Lady Elgin at the beginning of 1863, he started off in February, being given a public entertainment by the Europeans in the Calcutta Town Hall on the eve of his departure.

The arrangements for his tour mark a midway stage between the tedious boat journeys and the long and exhausting land marches of the Governors General during the first half of the 19th century, and the swift and organised comfort of the Viceroy's progress at the beginning of the 20th.   Lord and Lady Elgin went by train to Benares, thence by carriage *dak* to Allahabad, travelling in separate carriages drawn by horses and proceeding at a hand gallop by night, on by rail to Cawnpore (where the Viceroy consecrated the monument over the bodies of the Mutiny victims) and to Agra.   After a tour in the Punjab the party marched up to Simla, where the summer was spent. In the autumn a start was made on a journey through the hills to Kulu and Lahoul ; but Elgin, who in spite of a stout frame and a vigorous constitution had a weak heart, was seized with faintness while crossing a rope bridge[2] that swung violently over the Chandra

---

[1] " Men and Events of my Time in India," p. 230.
[2] In that neighbourhood these bridges were made of birch twigs.

2—P

River. It was soon apparent that the organ was fatally affected. The dying man sent a telegram of resignation to the Queen, and passed away peacefully on 20th November, the second of the British Governors of India to die in that country.

Two days after the news of Lord Elgin's death had reached London, Sir John Lawrence, then living in England in a retirement which he believed to be final (though he was a member of the Secretary of State's Council in the India Office), received and accepted, at the hands of Lord Palmerston, the appointment of Viceroy, and ten days later, with characteristic promptitude, he started to assume his new and magnificent charge. It was believed that his selection was mainly due to the fear that a war was impending on the North-west Frontier of India, and to the belief that his well-known peaceful tendencies would avert the calamity.

To the majority of persons it seemed that here was the crown of a great and glorious career. For the first time for nearly three quarters of a century a member of the Indian Civil Service had risen by his unaided abilities to the highest office open to a subject of the British Crown ; and this man was one who had served and helped to save his country in the hour of her supreme trial, who, unlike the majority of those who have made a great Indian reputation, was already a hero to his countrymen, and who now came back in the prime of life—for he was only fifty-two years of age—to rule a people whose language he spoke, whose character he knew, to whom his name was already a household word. Never, it seemed, had a Viceroy entered upon his office under happier auspices and with a more assured prospect.

Lawrence himself was fully alive to the splendour (though he cordially disliked the pomp) and the responsibility of the situation. He said to his son-in-law :

" It was a proud moment to me when I walked up the steps of Government House, feeling as I then did that without political interest or influence I had been chosen to fill the highest office under the Crown, the Viceroyalty of the Queen. But it will be a happier moment to me when I walk down the steps with the feeling that I have tried to do my duty."

And yet it cannot be denied that the next five years, though filled with much sincere and steadfast labour, were in many ways a disappointment, and showed that the qualities which had crushed a rebellion, or saved a province, or evolved order out of bloody chaos,

LORD LAWRENCE

From the painting by G. F. Watts, R.A.

were not precisely those that were required for the administrator on the exalted pinnacle of the Viceregal office of a mighty Empire.

We have already, in an earlier chapter, seen John Lawrence in the somewhat uncongenial surroundings of Government House and of Calcutta society, to both of which he found difficulty in adapting himself. But neither in his more public capacities as Viceroy and head of the administration did he add to the fame of earlier years. We may derive what is perhaps the most dispassionate impression both of his character and career if we study the writings of Sir Richard Temple, himself a man of great ability and a fervent disciple and admirer of his master, who was originally Secretary to Lawrence at Lahore and was afterwards Foreign Secretary and then Finance Minister during his Viceroyalty. Temple's appreciation of the character of his Chief in his Punjab days was couched in the following terms :

" The prevailing sentiment in his public life was a love for duty. Though his temper was strong, and on occasions warm, yet in his nature judgment and reason reigned supreme. As a subsidiary element caution was present with him in the highest degree, and there never was in India a more cautious statesman than he. It being an object of the first importance with him to foresee the course of all affairs, he remembered that prescience could be acquired only by careful reflection. . . . To weigh both sides of every question evenly and strike the balance, to eliminate passion, favour, prejudice or misleading sentiment, and fix the gaze on exact justice alone, were maxims uppermost in his mind. He acted according to this principle in judging of the conduct and character of officers whose fates he held in the hollow of his hand. . . . To those who, notwithstanding their gifts and accomplishments, lacked the fundamental condition of zeal for public duty, he would show no consideration. In equitable discrimination of the diverse moral and intellectual qualities of the numerous subordinates under his command, he has not been surpassed by any man of his generation in India. He did not at that time arouse so much enthusiasm as his brother (Henry) among large numbers of men, nor win so extensive a popularity. But he was respected by all, admired by most, and beloved by many." [1]

And yet it is impossible to read the same writer's narrative of the crowning quinquennium of Lawrence's career in India without some sense of disappointment, which Temple manifestly shared. For the first time in his life, being in a position that has always been the target

[1] " Men and Events of my Time in India," pp. 58-9.

of a criticism to which it is wellnigh impossible for the occupant to return an effective reply, or indeed any reply at all, he found himself misunderstood, misrepresented, assailed. Questions came up one after the other—the revision of tenant-right in Oudh, the Bhutan Treaty of 1865, famine in Orissa (which the Government of India was charged, not without justice, with not having taken in hand in time), the proposals for a licence tax with respect to trades and professions—his attitude upon which brought the Viceroy a widespread though passing unpopularity. His Frontier policy was stigmatised as one of " masterly inactivity." He was involved in disputes with his capable but unruly lieutenant in Bombay, Sir Bartle Frere. The proceedings of his own Council were far from harmonious, and the constant bickerings of his colleagues tempted the exasperated man more than once to contemplate resignation.

The fact is that Lawrence was unfitted both by temperament and training for work in the peculiar conditions by which the Viceroy is bound. Essentially a man of action rather than of speech, he was intolerant of discussion and debate, and could not accustom himself to the slow and ponderous procession of the departmental files. All his life he had been used to give orders and to be obeyed ; now he was in harness with a troublesome and fractious team whom he could not in general overrule, and moreover he found himself not merely thwarted but widely traduced. He was exceedingly sensitive under attack, had not the resilience of temper to make him react to the situation as it developed, and, in common with many other Viceroys, thought himself insufficiently supported at home.

Simultaneously, as I have shown in a previous chapter, his conduct of the social and ceremonial side of the Viceroyalty was much criticised, and he was accused of niggardliness and lack of dignity. His simple habits and tastes—such for instance as working in dishabille, coat and waistcoat, collar and tie, thrown off, and slippers on feet—were unfavourably commented upon by those who were used to the observance of recognised forms in Government House ; and the Viceroy did not improve matters by a temper which was both hasty and warm.[1]

---

[1] Sir Alfred Lyall once related to me an amusing anecdote of this foible. When a young Civilian, he was driving in a carriage with Lawrence, who was instructing him in the way in which he should go, and in particular admonishing him to be always very gentle and considerate to the natives of the country. Presently the carriage stopped and Lawrence began to descend, when the Indian servant, who opened the door, stumbled and nearly precipitated the future Viceroy on to the ground. The latter retaliated by a violent kick on the hinder parts of the offender !

Nevertheless a more conscientious and indefatigable worker never sat in the Governor General's chair. He was a hard taskmaster, but not harder on others than on himself. Strict and severe, but inflexibly just, he was, as has been said, "hard in rebuke, but swift in redress." He took an intense pride in his work, slaved at the task of administration, and devoted his energies with unsparing vigour to internal reforms.

Upon one point he took up a position which seems to me to have been absolutely right in both its aspects. Realising the impossibility of working with advantage throughout the hot season in Bengal, and the danger as well as drawbacks of a situation which separated the Viceroy for months from his colleagues and advisers, he invested with permanence the system, which his predecessors had informally practised for years, of moving the seat of Government from Calcutta to Simla in the summer months, threatening to resign if this proposal was not sanctioned. At the same time, though he personally disliked Calcutta and Calcutta life, he held that that city was prescribed by situation, trade, climate, and population as the winter headquarters of Government, and he would have resisted to the uttermost the ill-starred policy that, nearly half a century later, was to deprive the old capital of the British Empire in India of her pride of place and to banish the Government of India to the crumbling graveyards of Delhi.

The reign of Sir John Lawrence, honourable and strenuous as it was, was generally regarded as demonstrating the undesirability of raising even the most eminent of Indian Civilians to the Viceregal throne. Allowing that personal idiosyncrasies were the most potent factor in this particular case, the administration of Lawrence did incidentally suggest that the potential danger of the experiment exceeded its advantages, and it has never since been repeated.

While, for the various reasons which I have indicated, Sir John Lawrence's career as Viceroy was flecked by some disappointment, none, even among his critics, failed to remember the superlative services of the man in earlier times, or to question the intense and practical piety by which his actions were at all times inspired. No more deeply religious man ever reigned in Government House ; and when the time came for his final retirement, the remainder of his life was consecrated to activities that gave useful scope to these inclinations. His health had already shown signs of declining in the later years of his Viceroyalty, and he returned to England a tired and toil-worn man.

Somewhat later his sight began to fail, and his final speech in the House of Lords, in June 1879, was all but attended by collapse. He was not more than sixty when he died. Fitly indeed did Westminster Abbey receive his body ; his statue, next to that of Clyde, gazes upon those who pass through Waterloo Place on foot on their way to Whitehall.

The famous veteran was succeeded in India by an almost unknown man. Disraeli had selected as the successor to Lawrence an Irish nobleman, who as Lord Naas had three times been Chief Secretary for Ireland, and had earned a good reputation for bonhomie, sound sense and business capacity in the House of Commons, but who was far from being in the front rank of politicians at home. In 1867 Lord Naas had succeeded to the Earldom of Mayo. His appointment to India was much criticised at the time, but Disraeli adhered to his choice ; and although the Minister had fallen from power before his nominee reached India, the latter was without hesitation confirmed by Mr. Gladstone, who had assumed office in the interval.

Lord Mayo adopted a somewhat unconventional route in entering upon his charge. Landing at Bombay, he spent ten days there instead of the brief and perfunctory two days' sojourn of the ordinary practice ; thence he steamed down the coast to Beypur, and crossed by rail to Madras, thus making acquaintance with the two principal Provincial Governments before he landed at Prinsep's Ghat on 12th January, 1869.

One who was present at the " taking over " in Government House thus described the scene :

" John Lawrence stood near the head of the flight of steps, wearing full uniform ; calm in aspect, and conscious that he had, according to his own phrase, served his time and done all he could. He was somewhat pallid and careworn, reduced in body from protracted labour while in precarious health, and looking like a hoary weather-beaten rock round which the elements had oft-times roared and dashed. Lord Mayo, on the other hand, mounted the steps in plain morning dress, robust in frame, beaming with the brightness of health, buoyant in spirits, and elastic with hope. He won favour with everyone at first sight, and soon began to acquire a personal popularity which, with slight intermissions at Calcutta, grew and expanded as he became more widely known."

Eastern peoples are amenable to the physical endowment of their rulers, particularly those who come of an alien and governing race.

Nor is the British community in India exempt from a similar pre-possession. Lord Mayo's appearance was such as to satisfy the most exacting standards of both ; for he was a man of commanding stature, broad frame, and singularly handsome countenance, the habitual expression of which bespoke both geniality and resolution. Add to this that he was a fine rider and ex-master of the renowned Kildare Hunt in Ireland, an all-round sportsman, and a man in the prime of masculine vigour and strength—and we may judge of the favourable impression that was produced by the exterior attributes of the new Viceroy. When these were found to be combined with excellent qualities of head, a genuine love of work, and a faculty both of feeling and exciting enthusiasm, it may readily be understood that all sections of the population in India took their new ruler to their heart, and that, if all of his measures did not obtain great popularity,[1] this detracted not at all from the general esteem in which their author was held.

Lord Mayo's advantages of manner and mien stood him in good stead in his relations with the princes and potentates of the East. At the dawn of his Viceroyalty he established friendly relations at a meeting with the Afghan Amir, Shir Ali Khan, who if he did not obtain all that he desired, went away from Umballa with cordial feelings towards the British ruler, which in no way foreshadowed or were connected with his subsequent lapse. On the other hand, the Indian Princes recognised in Lord Mayo a nearer approach to the ideal representative of the Sovereign than any previous Viceroy ; and found in his love for sport, in his debonair but dignified manner, and in his genuine interest in the education of the princely class, a stimulus alike to their loyalty and to their personal esteem. The admirable Chiefs' Colleges at Ajmer in Rajputana and at Rajkot in Kathiawar, which have been visited and encouraged by every subsequent Viceroy, and which have turned out in their time a long series of worthy and patriotic rulers, are the direct and living legacy of Mayo's administration.

The second chief administrative predilection of the Viceroy was for what in India are commonly called Public Works. Roads, railways, canals attracted his keen interest, and he himself assumed charge of the Public Works Department in order to supervise and speed their

---

[1] The most conspicuous instance was the doubling of the income tax in 1869 and the trebling of it in 1870—a measure which, while intended to balance the budget by mulcting the rich trading classes, was the source of untold oppression by the native tax-gatherers. Lord Mayo lived to acknowledge his mistake, which was corrected by his successor.

development. He would have done as much for agriculture had he been permitted ; but his proposals for the erection of a special agricultural department were watered down by the India Office into a composite Department of Revenue, Agriculture and Commerce, and it was reserved for a successor, thirty years later, to seek to place both commerce and agriculture on an independent footing.

While pursuing these aims Mayo had a sincere regard for economy, and delighted his Finance Ministers by a punctilious determination to maintain equilibrium between revenue and expenditure, and by his orthodox regard for public accounts.

The enterprising spirit and physical energy of the Viceroy enabled him to indulge in more frequent and longer tours, very often on horseback, than any of his predecessors had done ; and thus in the short space of three years he created an impression of combined efficiency and power such as few of them have produced. It is always said that the last two years of a Viceroyalty are the real testing time, when, the applause and flattery of the opening period having died down, the ruler's policy must stand, so to speak, upon its own legs, and the harvest of meritorious effort, if such there has been, begins to be reaped. Whether Lord Mayo would have survived this ordeal it is impossible to say. It is at least true that the most competent and experienced of his colleagues thought that he would.

At Government House, Calcutta, the Viceroy dispensed an urbane and generous hospitality, and his régime gained by contrast with that which had preceded it. The fact that he was as ready as the youngest member of his Staff to attend a race meeting or to ride after a pig was far from diminishing the popularity thus acquired ; and if an illustration were needed of the extent to which ability and industry can be reinforced in public life by sportsmanship and personal charm, it could be found in the short Indian career of Lord Mayo.

It was a sad misfortune for India when this imposing and virile personality was struck down by the hand of a Pathan assassin in the penal settlement of the Andaman Islands in February 1872. The story has been so often told that it need not be reproduced here. But it is perhaps worth mentioning that the impression produced by the crime was so great, and the fear of a possible repetition so lasting, that when, thirty years later, I desired to repeat the visit, I was not allowed to do so. No other Indian Viceroy has ever been to the Andamans.

LORD MAYO AS VICEROY (1870)

Now that this fascinating group of islands has ceased to be a penal settlement, the prohibition will presumably be withdrawn.

We have witnessed in these pages the arrival and departure from the seat of Government of many of Mayo's predecessors. Very different was the last return of the Viceroy to Government House and his final exit therefrom to his distant Irish home. The body of the murdered man was brought in the "Glasgow" up the river to Prinsep's Ghat, whence it was followed through a dense native crowd by the entire European population of Calcutta on foot to Government House. There it was carried up the steps which we saw him ascend with such high hopes only three years before, and was borne into the Council Chamber where he had so recently presided over the debates. After the burial service had been read in the presence of his widow and principal colleagues, the coffin lay in state for some days in the Throne Room, until it was taken on board a man-of-war for conveyance to the family burial-ground in Ireland. So passed the third Governor General who was fated to die during his term of office, but the first, and happily so far the last, to perish by the hand of an assassin.

After an interregnum of three months the new Viceroy, Lord Northbrook, arrived upon the scene. He came to the office with a wider administrative experience than almost any of his predecessors ; and he was better acquainted with economic theory and practice, and with the science of finance, than any Viceroy before or since. In these respects he had the invaluable assistance of his relative and Private Secretary, Major Evelyn Baring, who at a later date was destined to make the name of Lord Cromer known throughout the world.

Lord Northbrook was a quiet sound man of what in England would be termed the Whig type of mind, just and humane in his administration and conscientious in all his acts. He was as unlike his predecessor as the latter had been unlike Lawrence, for he was diffident in manner, disliked all parade and pageantry, and was not a good speaker. I often heard him in later years in the House of Lords, where he was greatly respected but left no impression of power. He never lost his regard for India, and of all the ex-Viceroys was the one who showed the most continuous interest in Indian affairs, corresponding with me regularly during my term of office, as he had done with my predecessors, even though he had left the country for thirty years. Of all the British rulers of India he was also the one with the keenest taste for art.

Himself the owner in England of a fine collection of paintings, and possessing artistic susceptibilities of no mean order, he took seriously in hand the completion of the Government House collection of pictures and, under the mistaken idea that the Indian genius could be or ought to be trained in Western schools of painting, accumulated a number of European pictures in the Museum at Calcutta, which in the succeeding quarter of a century were gradually dispersed, having exercised no influence whatever upon the Eastern mind.

Northbrook obtained an early popularity both with the European and with the wealthier native community by abandoning the income tax which Mayo had imposed ; and this favourable impression was deepened by the laborious energy which he devoted to that which was the most notable incident of his administration, namely the Bengal and Behar Famine of 1874. Famine policy had not then assumed the scientific perfection which, fortified by long experience and profound research, it had attained when it fell to my lot to administer a much greater Indian Famine in 1899-1900 ; but the elaborate preparations made by Lord Northbrook, who spent an entire hot weather in Bengal and scarcely left Calcutta for eighteen months, and by the two successive Lieutenant Governors of Bengal, Sir George Campbell and Sir Richard Temple, enabled him to avoid the lamentable disasters of the Orissa famine of Lord Lawrence, and to cope with the visitation with greater success than had attended any previous effort. I subsequently sat in the House of Commons with both of the aforesaid lieutenants, whose parliamentary careers illustrated the now familiar phenomenon that success in Indian administration is no necessary prelude to political achievement in England.

Lord Northbrook had accepted and entered upon office under the Liberal Administration of Mr. Gladstone, to whom, until the Home Rule crisis supervened at a later date, he was closely attached. But when the Disraeli Government came into power in 1874, and Lord Salisbury succeeded the Duke of Argyll at the India Office, a breach of ideas between the two heads of Indian administration began to make itself felt and gradually widened until it ended in rupture. Differences of opinion arose about more questions than one—the trial of the Gaekwar of Baroda for the attempt to poison the British Resident, Colonel Phayre ; the remission of duties on Lancashire cottons ; and, most of all, the desire of the Home Government to send a British Mission to

Kabul, and to appoint Political Agents at Herat and Kandahar. It was obvious, indeed, that the home authorities were developing an Afghan policy in direct antagonism to the views of the Viceroy, who was a convinced adherent of the Lawrence school ; and the latter, who had already spent four trying years in India, found no alternative but to resign his office, although ill-health was alleged as the ostensible plea.

Lord Northbrook stayed in India long enough to receive the Prince of Wales, afterwards King Edward VII, in the memorable visit of the cold weather season of 1875-6 ; and when he finally departed, in the spring of 1876, he left behind him the reputation of a sage and cautious though in nowise brilliant ruler. It was in accord with his high sense of duty that he should continue to perform much useful public work both in office, in Parliament, and in his county, after his return to England.

When Mr. Disraeli on 23rd November, 1875, offered the Vice-royalty to Lord Lytton, at that time British Minister at Lisbon, he said that Lord Northbrook had resigned for " purely domestic reasons." This, as we have seen, was not the fact. The Conservative Government could not, however, have found a more supple or enthusiastic instrument to carry out their new Afghan policy, shrouded with disaster though it was destined to be. It is no part of my design to narrate here the course of the Afghan War which was the direct consequence of this new policy, or to apportion the praise or blame. My own opinion is that the policy was neither well judged nor well directed, and that Lord Lytton's aspirations for a scientific frontier which was to be identical with the Hindu Kush were mistaken. Russia, however, loomed upon the scene at that time with an almost overpowering menace, and the prospect of a Russianised Afghanistan struck an indefinable terror into the hearts of Indian soldiers and administrators.

A study of the papers, however, both as published at the time and later on in the official records in India, led me to admire the extra-ordinary ability and resourcefulness with which Lord Lytton conducted his case on paper, and the perfection of the English prose in which his Minutes and Despatches were clothed. Of all the Governors General and Viceroys, he seemed to me to have the greatest literary gift, not indeed excelling Warren Hastings or Dalhousie in lucidity of exposition or vigour of phrase, but superior to both in the artistic quality of his writing.

This was perhaps to be expected from one who was *par excellence* a literary man. Indeed the entire Indian career of Lord Lytton was a demonstration of temperament and abilities suddenly transferred to novel and unexpected surroundings, which attracted him by their exotic quality, and appealed forcibly to his exuberant imagination. He was unconventional from the very start. Arriving at Calcutta in April 1876, and having been conducted by his predecessor to the Council Chamber, he then proceeded, after his Warrant of Appointment had been read, to make a speech to the assembled Councillors and officials, which he flattered himself produced, as no doubt it did, an excellent effect. No incoming Governor General had ever thought it necessary to do this before, or has done it since ; although Lord Napier of Merchistoun, on coming up from Madras to assume charge after the assassination of Lord Mayo, had, in the peculiar circumstances of the case, made a few appropriate remarks. Lord Lytton then entered upon a correspondence with the Queen in the first person, the irregularity of which procedure was condoned in the eyes of Her Majesty by the candour and charm of the letters themselves. At Simla the traditions of this Bohemian Viceroy's social intimacies still survived in my day, and there were those who remembered his sallies and witticisms and talked of the unusual proceedings at Government House. There can be no doubt, however, that Lord Lytton was much liked by the Services, and won the warm esteem and regard of some of his principal colleagues, notably that remarkable man, Sir John Strachey ; and that the popular belief in the frivolity and lack of seriousness of the current régime was an inaccurate representation of the facts. The Viceroy was indeed most industrious in his devotion to official work, as witness his famine tour to Madras in the summer of 1877; and in later days when Ambassador in Paris, where his gifts were much and naturally appreciated, he expressed an amused surprise that in India he had been so much misunderstood. "I devoted my life to India, and everybody abused me : I come here, do nothing, and am praised to the skies."

In one respect Lord Lytton displayed a courage, in which I was proud at a later date to follow in his footsteps. This was his open condemnation of the harsh treatment sometimes meted out by a certain and unrepresentative type of white man to the dark-skinned man in India. His attempt brought him more obloquy than praise, and I

LORD LYTTON (1876)

cannot recall in my time that the Indians, as a body, ever showed any gratitude to those who had risked popularity and very likely incurred serious odium with their countrymen by a rigid vindication of justice in this respect.

Lytton had the invaluable assistance of a charming wife ; and the record of his Indian Administration,[1] as also a selection of his Private Letters, have since been given to the world by his gifted daughter, Lady Betty Balfour.[2] These will convey a more faithful impression of the tastes and talents of this uncommon man than any written critique. He had the gift of inspiring personal affection to a remarkable degree even in persons to whom he was most unlike. For instance, he kept up for years an intimate correspondence with Lord Morley, until the breach in their several policies and ideas became irreparable ; and I can recall the infectious gaiety of his social intercourse and abundant hospitality in his English home.

To such a man the Proclamation of the Queen as Empress of India appealed with as much force as it did to the Oriental vision of the Jewish Prime Minister ; and Lytton addressed himself with ardour to the marshalling of the Imperial Assemblage at Delhi which was to celebrate and commemorate the world-shaking announcement. His imagination bubbled over with plans for the creation of an Indian Privy Council of great Chiefs, an Indian Peerage, and an Indian Heralds' College, and he devoted himself with enthusiasm to the preparation of silken banners, containing the Royal Arms on one side, and the escutcheons, specially and fantastically constructed for the occasion, of the Indian Princes on the other. These trophies, which were so heavy as to require two men to lift them, were paraded at the Imperial Assemblage on 1st January, 1877, and were to be used at all State ceremonials in the future. The idea was foreign to the Indian mind ; and the banners have since reposed in silken idleness in the *Tosha Khanas* or Treasure Chambers of the respective chiefs. In his contemplation of an Indian Chamber of Princes or House of Lords, Lytton showed a prescience which has since borne practical fruit ; but the heraldic part of the scheme was incongruous and stillborn.

No Viceroy was ever more fiercely attacked in England than Lord Lytton, whose ambitious projects and glowing fancy were represented

---

[1] " The History of Lord Lytton's Indian Administration," 1899.
[2] " Personal and Literary Letters," 2 Vols., 1906.

as equal dangers to the Empire; and it was inevitable that as soon as the General Election of 1880 had taken place, with the return of the Liberal Party to power by a large majority, he should forward his resignation to the authorities at home. This he did to Lord Beaconsfield while the latter was still in office.

It has been said that this picturesque and poetic figure—for Lytton was picturesque in appearance as well as in fact—was in reality out of date, and that he ought to have been born and to have lived in Elizabethan times. There is pertinence in this observation, for certainly in the picture gallery of Indian Viceroys there is no more singular or indeed startling portrait than his. In the Embassy at Paris he found a more congenial stage for his social and diplomatic accomplishments.

Mr. Gladstone was resolved to send out to India a successor who should be in every sense an antithesis to Lord Lytton, and in Lord Ripon, a man of approved and orthodox Liberalism, simple tastes, and prolonged official experience of public and not least of Indian affairs, he found a man to his heart's liking. The exchange of office took place on this occasion at Simla, where Lord Ripon arrived in the month of June, the retiring Viceroy continuing to reside in a private house for three weeks before his final departure. Lord Ripon was a Roman Catholic, and brought out a priest with him from England. This worthy padre, unused to the torrid amenities of the Indian climate in summer, and gratified at the safe arrival of his Chief and himself at Peterhof, which was then the Government House, after the perils of the railway journey through the plains, left on record this naïve confession :

"Soon all had gone, leaving Lord Ripon and Staff in quiet possession of Government House. By midnight silence reigned throughout, and we had laid ourselves down with thanks—and with reason, for coffins are in readiness at every station along the line ; and the driver and the guard of the train that left Bombay on the night previous to us, were both taken out dead—heat apoplexy—at Khandwa, where we breakfasted the morning after—all well. *Laus Deo semper.*" [1]

The career of Lord Ripon in India provides the most startling illustration in its history of an upright, painstaking, and honourable man taking steps or embarking on policies of whose abstract rectitude

[1] "Memoirs of Father H. S. Kerr," by Mrs. Maxwell Scott, p. 180.

he was profoundly convinced, but which uniformly succeeded in arousing prolonged and embittered controversy. Trained in a rather narrow school of English Liberalism, he continued for four years with unabated ardour to pour the vintage to which he had been accustomed at home into the archaic bottles of Indian tradition and prejudice, and was quite surprised when they burst in his hand. It was perhaps only to be expected, in view of the violent revulsion of policy in England following upon Lord Beaconsfield's fall and Mr. Gladstone's return to power, that the new Viceroy should at once seek to extricate himself from the Afghan entanglement of his predecessor by ordering the evacuation of Kandahar (having to exercise his statutory right of overruling his Council for the purpose), and should hastily repeal the Vernacular Press Act of Lord Lytton. But the high tide of Westernisation—if such a term be permissible—as applied to Oriental life and institutions, was only reached when he introduced a great system of Local Self-government on European lines—an experiment which was certainly premature at the time, but once made could not be withdrawn, and which for more than a quarter of a century was attended in India with only the most sparse success. Still more was this the case when, quite unconscious of the explosive nature of the material which he was so rashly handling, the Viceroy blundered into the policy generally summarised under the title of the Ilbert Bill. The object sounded admirable when stated on paper—" to remove from the Code at once and completely every judicial disqualification which is based merely on race distinctions." But when in practice this was found to mean that Native rural magistrates were in future to try and decide criminal cases in which Englishmen were involved, there burst forth a veritable storm of agitation, racial animosity, and personal abuse. Neither Lord Ripon nor his Law Member, Mr. (afterwards Sir) Courtnay Ilbert, who introduced the Bill, nor his colleagues who sanctioned it, had the slightest idea of the tempest they were about to raise. The Viceroy was personally insulted in Calcutta, Government House was partially boycotted by the British community, the Services were exasperated and estranged, and a plot was hatched for kidnapping the Viceroy, hustling him on to a ship, and sending him off to the Cape. While these excesses were greatly to be deplored, there was an obvious lack of prudence in provoking controversy in so many forms; and it was not the least among the many regrettable results that, while the

British element in the community were outraged and indignant, the native element was proportionately elated, and racial fissures, always lurking below the stately façade of Anglo-Indian society, were for a time immeasurably widened and deepened. In a subsequent letter to Lord Northbrook, Lord Ripon with characteristic honesty frankly confessed that a great mistake had been made, and that he must take his due share of the responsibility. The Bill was only placed on the Statute Book in a greatly modified form.

Apart from these errors or extremes of political action, Lord Ripon was personally liked and esteemed, for he was an indefatigable worker, a conciliatory colleague, and a perfectly straightforward and consistent man. His friends trembled under the voluminous correspondence which he showered upon them ; but this was a feature of his willingness to argue and his anxiety to convince. He held rigidly to what he regarded as the orthodox and fundamental principles of Indian Government ; and many years later, when I was involved in the struggle to uphold the supremacy of the civil as against the military authority in Indian administration, he made, without any communication to me, a powerful speech in the House of Lords on my behalf, and must have suffered considerable pangs when his colleague, Lord Morley, hauled down the flag which a little earlier he had so defiantly planted on the walls of the fortress.

It is a rather curious fact that this equable and worthy but far from assertive man should have had as much trouble with the India Office as the most autocratic of his predecessors. He, who had once presided over that Office himself, was now always complaining as Viceroy that the interference of Whitehall had greatly increased and was becoming intolerable, and his letters contained many veiled threats of resignation.

The Viceroyalty of Lord Ripon only lasted for four years, and if its termination was viewed without regret by the British community, it excited the most fervid and overwhelming demonstrations from Indians of all classes, who have ever since canonised him as the foremost saint in their political calendar, and still regard him as the real author of that advance towards self-government and nationhood which has in recent times progressed at such a dizzy rate of speed.

It was obviously desirable that so disturbing a régime as that of Lord Ripon should be succeeded by a period of reconciliation and repose, and the Home Government could not have taken a wiser step than when they had recourse to the diplomatic experience and persuasive personality of Lord Dufferin for the execution of the task.   From a comparatively early age that nobleman had been employed in positions of trust which had given him an almost unique knowledge of world politics, not excluding the East.   He had been Ambassador both at Petersburg and Constantinople, and had served on Special Missions to Syria and Egypt.   He had been Governor General of a great Dominion. There was nothing in the conduct of affairs or the management of men that remained to be taught to this shrewd and versatile man.   When further it is remembered that he was an Irishman, of romantic descent, gifted with all an Irishman's qualities of wit, geniality, and imagination, it will be readily understood that he was an almost predestined instrument, not to cut the Gordian knot in India, but with cool and agile fingers to unravel its twisted folds.

Perhaps the greatest of Lord Dufferin's services was that he himself had no more ambitious conception of his own task.   Although he came out to repair the rents and seams that had been produced in the Indian social and political structure by the somewhat too precipitate actions of his predecessor, he never dissociated himself in the smallest particular from the latter, always expressed the utmost regard and admiration for him, and laid down categorically the doctrine of continuity of administration.   He took the earliest opportunity afforded to him, when replying to an Address from the Calcutta Corporation, to propound, as regards Local Self-government in India, the principles which he applied equally to every branch of the administration :

"In alluding to the subject of Local Self-government, and to the exceptional impulse it has received under the benign auspices of Lord Ripon, you have touched upon a matter which has already attracted my attention. If there is one principle more inherent than another in the system of our Indian Administration, it is that of continuity.   Nothing has struck me more than the loyal and persistent manner in which successive Viceroys, no matter what part they have played in the strife of party politics at home, have used their utmost endeavours to bring to a successful issue whatever projects their predecessors may have conceived for the benefit of the people.   It is by adherence to this principle that we have built up in this country the majestic fabric of our Government, and it is needless for me to assure you that I shall not fail to follow a line of conduct consecrated by the example of Cornwallis, Bentinck, Canning, Mayo and those who followed them.   The Marquis of Ripon and his predecessors have prepared the soil, delved, and planted.   It will be my more humble duty to watch, water, prune, and train."

2—Q

It will be observed with what a dexterous hand Lord Dufferin omitted the names of those rulers in the past who had conspicuously violated the principle which he thus laid down, how he conveniently forgot that Cornwallis and Canning could hardly be described as enthusiastic adherents to the policies of Hastings and Dalhousie, and how in mentioning Lord Ripon, who had done all in his power to reverse the policy of Lord Lytton, he threw in a vague but calculated reference to his predecessors which might be held to embrace anybody or everybody in its ample ambiguity. Nevertheless the principle enunciated by Dufferin is, within limits, which it is unnecessary here to define, essentially sound. It has guided the actions of the most experienced and successful Indian administrators; and the well-known instances in which it has been departed from, during the last quarter of a century, have been attended with notorious and natural disaster.

Lord Dufferin's administration was not marked by any startling events. It is true that it included the annexation of Upper Burma; but this was not the result of any deliberate policy of territorial absorption, such as might have been practised by a Wellesley or a Dalhousie. It was the inevitable and logical consequence of the steps that had preceded it in Lower Burma, and was brought about, not by any preconceived design, but by the untoward combination of gross misgovernment on the part of a native King and the ominous and deliberate intrigues of a foreign Power. In other matters of foreign policy Lord Dufferin pursued a policy of pacification, settling the Northern and North-western boundaries of Afghanistan with Russia and observing friendly relations with the formidable Amir. The latter many years later always spoke to me in friendly terms of his meeting with Lord Dufferin and the Duke of Connaught at Rawal Pindi in 1885.

In his conduct of affairs the Viceroy exhibited a curious mixture of application and indifference. He laboured hard to obtain a mastery of all essential features of the administration, and wrote or inspired long and eloquent Minutes and Despatches. He took a great deal of trouble about his public addresses, which in common with all his speeches were carefully elaborated. He devoted weary hours to the study of Persian, under the quite mistaken impression that it was the language of the educated classes and of the Indian Princes, with whom he hoped to be able to converse in their own tongue. But he was careless about detail,

LORD DUFFERIN (1889)

From the painting by F. Holl, R.A.

interfered very little in departmental business, and left the conduct of all minor matters to his Private Secretary and the officials.

Of a certain type of eloquence Lord Dufferin was a master. In later life, in a Rectorial Address to the students of St. Andrews University, he deprecated the use of metaphor and ornament in public speaking. But these were the arts that he had himself consistently and successfully practised for half a century : his rather magniloquent addresses in Canada had first awakened that Dominion to a consciousness of its true greatness ; his Report on Egyptian Government was not complete without a reference to Memnon and the Rising Sun ; and his speeches in India, and elsewhere about India, were characterised by many rhetorical graces which excited much applause at the time, but seem a little pallid and artificial now.

Lord Dufferin's administration was in reality a monument to the saving grace of tact. No other man could have so soon or so triumphantly smoothed the ruffled surface of Indian life ; and, as Lord Northbrook wrote to me, when Dufferin died :

" I almost think the greatest of the many services he rendered to his country was the quiet way in which he managed to restore the confidence between the Indian Civil Service and the Government of India, which had been seriously shaken at the end of Ripon's administration—and Dufferin did this without crowing over Ripon."

These natural gifts were assisted by an appearance and manner of undeviating courtesy and the greatest charm, by a slight lisp of the voice and a sudden elevation or dropping of the eyeglass, that lent point and humour to any conversation. Nor can I ever forget an evening which I spent as the guest of Lord Dufferin in the Paris Embassy on my return from my visit to Afghanistan in 1895, when far into the night we exchanged experiences about our common, or rather our very uncommon friend, Amir Abdur Rahman Khan.

In one respect Lord Dufferin adopted an attitude and left on record an argument with which I was afterwards to find myself in the closest sympathy. Rejecting the opinion of Lord Lytton, the single Governor General in Indian history to take the opposite line, he warmly defended the existing constitution of the Government of India in military matters, and denounced as a dangerous heresy the concentration of all military power, executive, administrative, and financial, in the hands of the Commander-in-Chief. This view, which had been entertained by every

Governor General of India with the above solitary exception, by every Government of India without exception, and by every Secretary of State and Indian Council also without exception, was subsequently overthrown by the successive Governments of Mr. Balfour and Sir Henry Campbell-Bannerman, with ulterior consequences which it was left to the Report of the Royal Commission on the Mesopotamian Campaign in 1917 to point out.[1]

The social reign of Lord Dufferin was one of unbroken success. The narrative has been written in an agreeable book, entitled " Our Viceregal Life in India," by his talented wife, who further rendered an inestimable service to the women of India by instituting the Fund for the supply of medical aid to them which has ever since borne her name, and has been maintained and added to by the labours of subsequent Viceroys' wives.

After four years of tranquil and successful service in India and of harmonious relations with Secretaries of State so diverse in character and outlook as Lord Kimberley, Lord Randolph Churchill, and Lord Cross, everyone was much surprised when at the beginning of 1888 Lord Dufferin laid his office down.   Already, in October 1887, he had indicated in correspondence with England his desire to retire at the close of his fourth year, on the ground that he was getting on in years— he was already nearly sixty-three and the oldest Viceroy that had ever administered the Government of India—and that he wanted to be with his children at home.   It further transpired that he hankered after the Roman Embassy which was about to fall vacant, though, as he said, he would of course prefer Paris.   As a matter of fact he was destined to occupy both.   On the eve of departure he wrote to Lord Salisbury (5th February, 1888) in the following modest terms :

" [Mine] is certainly not a very brilliant record as compared with what has been achieved by some of my predecessors.   But I never had any ambition to distinguish my reign by a sensational policy, believing as I did (and subsequent experience has only confirmed the conviction) that in the present condition of affairs it is best for the country that the administration should be driven at a low and steady pressure."[2]

This was quite a true description, for Lord Dufferin had undertaken

---

[1] *Vide* especially p. 99 of the Report, where the Commission said that " This astounding system [*i.e.* the concentration of all military authority in the hands of a single individual in India] has only to be described to be condemned."

[2] " Life of the Marquis of Dufferin and Ava," by Sir Alfred Lyall, Vol. II, p. 178.

no new departure and had left no enduring mark on Indian administration. Indeed, as his biographer points out, he was eminently cautious in temperament and slow in arriving at decisions. But he had done that which was better and more valuable than any constructive innovation. He had re-established peace, and he left India more contented than he found it. In his parting speech at the St. Andrew's Day celebration in Calcutta, he drew a picture of that country and its people which was picturesque in its literary form but not without an undertone of serious warning.

Lord Dufferin was succeeded by a Viceroy, Lord Lansdowne, who like him came to the Viceregal throne of India from that of Ottawa, sharing many of his talents and gifts, and who left in India, as in every office that he has filled, a reputation of the highest distinction. His arrival was made the occasion for an innovation in social and ceremonial practice, which it is surprising should have been postponed for so long. We have witnessed the many occasions on which the outgoing ruler lingered on at Government House as the guest of the man who had replaced him—a sort of diluted decapitation which can hardly have been agreeable to either party. Now was instituted the sensible practice by which the incoming Viceroy spent a few days as a guest in Government House, in order to profit by confidential interviews with his predecessor, but did not himself assume the Government until he had escorted the latter to the wharf and bidden him farewell.

I have now, however, reached a point in my narrative at which the ban which I laid upon myself at an earlier date in relation to still living men must take effect, and at which the destiny of subsequent Viceroys, of whom there were four before Calcutta was abandoned—namely, in chronological order, Lords Lansdowne, Elgin, Curzon, and Minto—must be left to other hands. Lords Elgin and Minto have, it is true, passed away, and I might find in this fact an excuse for passing in review their personalities or their administrations. But I hold the opinion very strongly that in public life no man can be a quite impartial judge of the work either of his predecessor or of his successor in the same office, particularly in such a post as the Viceroyalty of India ; and although the recent biographer of Lord Minto, while accepting this canon, has found some difficulty in observing it in practice, I shall not reciprocate by saying anything except that Lord Minto was a prudent and justly popular Viceroy, while of Lord Elgin I would remark that he was a much more sagacious administrator than the world knew or allowed.

As to their successors in Government House, Calcutta, the sequence which I have traced from Clive and Warren Hastings to the present day was abruptly broken in 1912 ; and although recent Viceroys have wisely resumed the practice of a yearly visit to the former Capital, the record of their character and achievements must be sought elsewhere. The concluding reflection may perhaps be permitted, that while the abandonment of Bengal as the seat of Government and the move to Delhi were defended at the time as an act of Imperial statesmanship, there is now hardly a living authority on India, English or Indian, who does not disapprove and deplore it.

My readers will, I think, have gathered from my narrative and from the relative amounts of space which I have devoted to particular appreciations that, if it be either possible or desirable to discriminate between individuals, I should place Warren Hastings and Dalhousie in a class apart from their fellows, as Indian administrators and rulers of men. Both had blemishes of character or temperament which emerge from their conduct or writings ; but both were men with a genius for government, of a pure and splendid patriotism, of dynamic personality, and of immense and glowing achievement. The one may be said to have founded and the other to have completed the structure of British rule in India. Other Governors General there have been who, like Wellesley and Lord Hastings, made vast additions to the Empire and consolidated its greatness, or who, like Cornwallis and Canning, reformed an administration or controlled a crisis. Others again have won enduring popularity by their sympathies or their measures. Some have been commonplace and a few only have been ill-chosen men. The general level both of capacity and of accomplishment has been high, and Great Britain may look not without pride upon the long line of those who have represented the Sovereign and had charge of the overwhelming destinies committed to their care.

In the future the probability seems to be that the Viceroy will lose in authority and power, as the Provinces become more and more autonomous, and as the administration passes increasingly into Indian hands. He may end by wielding little more direct power than the Governor General of an Overseas Dominion, and may become the figurehead of the ship rather than the commander of the vessel.

Personally I shall be very sorry if this should turn out to be the case ; nor must I refrain from adding that, in my judgment, it is still and will continue to be open to a man of the right mould, should such be forthcoming, to retain the greater part of the prestige and to exert a large measure of the authority of the Governors General and the Viceroys of the past.

My own task, however, is not yet complete. I have endeavoured to depict the Governors General and Viceroys as they were, and to give to my readers some idea of the conditions in which they worked, and of their relations both with the society around them and with their official superiors at home. It has been, as the sub-title of these volumes indicates, a story rather than a history, and it has admitted much which the historian, pure and simple, as a rule ignores or conceals. But I have sought to do more : I have endeavoured to show that the story is one not merely of service or of splendour but of self-sacrifice and even suffering, not merely of honour and recognition but sometimes of flagrant ingratitude and stark injustice. I use these words not in any spirit of reproach, but because I think it is only right that my countrymen at home should know the conditions in which their principal servants abroad have frequently been called upon to act, and should make some endeavour to realise the sentiments of the outwardly applauded but as often secretly harassed or overridden man on the spot.

Of the Governors or Governors General or Viceroys whose story I have told, we have seen that Clive was driven by the persecution that he endured, after his return to England, to take his own life ; that Warren Hastings was recalled and actually displaced when in India, and was driven repeatedly to insist on resignation, while after his return to England he was the victim of an impeachment that is one of the crimes of history ; that Wellesley was openly censured and recalled and narrowly escaped a similar fate ; that the first Lord Minto was overthrown by a gross political manœuvre ; that Lord Hastings was severely censured after his retirement ; that Amherst only escaped the ignominy of dismissal by a timely resignation ; that Auckland resigned to avoid a similar fate following upon a change of Ministry in England ; that Ellenborough was recalled in disgrace ; that Northbrook retired because of a disagreement with the Home Government ; that Lytton did the same as the result of a General Election ; that a subsequent Viceroy, though in his second term of office, was driven to a similar step because he and his entire Council were overruled by the British Cabinet on a fundamental principle of Indian administration, in which he was subsequently declared by a public enquiry to have been in the right.[1]

We have also seen the long and heated warfare and the often strident asperities that marked the official intercourse between the ruler in India, whether it was Wellesley, or Dalhousie, or Lawrence, or Ripon, and the authorities in Whitehall. We have read the anguished outpourings of the tormented man in India on receipt of the mail bag or the telegram, and, while a portion of this spleen may be discounted either by the confidential nature of the outburst or by the inherent circumstances of the case, we cannot shut our eyes to the facts that first the East India House and later the India Office have often behaved with a lamentable lack of sympathy and of understanding towards their agents, and that the Indian satrap has in many cases found the Viceregal throne an altar of sacrifice quite as much as a seat of glory.

And how often or how seriously does the outside world take note of the price that has had to be paid in physical suffering, in family severance, in domestic sorrow, even in the desperate issues where the gates of life and death swing on their cruel hinges?

In our long list, ill-health or constant pain has been the daily companion of more than one Proconsul. Though he lived to an advanced old age in retirement, Warren Hastings was habitually ailing while in the fevered climate of Bengal, which he never left for thirteen years. Minto's strength had been sapped by his labours in the Javan Expedition and elsewhere. Auckland died at the age of 64. Dalhousie's life was one of incessant and truly heroic combat with devouring and ever-increasing pain. Canning was turned in a few years into a prematurely old man, from whom all spirit and vitality had fled. Others have kept a smiling countenance in the face of constant physical suffering. No doubt these conditions have been greatly and progressively alleviated by the vastly improved conveniences of modern life in India, and we shall see much less in the future of shattered health as the price of service. But here I have been concerned to record the experiences of the past rather than to anticipate the potentialities of the future.

[1] " Report of the Mesopotamia Commission " (1917), Part XI, entitled, " Faulty Organisation of Indian Military Administration."

SECOND ARRIVAL OF LORD CURZON AT GOVERNMENT HOUSE (1904)

As to the sundering of friendly ties, this may be said to be a part of the inevitable drawbacks of foreign employment anywhere. But it has operated with especial severity in the case of a climate so trying and a locality so distant as that of India. In the days when the voyage could only be made by the Cape, and might occupy any length of time from six months to a year, the privation was constant and applied as much to a Governor General as to anyone else. Warren Hastings was ordered to send his wife home in order to escape a breakdown of her health. Sir John Shore was twice obliged to leave his wife behind because of the terrors of the long voyage by sea. The first Lady Minto was not able to go out to India at all, and, from the day when her husband started for his great charge, never saw him again until his body was carried into the gates of their Scottish home. Lord Hastings had to send his wife and their young children away from India. Dalhousie forfeited all sight of his children during the long years of his Satrapy until, in the evening of his time, he was joined by his daughter. When he heard of their illness at home he once wrote :

" The sweetest chapters in their lives are being written while we are far away, transported to this penal settlement."

We have seen Lord Dufferin resigning in order to be able to rejoin his family and take charge of their education.

But what are we to say when we come to the supreme sacrifice, and find ourselves standing at the side of the open and premature grave ? We have seen two Governors General, Cornwallis and the first Lord Elgin, who never returned to England at all, having laid down their lives, where their bodies now rest, on Indian soil. A third, Lord Mayo, came back to the home of his birth a dead and murdered man in his coffin. A later Viceroy, Lord Hardinge of Penshurst, narrowly escaped by the mercy of Providence from a similar fate. The first Lord Minto, Dalhousie, and Canning only returned, worn out, to die.

Nor is this all. An even more poignant note of anguish remains to be struck. The first Lord Minto, a most devoted parent, heard while in Java in 1811 of the death of his youngest son, William, with whom he had parted just before at Madras. We have read in these pages of a similar bereavement of Lord and Lady Amherst, whose son and Aide-de-camp lies in the military cemetery at Barrackpore.

But deeper cups of misery have also been drained. We have seen Dalhousie stunned by the awful news of the death at sea of the beloved wife whom he had sent home to recover, but bracing himself with a martyr's fortitude to a continuance of the lonely struggle for three more years. We have seen the bowed form of Canning following his beautiful wife to her grave by the bamboos that quiver above the tranquil river-reaches of Barrackpore. A later Viceroy lost the partner and main author of his happiness in India a few months after they had left the shores of that country, to whose climate the recurrence of the illness which terminated her life was largely due. The last Viceregal mistress of the Government Houses of Calcutta and Barrackpore, the charming Lady Hardinge of Penshurst, came back to England for a holiday and died while her husband was still at his post in India.

It is not surprising that the already bereaved Dalhousie should have written as follows to his friend Couper, when contemplating the arrival of Lord Elgin :

" If Elgin cannot properly bring his wife to India he will be a fool if he comes without her and a maniac if he runs the risk of bringing her after all. I am poor, like Elgin, and, however he may like reputation and honour, I like them too. But seven years' heavy experience enables me to declare that emoluments, honours and reputation are as a feather against what must be set in the other balance in India." [1]

But I would go to another source—to the moving testimony of Thackeray, himself born in India and speaking through the voice of the old Indian soldier, Colonel Newcome—if I desired an impartial witness to the tragic possibilities of the scene. " I would rather be the author of a work of genius than the Governor General of India," exclaims the old man on one occasion. And on another :

" What a strange pathos seems to me to accompany all our Indian story ! Besides that official history which fills Gazettes and embroiders banners with the name of victory, which gives moralists and enemies cause to cry out at English rapine, and smaller patriots to boast of invincible British valour— besides the splendour and conquest, the wealth and glory, the crowned ambition, the conquered danger, the vast prize, and the blood freely shed in winning it—should not one remember the tears too ? Besides the lives of myriads of British men, conquering on a hundred fields from Plassey to Myanee, and

---

[1] " Private Letters," p. 329.

bathing them *cruore nostro*, think of the women and the tribute which they perforce must pay to those victorious achievements."

True it is that the tribute has had to be paid for nearly two centuries, not by Governors General and Viceroys alone, but by English men and English women of every class of life and service in India.[1] But I have sought to show here that even the most highly placed cannot escape, and that over the Viceregal throne there hangs not only a canopy of broidered gold but a mist of human tears. I think that the majority of those who have suffered have done so without repining ; they have thought the price worth paying ; perhaps even they would do it again. But at least let their countrymen know that they pay it, and remember that the foundation stones of the Indian Empire which they vaunt so loudly have not merely been laid in pride and glory, but have been cemented with the heart's blood of stricken men and women. And equally would I say to the Ministers who sit in state in Downing Street and the officials who rule and overrule from Whitehall, and to the legislators at Westminster who are often so ready with criticism and so glib with censure—that they may derive some profitable lessons from the history of the past, and may learn that the government of India is not a pastime but an ordeal, not a pageant alone but as often a pain. As for the Governor General or the Viceroy who has laboured there, peradventure as he leaves those shores for the last time he may find solace in the words of Edmund Burke :

" If I were to call for a reward it would be for the services in which for fourteen years without intermission I showed the most industry and had the least success. I mean the affairs of India. They are those on which I value myself the most : most for the importance ; most for the labour ; most for the judgment ; most for constancy and perseverance in the pursuit."

[1] I do not know of a more poignant testimony to the sorrows and risks of Indian life—at least as they used to be—than the avowal of Samuel Brown's wife in the 11th chapter of " Cranford " :
" 'Have you been in India ? ' said I, rather astonished. ' Oh, yes ! many a year, ma'am. Sam was a sergeant in the 31st ; and when the regiment was ordered to India, I drew a lot to go, and I was more thankful than I can tell ; for it seemed as if it would only be a slow death to me to part from my husband. But, indeed, ma'am, if I had known all, I don't know whether I would not rather have died there and then, than gone through what I have done since. To be sure, I've been able to comfort Sam, and to be with him ; but, ma'am, I've lost six children,' said she, looking up at me with those strange eyes, that I have never noticed but in mothers of dead children—with a kind of wild look in them, as if seeking for what they never more might find. ' Yes ! six children died off, like little buds nipped untimely, in that cruel India.' "

PUBLISHERS' NOTE

At the time of his death, Lord Curzon had read the proofs of this work as far as page 148 of the Second Volume, and had indexed it to page 140. In accordance with his Lordship's wishes, the remaining proofs have been examined by Sir William Foster, C.I.E., who has also completed and passed through the press the Index.

INDEX

PRINTED BY CASSELL & COMPANY, LIMITED, LA BELLE SAUVAGE, LONDON, E.C.4
5.525